Moving from C to C++

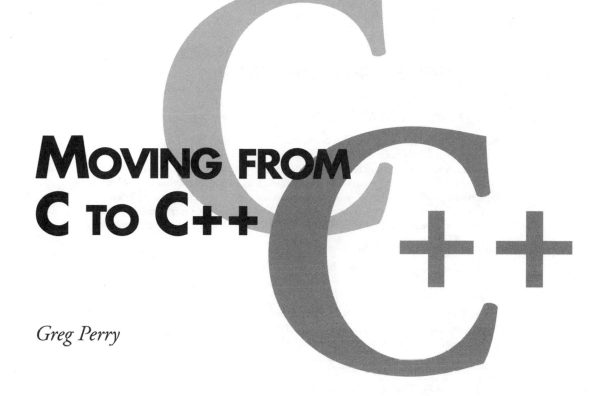

MOVING FROM
C TO C++

Greg Perry

PUBLISHING

A Division of Prentice Hall Computer Publishing
11711 North College, Carmel, Indiana 46032 USA

For Bruce Eckel, a friend, teacher, author, and the unchallenged king of C++.

© 1992 by Sams Publishing

International Standard Book Number: 0-672-30080-X

Library of Congress Catalog Card Number: 92-82872

95   94   93   92   4   3   2   1

Interpretation of the printing code: the rightmost double-digit number is the year of the book's printing; the rightmost single-digit, the number of the book's printing. For example, a printing code of 92-1 shows that the first printing of the book occurred in 1992.

Composed in AGaramond and MCPdigital by Prentice Hall Computer Publishing

Printed in the United States of America

Trademarks

Publisher
Richard K. Swadley

Acquisitions Manager
Jordan Gold

Managing Editor
Neweleen A. Trebnik

Acquisitions Editor
Gregory Croy

Development Editor
Stacy Hiquet

Editors
Gayle L. Johnson
Tad Ringo

Editorial Coordinators
Rebecca S. Freeman
Bill Whitmer

Editorial Assistants
Rosemarie Graham
Lori Kelley

Technical Editor
Bob Zigon

Cover Designer
Tim Amrhein

Cover Artist
George Harris

Director of Production and Manufacturing
Jeff Valler

Production Manager
Corinne Walls

Imprint Manager
Matthew Morrill

Book Designer
Michele Laseau

Production Analyst
Mary Beth Wakefield

Proofreading/Indexing Coordinator
Joelynn Gifford

Graphics Image Specialists
Dennis Sheehan
Jerry Ellis
Sue VandeWalle

Production
Katy Bodenmiller, Alys Brosius,
Michelle Cleary, Christine Cook,
Lisa Daugherty, Sandy Doell,
Terri Edwards, Carla Hall-Batton,
John Kane, Betty Kish,
Tom Loveman, Roger Morgan,
Juli Pavey, Angela Pozdol,
Linda Quigley, Linda Seifert,
Michelle Self, Susan Shepherd,
Kelli Widdifield, Alyssa Yesh

Indexers
John Sleeva
Jeanne Clark

OVERVIEW

CONTENTS

ACKNOWLDGMENTS

The people at Sams and Prentice Hall are not editors, proofreaders, artists, and publishers first and foremost. First and foremost, they are wonderful friends who love their work, and it shows in quality books. They perform a service for the computer community that is unequaled anywhere else.

In particular, I'd like to thank the people who directly worked on this book. The epitome of "nice to work with," Stacy Hiquet, always has a smile in her voice. My appreciation to Gregory Croy, who trusted me with yet another project. Also, Gayle Johnson, Tad Ringo, and Bob Zigon took my manuscript and, somehow, made a good book out of it.

I also want to thank the top-notch people at Borland International, Inc., for supplying the excellent C++ software used throughout this book.

My students teach me much more than I teach them. Nobody really knows a subject until he or she teaches it at least once to someone else. I love the C and C++ languages, I suspect, because of how much I enjoy teaching them to others. My all-time favorite "continuing education" student, Christine Chambers, still wants to learn eight years after her first lesson with me.

I'm not really sure how or when I learned C++. The learning process spanned a year or more, and although many sources helped put the pieces together, my beautiful bride Jayne kept telling me I could do it. Since then, Jayne has kept me motivated to master the much more advanced computer topics in this ever-changing field. In addition, I suspect that my parents, Glen and Bettye Perry, will beam as brightly at this book as they have for 13 other books. It amazes me how lucky I am to be around so much love.

ABOUT THE AUTHOR

Greg Perry has been a programmer and a trainer for the past 14 years. He received his first degree in computer science, then he received a master's degree in corporate finance. He currently is a professor of computer science at Tulsa Junior College, a computer consultant, and a lecturer at programming conferences across the country. Perry is the author of 13 other computer books, including *C++ By Example; C By Example; QBasic By Example; Turbo Pascal By Example;* and with Marcus Johnson, *Turbo C++ By Example.* In addition, he has published articles in several publications, including *PC World, Data Training,* and *Inside First Publisher.* He is fluent in nine computer languages.

INTRODUCTION

Because you have this book, you must be a C programmer wanting to get in on the C++ action. No problem! This book was designed for you.

Many C programmers who have attempted to learn C++ have had only limited success. It seems as if authors and teachers want to teach C++ to current C++ programmers, or they want to teach C++ to beginning programmers. Current C programmers, of which there are many, need help moving from the world of C to C++. C++ requires a change in thinking and a different approach from the regular procedural programming languages such as C, Pascal, COBOL, FORTRAN, or BASIC.

This book takes what you already know, the C programming language, and eases you through the transition into C++. You are not thrown a bunch of silver-dollar words such as *polymorphism, encapsulation,* and *abstract base classes* until you see the need for the concepts behind the words.

As much as possible, when this book teaches you a new concept, it uses what you already know in C, shows the way you now achieve the same C result, points out the problems inherent in C, and describes how C++ better handles the programming task. This book does not put the C programming language into a bad light; actually, without C, C++ would be nonexistent. Rather, this book attempts to show you the new methods that C++ brings to the programming bag of tricks.

Overview

This book is for current C programmers. Chapter 1, "Welcome to C++," discusses the actual C prerequisites for the reader, but if you have written programs in C, and fairly well understand the C way of coding, you will be fine with this book. No time is spent describing the C language in detail. No time is spent describing what a program is, or what a compiler does with a program. If you know some C, you are past the novice point, and this book treats your current knowledge with respect.

If you are an expert C programmer, this book is also aimed at you. You spent much of your C career learning about the ins and outs of file I/O, defined macros, structures, passing arguments between functions, and dynamic memory allocation. Now that you have mastered those concepts, C++ turns the tables by performing each of them differently from C! Do not despair yet. That advanced C knowledge will help you move into the C++

programming mode quickly, as you will understand why C++ is considered to handle those programming topics much better than C.

This book is divided into five sections. The first section describes many of the C++ programming constructs that improve upon C. You probably have heard the phrase *object-oriented programming* (*OOP*), and Part I, "Non-OOP C++ Basics," has nothing to do with OOP. If you read only Part I, you would immediately want to switch to C++ for the rest of your C programming.

Part II, "Objects and Classes," introduces you to the object-oriented world. You will see a shift in the way you view your program's data. Your C++ variables become active, taking over a lot of work that the rest of your program used to have to do.

Part III, "Operators and Friends," is the first part that really exploits the power of OOP. With defined macros, you already know that you can rewrite the way the C language behaves. You can define your own command names instead of using those that come with C. Unlike with defined macros, which do little but produce unreadable and error-prone code, you can extend the way C++ operates in a safe and uniform manner.

Part IV, "Inheritance and Virtual Functions," takes the concept of program extension and reusability to new levels unknown in non-OOP languages. For the first time, you can take existing code, even if you have no access to the source code, and use functions and data in your own programs. No more copy/paste operations with source code, no more recompiling entire systems when you make a change to a piece of code. With inheritance, C++ does the work for you.

Part V, "Advanced Object-Oriented Programming," wraps up the book, not with difficult topics, but with additional C++ features that you might not need right off the bat, but that you will use when you start developing complete systems.

This book stresses more than any other concept the importance of C++ for producing more correct code in less time than is possible in C or in any of the other non-OOP programming languages.

Required Programming Tools

You need a computer and a C++ compiler to use this book. Because the sample program listings all contain the program's output, you can learn C++ without a computer, but seeing the programs operate and playing "what if?" on C++ source code is the best way to learn C++.

This book does not target a specific C++ compiler. Because the ANSI committee has yet to adopt a standard, there is not really "one" C++ standard. As discussed in Chapter 1, "Welcome to C++," AT&T has promoted the C++ de facto standards ever since C++'s inception. If your compiler conforms to the AT&T C++ 2.1 standard, you will be able to master C++ without worrying much about any compatibility issues. (You must have a compiler that conforms to AT&T C++ version 3.0 to use templates, discussed in Chapter 19, "Templates.")

If you purchased your C compiler within the last year and a half, chances are good that the compiler also includes C++. The two most popular PC compilers, Borland International's Turbo C++ and Borland C++, run every program in this book because they were the development compilers used for the code examples. Nevertheless, the Microsoft C/C++ 7.0 compiler should also handle the programs with little or no trouble, as should any UNIX or mainframe C++ compiler that conforms to an AT&T standard.

Companion Disk

A low-cost companion disk is available through the order form at the back of this book. This book contains approximately 100 programs, and the disk will save you a lot of typing time. To keep the price of this book down, the disk is offered to you as an option and not bound into the book itself.

If you choose to order the disk, it will be sent to you quickly so that you can begin using it as soon as possible.

Conventions Used in This Book

This book uses certain typographic conventions:

- New terms appear in *italic*.

- Keywords, function names, variable names, class names, code lines, and so on appear in `monospace`.

- Placeholders appear in *`italic monospace`* (for example, `class` *`tagname`* `{`).

Each chapter of *Moving from C to C++* begins with a quote. These are not real-life quotations, but they are always applicable to the chapter, sometimes in a humorous way. In addition, each chapter includes a list of topics discussed, and each chapter ends with a summary.

Certain information is highlighted in a way designed to catch your attention. Margin notes emphasize important concepts from the text. Notes, tips, and cautions appear in sidebars, with the appropriate icons next to them. A program that shows the C way of doing something, followed by a program that shows the C++ way of accomplishing the same task, has a special "C Version" or "C++ Version" icon next to it.

Part 1

Non-OOP C++
Basics

WELCOME TO C++

1

"C++ is a better C."

Congratulations! You are now taking the first step to learning C++, the "next generation" for C programmers. C++ is one of the newest programming languages available. Like its predecessor, C, C++ is rapidly taking the programming world by storm. Throughout the programming community, people are learning and adopting C++ because of its superiority to other languages. Several software companies offer C++ compilers. In the world of PCs (personal computers), both Borland and Microsoft, two of the leading names of PC software, offer full-featured C++ compilers. The fact that these two software giants pledge so much time and development dollars for perfecting their C++ compilers demonstrates the language's significance.

Some choose to call C++ an extension of C. Some see C++ as a replacement of C. C went against all odds in the 1980s to become one of the world's foremost computer languages—not just on personal computers, but on minicomputers and mainframes as well. C++ promises to do in the 1990s what C did in the 1980s. C++ is not just another programming language; its programming elements, especially its *object-oriented programming* (*OOP*)

capabilities, make C++ the language of choice among programmers and programming shops who need to produce code faster while also making it more maintainable. In most companies, the programming backlog is tremendous. C++ promises to reduce some of the backlog, thanks to its better programming elements as compared to its non-OOP predecessors.

The AT&T Standard

C++ is defined by AT&T to achieve conformity between versions of C++.

Several companies have written different versions of C++, but almost all C++ languages available today conform to the AT&T standard. *AT&T-compatible* means that the C++ language in question conforms to the standard defined by the company that invented the language—namely, American Telephone & Telegraph, Incorporated.

In the 1980s, Bjourn Stroustrup, working for AT&T, took the C language to its next progression. He added features to correct some of the problems in the C language, while changing the way programmers view programs by introducing object orientation to the language. The object-oriented aspect of programming got its start in other languages, such as Smalltalk. Stroustrup realized that C programmers needed the flexibility and power offered by a true object-oriented programming language.

AT&T understands that C++ is still new and is not a fully mature language. They have just completed the AT&T C++ 3.0 specification to which software companies will begin to conform. Developing a uniform C++ language helps ensure that programs you write today will probably be compatible with the C++ compilers of tomorrow.

The AT&T C++ specification is only a suggestion. Software companies do not have to follow the AT&T specification, although most choose to do so. No typical computer standards committee has yet adopted a C++ language. The ANSI committee is working on the issue, but they are waiting for C++ to get more of a firm hold in the programming community before settling on a standard. They will not have to wait much longer. C++ is rapidly gaining acceptance, and the AT&T specification is the de facto standard in use today.

Although not all companies follow the AT&T C++ specification, many do. Most C++ compiler writers also add their own extensions to the language, making their version do more work than the AT&T specification requires. If you program using the AT&T C++

specification, your program should successfully run on any other computer in the world that also uses AT&T-compatible C++.

AT&T developed C++ as an improved version of the C programming language. C has been around since the 1970s and has matured into a solid, extremely popular programming language. The ANSI (American National Standards Institute) committee has set forth a standard C programming specification called ANSI C. If your C compiler conforms to ANSI C, your program should work on any other computer in the world that also has ANSI C. This compatibility between computers is so important that AT&T's C++ specification includes almost every element of the ANSI C and more. In fact, the ANSI C committee often requires that a C++ feature be included in subsequent versions of C. For instance, function prototypes, a feature not found in older versions of ANSI C, are now required for approval by the ANSI C committee. C function prototypes did not exist until AT&T included them in their first C++ specification.

C and C++ Today

The importance of C++ cannot be overly stressed. Throughout the years, several programming languages have been developed that were designed to be "the only programming language you will ever need." PL/I was heralded as such back in the early 1960s. It turned out to be so large and it took so many system resources that it became simply another language programmers used, along with COBOL, FORTRAN, and many others. In the mid-1970s, Pascal was developed for smaller computers. Microcomputers had just been invented, and the Pascal language was small enough to fit in their limited memory space while still offering advantages over many other languages. Pascal became very popular and is still often used today, but it never became *the* answer for all programming tasks, and it failed at being "the only programming language you will ever need."

When C became known to the mass computer markets in the late 1970s, it too was promoted as "the only programming language you will ever need." What surprised so many skeptics (including this author in the beginning) is that C almost fulfills this promise! An incredible number of programming shops have converted to C. The appeal of C's efficiency, combined with its portability between computers, makes it the language of choice. Most of today's familiar spreadsheets, databases, and word processors are written in C. Now that C++ has improved on C, programmers are retooling their minds to think in C++.

The computer professional help-wanted ads seem to seek more and more C++ programmers every day. By learning this popular language, you will stay with the programming crowds and keep your skills current. You have taken the first step: With this book, you will

learn the C++ language particulars, as well as many programming tips to use and pitfalls to avoid. This book attempts to make you not just a C++ programmer, but a better programmer in general by applying the structured, long-term programming habits that professionals require in today's business and industry.

C++ Compared to C

Before learning the C++ language specifics, you should understand a little about how C++ differs from other programming languages on the market, and how it is similar to C. C++ began as a *language translator*. The original C++ language was not a compiler, but a pre-compiler program called *cfront*. Cfront was similar to the C preprocessor that translates the directives such as #include. Cfront translated C++ code into regular C code; the regular C compiler at hand would then finish the compilation. Because the original C++ language was not a compiler, C++ was not as efficient in the beginning as C. Today, most C++ languages are fully compiled directly from C++ into machine language, so today's C++ compilers are about as efficient as, and sometimes more efficient than, C compilers.

C++ requires more stringent data type checking than C.   C++ is very efficient and has much stronger data typing than C. C is known as a *weakly typed* language; that is, variable data types do not necessarily have to hold their declared type of data. For example, if you declare a floating-point variable and then decide to put a character value into it, C enables you to do so. Consider this code:

CTYPE.C. Illustrates C's weakly typed data.

```
/* Filename: CTYPE.C */
/* Illustrates C's weakly typed data */
#include <stdio.h>
void main()
{
   float x=56.98;  /* Defines a floating-point variable */
   printf("The value of x is %.2f \n", x);

   x = 'A';
   printf("The value of x now is %c \n", x);  /* Attempts to print A */
                                   /* An 'A' did not just print! */
   return;  /* Returns to the operating system */
}
```

The data in x might not be in the format you expect, but C does its best to accommodate your requests. This is much different than stronger-typed languages such as COBOL and

Pascal. A Pascal compiler would never enable you to assign a character value to a floating-point variable.

When you begin using C++'s OOP features, you can get into trouble with the freedom possible in C. The designers of C++ decided to make C++ more stringent in its data type checking. C++ still enables you to mix data types, but there are times when you must show your intent to do so with a typecast before the value. Get into the habit of typecasting all data types you mix, such as when you store a character value into a floating-point location. Strong type checking is especially apparent when passing values to functions; C++'s required prototypes strictly require that data types match.

A Note to the Reader

All the programs in this book are available on a separate diskette (see the order form in the back of this book). The price was kept extremely low and covers the cost of the disk's production and shipment. You might prefer to order the disk instead of typing these programs yourself. If you do, the disk's programs are stored under filenames designated by the first line's comment. For example, the program just shown is stored under the filename CTYPE.C on the disk.

C++, unlike C, treats character data differently from integer data. (Regular C promotes character data into integer storage automatically, enabling you to use them interchangeably.) The upcoming chapters take these things much more slowly and provide lots of examples to clarify them. You can still be sloppy with C++—forgetting to typecast mixed data types—but you can get into more trouble with C++ than C if you do so.

Like C, C++ is a small, block-structured programming language. It has about 45 keywords, only a few more than C has. As with C, to make up for its small vocabulary, C++ has one of the largest assortments of *operators* (second only to the APL programming language). The large number of operators in C++ could tempt programmers to write cryptic programs that do a lot with a small amount of code. As you will learn throughout this book, making the program readable is more important than squeezing out bytes. The tricks and shortcuts you learned as a C programmer do not always make for good C++ programs.

C++, as with C, has no input or output statements. Unlike C, most C++ programs use operators to perform input and output. The old standbys, `printf()` and `gets()`, are still available in C++, but C++ programmers rarely use them. As you learn more about C++, you will want to start converting some of your existing C code into C++ code. Because C++ is primarily a superset of C, most C++ compilers have no problems compiling regular C code. If you want to mix C and C++ code, your C++ compiler has ways of handling the mixture, as this book demonstrates.

Your C++ compiler will compile your C programs with very few problems.

7

> Because C++'s rules are so much stricter than C's, some present-day C programmers, when faced with a logic bug they cannot find, often run their C programs through a C++ compiler. The C++ compiler warnings and errors that go undetected by C compilers can help the C programmer spot hidden bugs such as uninitialized variables and incorrect (or ignored) typecasting.

This Book's Approach

This book shows you how to program in C++. Many examples, especially those in the early chapters, compare the new C++ concepts to the C way of doing things. This should speed your understanding of C++ because you already have a fundamental grasp of C. As this book progresses into the more advanced aspects of C++, fewer concepts are based on C because nothing in the C language conforms to these areas of C++. Nevertheless, C is a perfect stepping-stone for learning C++.

All programs in this book conform to the AT&T C++ 2.1 standard. The differences between AT&T 2.1 and the new AT&T 3.0 are relatively minor for beginning and intermediate C++ programmers. Many compiler writers have yet to adopt the AT&T 3.0 specification. (As you progress in your programming skills, you will want to tackle the more advanced aspects of C++, and 3.0 might come more into play later as compiler writers implement 3.0 in their product.) If a topic in this book behaves differently under 3.0 than under 2.1, I explain how the later version differs from version 2.1. Whether you use a PC, a minicomputer, a mainframe, or a supercomputer, the C++ language you learn here should work on any compiler that conforms to AT&T C++ 2.1 and later versions. Most of today's C++ compilers guarantee full AT&T 2.1 compatibility. There seems to be some debate over what makes a compiler 3.0-compatible, but again, the differences between 2.1 and 3.0 are minor and should not concern most C++ programmers.

There are arguments in the programming community about whether a person should learn C before C++ or just start with C++. Because C++ is termed "a better C," many feel that C++ is an important language in its own right that can be learned just as easily as C. Almost every veteran C++ programmer started with C. The original author of the C++ programming language wrote C++ using C as a basis, attempting to overcome some of C's shortcomings. To learn C++ without first learning C probably would hinder people more than aid them. The cryptic nature of the C style of coding is difficult to learn at first, as you might well remember. Because you already know C and have overcome the anxiety of C, you should be able to pick up C++ faster.

Some of you have read, or attempted to read, other books on C++ and never really quite "got it." Many frustrated C programmers want to move to C++ but cannot make the transition. This book hopes to fill the niche left by so many other C++ tutorials. This is not an advanced programmer's guide to C++. You will not find hundreds of pages devoted to C class libraries, container classes, and the like. What you will find is a solid C++ tutorial, one that takes the C programmer by the hand, respecting his or her prior C programming knowledge, and explains the *why* behind a new concept before explaining the *how*. So many C++ tutorials throw object-oriented programming statements at you before they teach the reason for OOP. They feel that as soon as you program in OOP for a while, it becomes second nature. This is true, but you need to know the importance of moving from C to C++ all along the way or you lose sight of the advantages of C++.

The primary goal of this book is to present the reasons for moving from C to C++.

Here, you will not even read OOP-heavy words such as *polymorphism, inheritance,* and *data hiding* until you learn the concepts behind them. You will learn the names of these and other extended C++ concepts almost as an afterthought. Too many C++ students are thrown descriptions, definitions, and code before they see the meaning behind the concepts. If anything, this book's approach makes the beginning C++ programmer want more information faster, especially the early OOP concepts. If you grasp the fundamentals of OOP, C++ poses no problems for you whatsoever.

C++ is *not* difficult! You can learn C++ as well as you know C. Object-oriented programming is just a different way of approaching parts of programming problems. C++ is not all OOP, either. A large percentage of the code you write in C++ will look exactly like C code, because that is what it will be. C++ programs contain for loops, while loops, if statements, return statements, function names, braces for blocks, and all the other regular C programming statements you are used to. Not all programming problems lend themselves to OOP concepts, and not all C++ programs have to include OOP.

This book begins where you are most comfortable—in C. The opening chapters have nothing about OOP in them. The entire first part of this book begins by teaching you the fundamental differences between C and C++ and the advantages of C++ concepts over their C counterparts. Only after introducing you to C++ are OOP concepts presented, and only after thoroughly explaining the need for OOP and why OOP offers possibilities unavailable in non-OOP languages such as C.

Your C Background

As you know by now, this book assumes that you have written C programs. To "know C" means different things to different programmers. It is difficult to determine how much C you need before learning C++. You do not have to be a C expert, or have programmed in C for many years, to learn C++ from this book. Nevertheless, you should have a fundamental grasp of a few basic constructs and elements from the C language before starting this book.

A short rundown of things you should already know before learning C++ follows. Don't fret if you still need your C reference manual for some of the following concepts before you use them in a program. C takes a while to master, and few people are as expert in C as they would like. Even fewer are expert in C++. C++ is still new, and if you are just now learning C++, you are still on the ground floor of C++ programmers.

This book assumes that you have exposure to, and have at times used, the following elements of C:

- All programming construct statements, such as `for`, `if`, `while`, `do while`, and `goto`

- The many operators of C, such as `++`, `?:`, `<`, and `/`, along with their precedence and associativity with each other

- Preprocessor directives, especially `#include` and `#define`

- Data and variable type differences, such as integers, characters, and floating-point numbers

- Simple input/output functions such as `printf()`, `scanf()`, `gets()`, and `fprintf()`

- Arrays

- The block-structured nature of C, including local and global variables and their scope and visibility considerations

- Calling and returning from functions

- Passing and returning values between functions

- Structure definitions using the `struct` statement

- Dynamic memory allocation using the functions `malloc()` and `free()`

Summary

C++ is an efficient, powerful, and popular programming language. This book takes your current working knowledge of C and uses it as a stepping-stone to teach you C++. C++ is all you need to produce computer programs that make the computer work the way you want it to.

This chapter presented the background of C++ by walking you through its history and explaining its predecessor, the C programming language. C++ adds to C by offering some of the most advanced programming language commands that exist today. Although object-oriented elements exist in other languages such as Turbo Pascal and Smalltalk, C++ sits by itself as the OOP language most widely in use today, despite its infancy in the marketplace and in programming shops around the country.

The rest of this book is devoted to teaching you C++. Put on your programming training hat and set your sights for mastering C++.

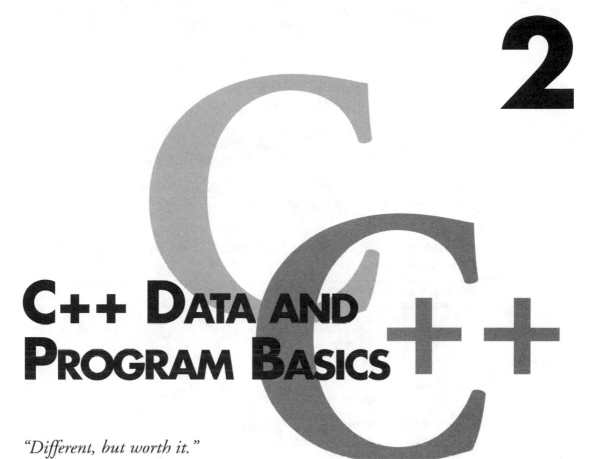

C++ DATA AND PROGRAM BASICS

"Different, but worth it."

This chapter gets you started using your C++ compiler right away. There are a few preliminary basics of C++ you should learn before moving on to the heart of the language. This chapter explains the C++ style comments and then goes directly to the fundamentals of C++ data.

In this chapter, you will learn about:

- The // comment prefix

- How C++ stores character data types

- Clearer typecasting

- C++ scope considerations

- How to use the const keyword

- inline functions

- The C++ prototyping specifics

C++ Comments

If you look at a C++ program, you might first notice its different commenting style. C++ compilers still support the /* and */ enclosing comment sections that you are used to. However, C++ has its own method of commenting that you should begin to use.

In C++, a comment begins with two forward slashes (//) and continues until the end of the line. Look at the following program:

COMMENT.CPP. Contains both old C-style comments and the new C++ style.

```
/* Filename: COMMENT.CPP */
// This program contains both old C-style comments and
// the new C++ style. C++ compilers enable you to use either.
//
#include <stdio.h>
void main()
{
   int age = 30;
   printf("Your age is %d years old.\n", age);  /* Prints */
                                                // the age

   printf("%d is still young!\n", age);
   return;
}
```

Although this program mixes the two commenting styles to show you both of them together, C++ programmers rarely use comments between /* and */. It is easy to forget to end these older comments. Without the closing */, you might comment out several lines of code, requiring extra debugging and compiling time to fix the problem. You never have to worry about ending C++ comments, because C++ considers only the rest of the line to be the comment.

If you have ever programmed on a mainframe computer, you might have seen comments that look like these C++ comments. *JCL* (Job Control Language) is a batch processing language similar to the batch file commands used on PCs. JCL programmers use // to begin all lines of JCL comments.

Inadvertent problems creep into code when you comment more than one line of code with the older style. There might be times when you want to comment out several lines of a program so you can watch the execution of another part of the code. How would you comment out the first two printf() calls in the COMMENT.CPP program? You couldn't put a /* before the first printf() and a */ after the second because there is already a /* */ comment on one of the lines. The compiler would get confused, thinking that the first comment ended early. Commenting out several lines with the new style of C++ comments is less error-prone. Insert two forward slashes before the lines you want to comment. Nothing else on the lines, including other comments, will interfere with the lines you commented out. Here is the same program with the first two print() statements properly commented out:

NEWCOMM.CPP. Contains both old C-style comments and the new C++ style.

```
/* Filename: NEWCOMM.CPP */
// This program contains both old C-style comments and
// the new C++ style. C++ compilers enable you to use either.
//
#include <stdio.h>
void main()
{
   int age = 30;
// printf("Your age is %d years old\n", age);   /* Prints */
//                                              // the age
   printf("%d is still young!\n", age);
   return;
}
```

Now that you are becoming a C++ programmer, you should refrain from using the old C-style /* */ comments at all.

Filename Extensions

C++ programs almost always end with the *.cpp* extension (C programs end with the *.c* filename extension). This book follows this convention, so you can tell by the filename which programs contain straight C code and which contain C++. Soon, you will know at a glance, without looking at the filename, which programs are C++ programs.

continues

> *continued*
>
> Both C and C++ programs generally use *.h* for included header filename extensions, although some C++ programmers prefer to use *.hpp* for C++ header filename extensions. Because more C++ compilers adopt the *.h* filename extension for header files than adopt *.hpp*, this book uses *.h* for both C and C++ header files.

Storing Data Types

In Chapter 1, "Welcome to C++," you learned that C++ treats data differently than regular C does. You will first notice this difference in the way C stores integer and character data. C promotes character data to an integer format before storing it. You might not realize C does this.

No C programmer can accurately predict storage requirements for various types of data. You might happen to know that *your* C compiler uses 4 bytes of storage to store a floating-point value. Knowing how many bytes a floating-point value takes should have no bearing on your programs. Some compilers might use 6 or 8 bytes to store floating-point values. If you want your programs to work on other computers (and on your own after a compiler upgrade), blind yourself to the data-storage limits of your particular compiler. Use the sizeof() operator at all times when you need to work with the byte sizes of data.

Consider this program:

CDATA.C. Prints the number of bytes needed to store different types of data.

```c
/* Filename: CDATA.C */
/* Prints the number of bytes needed to */
/* store different types of data.        */
#include <stdio.h>
void main()
{
    double d = 12.34;
    float f = 5.6;
    int i = 7;
    char c = 'C';

    printf("Double values take %d bytes\n", (int)sizeof(d));
```

```
    printf("Float values take %d bytes\n", (int)sizeof(f));
    printf("Integer values take %d bytes \n", (int)sizeof(i));
    printf("Character values take %d bytes \n", (int)sizeof(c));
    return;
}
```

On many computers, this program produces the following output:

```
Double values take 8 bytes
Float values take 4 bytes
Integer values take 2 bytes
Character values take 2 bytes
```

Your C compiler may or may not give you these exact results, but many do. The surprising part of the output may be its last two lines, unless you already understand C's promotion of character data to integers. Weren't you always taught that a character is the same as a byte and that a byte always takes one byte of storage? This output shows that a character takes *two* bytes of storage. However many bytes the integer takes in regular C compilers, the character data usually takes the same amount as well, even though you treat the character as if it were a single byte and you store single characters in them. C compilers promote characters to integers before storing them.

As the program CDATA.C shows, typecast all `sizeof()` values to `int` before printing them using the integer `%d` print specifiers. `sizeof()` produces a `size_t` data type (usually the same as `long int`) and not `int`. Typecasting values to their needed types becomes most important in C++ programs.

C++ compilers change the rules for character data storage. Although you must still use the `sizeof()` operator to learn the machine's storage requirements for all other data types, C++ compilers store character data using a single byte of memory. The preceding program run on a C++ compiler might produce the following result:

C++ compilers use only one byte of storage for character data.

```
Double values take 8 bytes
Float values take 4 bytes
Integer values take 2 bytes
Character values take 1 bytes
```

Again, the length of doubles, floats, and integers is open to change, depending on the compiler and target computer, but C++ compilers always treat characters as single bytes and never promote them to integers unless you specifically typecast them into integers.

Figure 2.1 helps illustrate this point. As you learn more about C++, you will see why the distinction between characters and integers is important.

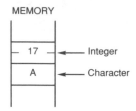

Figure 2.1. Whereas an integer may take 2 bytes, a character always takes one in C++.

Declaring Variables

There are only two places that you can declare variables in C: globally before a function name, and locally after the opening brace of a block. In C++, you can declare local variables almost anywhere in a program *as long as you declare them before you use them.*

Consider the following C program. Even though net_pay is not used until the end of the program, its declaration must reside toward the top of main():

VARLOC.C. Illustrates the declaration of C local variables.

```
/* Filename: VARLOC.C */
/* Illustrates the declaration of C local variables. */
#include <stdio.h>
void main()
{
   float pay, taxes, net_pay;
   int hours;

   printf("How many hours did you work? ");
   scanf(" %d", &hours);

   pay = 5.75 * (float)hours;  /* Gross pay */
   taxes = .28 * pay;     /* Computer taxes */
   net_pay = pay - taxes;  /* Take-home pay */

   printf("Your take-home pay is $%.2f", net_pay);
}
```

Although this example is short, you can see that net_pay is used several lines after it is declared. Some programmers feel that they lose track of their variables when they have to declare them so far away from the variable's actual use. Other programmers feel that all variables should be declared together. To give you the choice, C++ enables you to declare variables anywhere in the program. Here is the C++ version of the preceding program, with net_pay declared right before it is used the first time:

VARLOC.CPP. Illustrates the declaration of C++ local variables.

```
// Filename: VARLOC.CPP
// Illustrates the declaration of C++ local variables.
#include <stdio.h>
void main()
{
   float pay, taxes;  // net_pay NOT declared here
   int hours;

   printf("How many hours did you work? ");
   scanf(" %d", &hours);

   pay = 5.75 * (float)hours;    // Gross pay
   taxes = .28 * pay;            // Computer taxes
   float net_pay = pay - taxes;  // Take-home pay with newly
                                 // declared net_pay
   printf("Your take-home pay is $%.2f", net_pay);
}
```

There is much debate as to the usefulness of such declarations. It is difficult to find variables declared in the middle of a program, and during debugging you might wish that all your variables were declared in one place so that you can see their data types at a glance.

The most common use of close variable declarations is for loop control. The following variable, ctr, is declared within the for loop that uses it. Because loop counters rarely are important variables, declaring them close to their loop takes the clutter out of more important variable declarations at the top of the block.

```
for (int ctr=0; ctr<100; ctr++)  // Rest of loop would follow
```

Assigning Aggregate Character Arrays

C allows the following aggregate assignment of a string to a character array. A problem can occur if you treat the array as though it holds a string:

```
char name[5] = "Tulsa";  /* No room for null! */
```

This is a dangerous definition if you use name as a string. As long as you treat the array as an array of five individual characters, you can define name as shown here. Nevertheless, the definition is misleading, because it appears that you want to make room for a string with five letters, even though the string to assign to name has six characters (the null zero is the sixth character).

C programmers wanting to define a character array of five characters with 'T', 'u', 'l', 's', and 'a' in each element would be more clear if they did this:

```
char name[5] = {'T', 'u', 'l', 's', 'a'};  /* Single characters
```

Because the first definition is misleading, C++ does not allow it. C++ will complain because you did not declare enough array elements to hold the string on the right of the assignment. Of course, both C and C++ will count the number of elements for you if you want to assign a string to a character array upon initialization, like this:

```
char name[] = "Tulsa";  /* C and C++ make room for null */
```

Clearer Typecasting

The C typecasting method looks like this:

```
factor = (float)i * 2.5;  /* Typecasts i to floating-point */
```

The designers of C++ decided that this method looks awkward. The data type in parentheses is somewhat cumbersome. C++ still respects the C style of typecasts, but C++ offers a much cleaner method of typecasting variables. C++ typecasts look like function calls. The preceding line looks like this in C++:

```
factor = float(i) * 2.5;  // Typecasts i to floating-point
```

float is *not* a function call. Despite their appearance, all typecasts are operators, having precedence among other operators just like + and && do. Even though typecasts are not

functions, they act almost like functions, returning values of whatever data type the cast dictates. Most people like the "look and feel" of C++-style typecasts better than C's.

Scope Considerations

When you declare a local variable, whether at the top of the block or in the middle, that variable is available for use only within the block in which it is defined. Consider the following program:

VARSCOPE.CPP. Declares variables in two different places within the same block.

```
// Filename: VARSCOPE.CPP
// Declares variables in two different
// places within the same block.
#include <stdio.h>
void main()
{
   int var1 = 5;  // Visible until the end of main()'s block

   for (int var2=0; var2 < 10; var2++)  // var2 also visible
   {
      int var3 = 15;  // Visible ONLY within for's block
      printf("var1, var2, and var3 are %d, %d, and %d\n",
             var1, var2, var3);
   }                             // var3 loses visibility here

   // Both var1 and var2 are still visible here

   return;
}     // Because block ended, var1 and var2 lost their scope
```

Although var2's scope ends at the end of main()'s block, var2 could never be used before the for statement in which it is defined. var2's scope extends from its point of definition until the end of its block.

If you write a C program with two or more variables of the same name, only the innermost variable is visible at any one time. C++ uses a new operator named the *scope resolution operator* (::) to resolve scope conflicts between variables with the same name. Without using the scope resolution operator, the following program's printf() prints the value of only the innermost occurrence of avar:

The :: is the scope resolution operator.

21

AVAR1.CPP. Program with four variables of the same name, all with different scopes.

```
// Filename: AVAR1.CPP
// Program with four variables of the same name,
// all having the same name but different scopes
#include <stdio.h>
int avar = 5;  // Global variable
void main()
{
   int avar = 10;  // Outer local variable
   {
     int avar = 20;  // Another local variable
     {
        int avar = 30;  // Still another
        printf("%d %d %d %d\n", avar,avar,avar,avar);
     }        // Innermost variable loses its scope
   }        // Second innermost variable loses its scope
}        // First local variable loses its scope and so does global
```

This program produces the following output:

```
30 30 30 30
```

Even though there are three other variables with the same name and with different values, the `printf()` prints only the innermost variable, or the one *most local* to the `printf()`.

The scope resolution operator gives you a way to access global variables that have the same name as local variables. By preceding the variable with a scope resolution operator, you instruct C++ to access the global variable.

The only difference between the next program and the preceding one is the `printf()`. Notice that the second and third variables print the value of the global variable `avar`.

AVAR2.CPP. Program with four variables of the same name, all with different scopes.

```
// Filename: AVAR2.CPP
// Program with four variables of the same name,
// all having the same name but different scopes
#include <stdio.h>
int avar = 5;  // Global variable
void main()
{
   int avar = 10;  // Outer local variable
```

```
    {
       int avar = 20;   // Another local variable
       {

          int avar = 30;   // Still another
          printf("%d %d %d %d\n", avar,::avar,::avar,avar);

       }        // Innermost variable loses its scope

    }        // Second innermost variable loses its scope

}        // First local variable loses its scope and so does global
```

The output is the following:

```
30 5 5 30
```

There is no way to access the second and third `avar` variables, only the innermost local variable and the global variable. Although you should shy away from using the same name for two different variables, loop counter variables might be a useful place for them.

Accessing global variables is not really the primary purpose for the `::` operator. You will learn much more about its other uses as you tackle the OOP programs later in this book.

Use *const* and *inline* Functions Instead of *#define*

Now that you are moving from C to C++, resist the urge to use the `#define` preprocessor directive that is so common in C. `#define` gives names to constants (sometimes called *literals*). Suppose that you wrote a program that keeps track of profits. If your profit margin is .34, you have two choices: Either use .34 throughout the program, or `#define` it once at the top of the program with the following preprocessor directive:

```
#define MARGIN .34
```

From then on, you would use `MARGIN` instead of .34 everywhere in the program that you computed profits. If the profit margin percentage changes, you have to change only the one line that defines the constant instead of changing the number throughout the program. The `#define` also does no type checking. Whatever value `#define` defines gets replaced throughout the program without regard to proper type checking.

*const is better
than #define
when program-
ming constants
in C++.*

C++ programmers use `const` instead of `#define` for declaring constants and string literals. `const` reserves storage for data and makes the data read-only. (Current ANSI C compilers now support `const` as well.) To declare a constant with `const`, place `const` before a variable's definition, as in the following:

```
const int AGE_LIMIT = 18;
```

After its definition, the value does not change in the program. If you attempt to assign a value to a `const` variable after the variable is initialized, the compiler issues an error message. (You cannot assign `AGE_LIMIT` a value such as 21 in the middle of the program.) `const` also provides better type checking on the data, because a data type must precede the constant's name.

> Not all C++ programmers put constant names in uppercase letters. There is debate about the merits of using uppercase constant names. C programmers almost universally use uppercase characters for `#define` constant literals. Therefore, many C++ programmers use lowercase names for `const`, because `const` values have data types and can be used everywhere variables can be used except as *lvalues* (values that can change during program execution). The rest of this book uses lowercase names for `const` values.

Because of the heavy use of `const` in C++ programs (and in newer C programs that use `const`), programmers are beginning to call directly explicit data *literals* and data declared with `const` *constants*. Using this terminology, the data inside the quotation marks represents a string *literal*:

```
strcpy(message, "This is a string");
```

Furthermore, `message` is a string *constant* in this line of code:

```
const char message[] = "This is a string";
```

Always specify an initial value when declaring constants. The following is not allowed:

```
const float net_sales;   // Invalid
```

If you fail to initialize a constant in C, the compiler issues no error message. C initializes the constant with whatever value happens to be in memory at the time, which is unpredictable—any value could be in the constant. C++ does not initialize constants for you because too many errors appear when uninitialized constants creep into C programs. To make the preceding constant declaration valid in C++, put an initial value into `net_sales`, such as this:

```
const float net_sales = 2000.0;   // Valid
```

You should be able to see why constants require initial values. Because you can never change a constant after you declare it, you cannot assign a value to a constant after it is declared.

Constants for Declaring Arrays

Use const values for array subscripts when declaring arrays. The following section of code illustrates the use of const for array declarations:

```
main()
{
   const  int inv_limit = 1000;
   float sales[inv_limit];      // Not allowed in C
   int    quantity[inv_limit];  // Not allowed in C
// Rest of program follows
```

If the array limits change, you have to change only the constant's value instead of changing 1000 everywhere it appears in the program.

There is a const shortcut allowed by C that C++ still supports. If you do not specify a constant data type, C++ treats the constant as an integer literal. The following two constant declarations are the same:

```
const int age_limit = 18;
```

```
const age_limit = 18;   // C++ assumes integer
```

Despite this shorter method, modern programming practices are moving toward more readable code and away from tricky code that is difficult to maintain. Even though C++ enables you to specify integer constants without the int keyword, always include int to make clear your intentions for the integer constant.

From your C background, you know that #define defines macros as well as constants. The following program contains a macro defined with #define:

MACRO1.C. A C program with a macro that computes the cube of a number.

```c
/* Filename: MACRO1.C */
/* C program with a macro that
   computes the cube of a number */
#include <stdio.h>

#define CUBE(x) x*x*x

void main()
{
   int num, c_num;
   printf("Please type a number ");
   scanf(" %d", &num);

   c_num = CUBE(num);   /* Executes the macro */
   printf("\nThe cube of %d is %d\n", num, c_num);
}
```

Here is the output for this program:

```
Please type a number 3
The cube of 3 is 27
```

Although CUBE looks like a function, it is not one. Because #define is a preprocessor directive, the code for CUBE is substituted for the word CUBE in the body of the program. The next-to-last line in main() looks like this to the compiler:

```c
c_num = num*num*num;   /* Executes the macro */
```

Despite its widespread use in C, #define produces serious drawbacks at times. Suppose that you wanted to compute the cube of the user's number and the next two cubes in sequence. The following program appears to do just that:

MACRO1.CPP. A C++ program with an inline function that computes the cube of a number and its two cubes in sequence correctly.

```cpp
// Filename: MACRO1.CPP
// C++ program with an inline function that computes the cube
// of a number and its two cubes in sequence correctly
#include <stdio.h>

#define CUBE(x) x*x*x
```

```
void main()
{
   int num, c_num;
   printf("Please type a number ");
   scanf(" %d", &num);

   c_num = CUBE(num);      // Executes the macro
   printf("\nThe cube of %d is %d\n", num, c_num);
   c_num = CUBE(num+1);  // Cubes the next number
   printf("\nThe cube of %d is %d\n", num+1, c_num);
   c_num = CUBE(num+2);  // Cubes the next number
   printf("\nThe cube of %d is %d\n", num+2, c_num);
}
```

This program produces the following output:

```
Please type a number 3
The cube of 3 is 27
The cube of 4 is 10
The cube of 5 is 17
```

This output obviously is incorrect. The cube of 4 is *not* 10. #define preprocessor directives do nothing more than find and replace code. The line that attempts to calculate the cube of the user's number plus one looks like this to the compiler:

```
c_num = num+1*num+1*num+1;   /* Attempts to cube the next number */
```

Because multiplication has precedence over addition, the results do not compute correctly, as the output shows. Using #define forces you to think ahead about possible side effects and attempt to correct them before they occur. You can fix this problem by coding the #define as follows:

```
#define CUBE(x) (x)*(x)*(x)
```

The parentheses ensure that no matter what expression x happens to be, the multiplication will be performed accurately, cubing whatever is passed to the CUBE. Even though you can free #define from this precedence side effect using parentheses, you should not have to. C++ contains a new feature called *inline functions*. Inline functions offer advantages of defined macros without their side effects. The C++ compiler attempts to replace an inline function call with the code for the function. This eliminates function call overhead.

To turn a function into an inline function, place the inline keyword before the function name. The C++ compiler may choose to ignore your inline request (similar to the way C compilers do not have to honor your register requests). Reserve the use of inline

functions for small functions only, such as those three to five lines long. C++ compilers begin to ignore `inline` requests as functions get longer. Although there is no set limit, functions with 10 or more lines of code almost always compile as stand-alone functions whether or not you specify `inline`.

Most C++ compilers warn you if they cannot honor your `inline` function request.

Here is an example of the cube-calculation program using an inline function:

MACRO2.CPP. A C++ program with an inline function that computes the cube of a number and its two cubes in sequence correctly.

```
// Filename: MACRO2.CPP
// C++ program with an inline function that computes the cube
// of a number and its two cubes in sequence correctly
#include <stdio.h>

inline int cube(int x)
{
    return x*x*x;
}

void main()
{
    int num, c_num;
    printf("Please type a number ");
    scanf(" %d", &num);

    c_num = cube(num);   // Executes the macro
    printf("\nThe cube of %d is %d\n", num, c_num);
    c_num = cube(num+1);  // Cubes the next number
    printf("\nThe cube of %d is %d\n", num+1, c_num);
    c_num = cube(num+2);  // Cubes the next number
    printf("\nThe cube of %d is %d\n", num+2, c_num);
    return;
}
```

Because the compiler detects and compiles inline functions, it knows how to handle the function's arguments so that `#define`'s precedence problem is not a problem for `inline`

functions. Despite the appearance of this program, the compiler treats the cube() function call as an inline function, replacing the function call with the inline function's actual code. For instance, the last function call becomes

```
c_num = (num+2)*(num+2)*(num+2);
```

before the compiler compiles it. No function call actually takes place. Inline functions become very important when you begin object-oriented programming.

> Both const values and inline functions work with symbolic debuggers supplied with most C++ compilers, unlike #define constants and macros. Being able to debug the code interactively gives yet another reason to move toward the C++ standard and away from #define.

The more inline functions you have, the larger your compiled programs will be. If you have too many inline functions, the program's disk storage or loading time might become too great to justify advantages of regular function call overhead.

C++ ignores the inline designation for recursive functions. Recursive functions must be stand-alone functions.

Global Constants Have File Scope

Unlike C, global const values, those const values declared outside of functions, have file scope (sometimes called *internal linkage*) and cannot be referenced by other programs. If you separately compile several programs and then link them together into one module, you must use extern before the const declaration if you want other files to have access to one file's global const values. For example, in the following section of code:

GLOC1.CPP. Global constant value.

```
// Filename: GLOC1.CPP
#include <stdio.h>
```

continues

GLOC1.CPP. continued

```
const int part_max = 1500;   // Global constant value

main()
{
   // Rest of program follows
```

only this file, GLOC1.CPP, can use the part_max constant value. Any function in this file can refer to part_max because part_max is globally defined. However, other files linked to GLOC1.CPP cannot use part_max. Its use is limited to this file due to its file scope.

To make part_max global to any file linked to this one, you would have to precede the const definition with the extern keyword, in effect telling the compiler to give the constant *external linkage,* or scope outside the current file. Here is the revised program section with part_max defined for external linkage:

GLOC2.CPP. Global constant value with external linkage.

```
// Filename: GLOC2.CPP
#include <stdio.h>

extern const int part_max = 1500;   // Global constant value
                                    // with external linkage
main()
{
   // Rest of program follows
```

Another file linked to GLOC2.CPP could use the constant value part_max if it contained the following line:

```
extern const int part_max;   // Value defined elsewhere
```

C++ Prototyping

Prototype all C++ functions before they appear in your program. The only exception to this rule is main() (if it appears first in the program, as it should by convention) because main() is self-prototyping. That is, because no function calls main(), its declaration is all the prototype the compiler needs.

In C, sometimes you can get away without prototyping functions. Even the built-in C functions such as `printf()` usually work correctly if you do not prototype them. The following short program works on almost every C compiler:

CPRINTF.C. Demonstrates that no header file with prototypes is needed to use `printf()`.

```
/* Filename: CPRINTF.C */
/* Demonstrates that no header file with
   prototypes is needed to use printf(). */
main()
{
   printf("Here is a program without prototypes.");
}
```

Although this program works with C compilers, it would not work with C++ compilers. C++ compilers would issue an error because `printf()`'s prototype, appearing in stdio.h, does not appear in the program. C++ takes prototypes very seriously, and you cannot avoid them.

C is also more relaxed in its use of the function return type. If a function returns a value, you must declare that return value to the left of the function name in both C and C++. Here is a function that returns a floating-point value:

```
float CalcIt(int i, float y)
```

If you do not specify a return type, C and C++ assume `int`. Both of the following are equivalent:

```
int GetHours()
```

and

```
GetHours()
```

If a function does not return a value, you should precede the function name with `void`, as in

```
void GetHours()
```

C++ differs from C in the way it handles functions that do not return values. With C, if you declare that a function returns an integer value, preceding its name with `int` or leaving off the return type altogether gives you the option of returning an integer, or not returning an integer. The following program compiles and runs under regular C:

RETURN.C. C ignores the integer return type if you do not return a value.

```c
/* Filename: RETURN.C */
/* C ignores integer return type if
  you do not return a value. */
#include <stdio.h>
main()
{
   pr_it(5);  /* Calls a function and passes it 5 */
}

pr_it(int num)   /* Assumes that an integer */
{                /* value will be returned */
   printf("You passed %d\n", num);
   return;       /* !! Nothing is really returned */
}
```

C ignores integer return type declarations if you do not return a value. This program works identically if you completely remove the `return` statement. (Some C compilers issue a warning message, but they never consider the lack of return value an error.) You can *never* get away with such mismatches of return types in C++ programs. Because the `return` statement in the preceding program returns no value, C++ requires that you precede the function name with `void`, like this:

RETURN.CPP. C ignores the integer return type if you do not return a value.

```cpp
// Filename: RETURN.CPP
// C ignores integer return type if
// you do not return a value.
#include <stdio.h>
void pr_it(int num);
void main()
{
   pr_it(5);  // Calls a function and passes it 5
}

void pr_it(int num)   // Void required because function
{                     // returns nothing
   printf("You passed %d\n", num);
   return;            // Nothing was returned
}
```

The designers of C++ are attempting to make programmers less sloppy in their work. Prototypes protect you from potential errors and cut your debugging time by requiring explicit function parameters.

C++ and C also treat empty argument lists differently. When you leave out arguments from a C prototype, you leave an *unspecified argument list* in the prototype. In C, the following prototype with an unspecified argument list describes a function named fun1() that returns a long integer value:

```
long int fun1();  /* Prototype */
```

Nothing about this prototype defines the arguments passed *to* the function. Because no arguments are specified, this is an incomplete prototype; only the return value is stated. C does not care whether or not fun1() contains arguments. Both of the following C programs compile and run:

RETURN1.C. Shows how to return the doubled value.

```
/* Filename: RETURN1.C */
#include <stdio.h>
long int fun();  /* Notice no specified arguments */

void main()
{
   long int i;
   i = fun(2L);  /* Passes a long integer constant to fun() */
   printf("\ni is %d\n", i);  /* Prints the return value */
}

long int fun(long int n)
{
   return (n * 2L);  /* Returns the doubled value */
}
```

The next C program contains the identical fun() prototype as RETURN1.C, but sends it no arguments:

RETURN2.C. Shows the return.

```
/* Filename: RETURN2.C */
#include <stdio.h>
long int fun();  /* Notice no specified arguments */
```

continues

RETURN2.C. continued

```
void main()
{
   long int i;
   i = fun();  /* Passes nothing to fun() */
   printf("\ni is %d\n", i);  /* Prints the return value */
}

long int fun()
{
   return (2L);  /* Returns 2 */
}
```

C++ does not consider empty prototype argument lists *unspecified*. C++ acts as if you do not want any arguments passed when you fail to put arguments in a prototype, in effect treating empty argument lists the same as void. Both of these prototypes are the same in C++:

```
float MyFun1();  // Prototype with void arguments
```

and

```
float MyFun2(void);  // Prototype with void arguments specified
```

See if you can spot the error in the following C++ program:

RETURN1.CPP. Shows how to return the doubled value.

```
// Filename: RETURN1.CPP
#include <stdio.h>
long int fun();  // C++ assumes void

void main()
{
   long int i;
   i = fun(2L);  // Passes a long integer constant to fun()
   printf("\ni is %d\n", i);  // Prints the return value
}

long int fun(long int n)
{
   return (n * 2L);  // Returns the doubled value
}
```

34

Because the prototype for `fun()` contained no arguments, C++ assumes that no arguments will be passed to `fun()`. When `main()` passes the long integer literal 2L, C++ issues an error because the argument does not match the `void` prototype.

> If you want an unspecified argument list, you must use ellipses (...) in the prototype (this is also allowed in C). C++ then enables you to include any number and type of arguments in the function's final argument list. These kinds of unspecified argument lists are best reserved for variable argument lists in which you pass a different number of arguments to the function at different places in the program.

Summary

You now have a taste of the differences between C and C++. C++ is stricter than C, requiring more awareness of prototypes and argument lists. Along with this strictness, C++ offers safer programming conventions and quicker program development. If you are more attuned to your data types, your programs work more accurately and you spend less time debugging.

You can quickly spot C++ programs from their // comment styles. As you learn other C++ program elements, you will see that C++ programs can look quite different from C programs. One of the most important differences between C and C++ is C++'s use of operators for input and output. The functions such as `printf()` and `scanf()` go out the door, being replaced by more readable and more reliable I/O routines. Chapter 3, "Introduction to C++ Input and Output," explains the improved C++ input and output features.

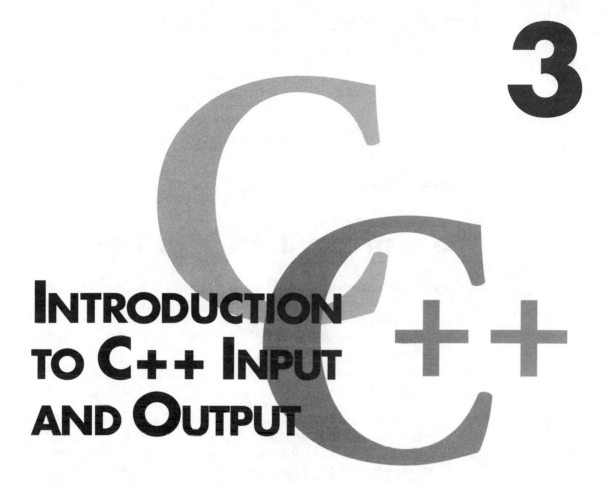

INTRODUCTION TO C++ INPUT AND OUTPUT

"I/O, I/O, it's off to work we go."

C++ programs almost universally use different input and output methods than regular C. There is nothing inherently wrong with printf(), scanf(), and all the other functions you are used to. As a matter of fact, all C++ compilers support the use of the stdio.h header file and the input/output functions and macros of C. When you begin writing more advanced C++ programs, especially when you begin using the object-oriented features of C++, you will find printf() and the other C functions lacking in their capability to supply the I/O you need.

This chapter introduces some of the C++ I/O features. As soon as you master some of the more advanced OOP concepts, you will be ready for additional I/O features.

In this chapter, you will learn about:

- The use of the iostream.h header file

- The advantages of C++ I/O objects cout, cin, cerr, and clog

- C++ I/O operators << and >>

- Manipulator formatting

The iostream.h Header File

C++ uses operators to perform standard input and output. To use C++ I/O operators, include the iostream.h header file. (This file is called stream.h in C++ compilers earlier than Version 2.0.) The iostream.h file does not contain prototypes for printf() and the other I/O functions. If you still want to use any of those, along with C++'s newer I/O operators, you still must include stdio.h.

Almost every C++ program contains the following #include preprocessor directive:

```
#include <iostream.h>
```

Use the iostream.h header file for C++ I/O.

The iostream.h file is more than just a header file with prototype declarations. The iostream.h file contains definitions for input, output, and error I/O data streams so that C++ knows how to route I/O. In C++ terminology, the file contains *class* descriptions. A class is a special compound data type in C++, similar to the struct with which you are already familiar. The details of classes are covered in later OOP chapters (see Part II, "Objects and Classes"). You do not have to understand the inner workings of classes of the iostream.h header file to become proficient at C++ standard input and output. Even if you never program with OOP techniques, the C++ I/O operators offer many advantages over C's I/O functions.

The biggest problem with the C standard I/O functions is their inability to work with objects you create, such as windows. printf() was designed many years ago when the two most common output devices were text screens and printers. With the graphical nature of I/O today, printf() just doesn't respect the new kinds of output you might want. Graphical environments are not the only reason for new I/O methods, either. printf() and the others fail to work with data the way your programs usually require. In the past, whenever you needed to print the contents of a structure, you had to write several lines of code to print the structure to the screen, printer, or any other output device.

Not only are the I/O functions more limited in C than they are in C++, but they are more difficult to use as well. You are about to see that the C++ style makes input and output much easier than using those printf() format codes you have used for so long.

The Objects *cin, cout, cerr,* and *clog*

There's that word—*objects.* The same as the "object" in "object-oriented programming." cin, cout, cerr, and clog are examples of C++ objects. Rest assured that you don't have to know anything about C++ objects, or OOP, to use cin, cout, and the others. The only reason you're learning that these are objects now, instead of in the later OOP chapters, is that there is no other label for them. Just as printf() is a function and while is a keyword, cin is an object. Now that you know what it is called, you will see how easy it and the other I/O objects are to use.

Table 3.1 shows the I/O objects, their default devices, and their descriptions.

Table 3.1. C++ I/O objects.

Object Name	Default Device	C Equivalent	Description
cin	Keyboard	stdin	Standard input device
cout	Screen	stdout	Standard output device
cerr	Screen	stderr	Standard error device
clog	Screen	none	Standard error device (buffered)

If you do nothing special to redirect these objects, their input or output comes from or goes to the keyboard and screen. As with C's standard input and output devices, you can redirect the I/O to other devices from your operating system or from within a C++ program. C++ programmers use cin and cout much more often than they use the other two.

Generally, C++ programmers rarely use the cerr error device. When an error occurs, such as a bad disk read or a printer fault, you want to see the error message immediately. The unbuffered error device cerr ensures that you see the error message immediately, whereas clog buffers error messages and displays them later, sometimes too late.

These I/O objects make much more sense when you combine them with the C++ stream operators described in the next section.

The Stream Operators << and >>

<< *is the insert operator and* >> *is the extractor operator.*

The two operators (<< and >>) are called the *insert* operator and the *extractor* operator, respectively. You have seen these operators before, but they were not I/O operators. << and >> are bitwise shift operators, and are still available as bitwise shift operators in C++. They perform double duty in C++, and because they do, they are called *overloaded operators*. Overloading is a fancy name given to operators (and functions, as you will see in Chapter 5, "C++ Function Advantages") that do two or more different things. C++ knows from the context of the operator's arguments (the values on either side of the operator) when to perform bitwise shifting and when to perform input and output.

When you combine >> and << with cin and cout, input and output occur. The following examples show that the insert and extractor operators are very easy to use.

<< and >> are Flexible

<< and >> work with all the standard data types such as char, int, and float. Later you learn how to perform input and output on your own aggregate data types such as structures. One of the most important advantages of cout and cin is that they work with *any* data type, including ones you create, unlike printf() and scanf(), which work only with built-in data types.

Using the Insert Operator

Here is a simple C program that prints a message to the screen:

CPRINT.C. Prints a string to the screen.

```
/* Filename: CPRINT.C */
/* Prints a string to the screen. */
#include <stdio.h>
void main()
{
 int years = 4;
 char mesg[] = "I want to learn C++\n";
 printf("I've known C for %d years. %s", years, mesg);
}
```

The printf() in this program contains two format characters: %d for the integer years and %s for the character string mesg. Without the format characters, printf() does not know the data types of the items you want to print. Therefore, you have to specify the data type of your data twice: once when you declare it and once when you print it so that printf() knows how to print the data.

Because C++ uses operators to perform I/O, not functions, the operators already know the data type of the data they are printing. Therefore, you do not have to tell the C++ compiler the data type of everything you print. Here is the equivalent C++ program (notice the use of the iostream.h header file instead of stdio.h):

CPRINT.CPP. Prints a string to the screen.

```
// Filename: CPRINT.CPP
// Prints a string to the screen.
#include <iostream.h>
void main()
{
 int years = 4;
 char mesg[] = "I want to learn C++\n";
 cout << "I've known C for " << years << " years. " << mesg;
}
```

This program produces the following output:

```
I've known C for 4 years. I want to learn C++
```

Study the line with the cout << code. You probably can see at a glance how to use cout and <<. Because cout is the screen object unless you reroute it (people rarely do), the output stream goes to the screen. Think of cout as actually being another name for your screen. (This is why cout is called an object. It closely represents a real-world object.) The << insert operator is *inserting* something into the cout object, or sending something to the screen. The remaining << and data values go to the screen as well. Notice the embedded newline character (\n) inside the last string printed. C++ recognizes all of C's control codes, such as \t, \r, and \a.

The cout screen device (object) knows that years and mesg are variables, an integer and a character array respectively. Therefore, they print correctly. Taking this one step further, the following C++ program correctly prints several different types of variables:

CVALPRNT.CPP. Prints several different types of values with <<.

```cpp
// Filename: CVALPRNT.CPP
// Prints several different types of values with <<.
#include <iostream.h>
void main()
{
 char c = 'C';
 char cara[] = "A message.";
 int i=95;
 long int l = 92343;
 float x=22.619;
 double d = 3.14159;

 cout << "c is " << c << '\n';
 cout << "cara[] is " << cara << '\n';
 cout << "i is " << i << '\n';
 cout << "l is " << l << '\n';
 cout << "x is " << x << '\n';
 cout << "d is " << d << '\n';
}
```

Although this program prints six different types of data, no formatting characters exist. C++ correctly outputs the following:

```
c is C
cara[] is A message.
i is 95
l is 92343
x is 22.618999
d is 3.14159
```

Although the double floating-point variable x printed with a little rounding problem, C++ performed the output well. There are ways to control rounding precision with cout, as you learn later in this chapter.

Using the Extractor Operator

The extractor operator is as easy for input as the insert operator is for output. Instead of inserting to the output device, you extract values from the input device (typically, the keyboard). You can throw the drawbacks of scanf() out the door—no more format characters or & operators before your input variables. Here is a C program that uses scanf() and gets() for input:

COLDIN.C. Inputs values from the keyboard.

```
/* Filename: COLDIN.C */
/* Inputs values from the keyboard. */
#include <stdio.h>
void main()
{
 char name[25];
 int age;
 float salary;

 printf("What is your name? ");
 gets(name);
 printf("How old are you? ");
 scanf(" %d", &age);
 printf("How much do you make? ");
 scanf(" %f", &salary);
}
```

This program asks for three values of three different data. The same C++ program, using cout and cin, appears as follows:

CIN.CPP. Inputs values from the keyboard.

```
// Filename: CIN.CPP
// Inputs values from the keyboard.
#include <iostream.h>
void main()
{
 char name[25];
 int age;
 float salary;

 cout << "What is your name? ";
 cin >> name;
 cout << "How old are you? ";
 cin >> age;
 cout << "How much do you make? ";
 cin >> salary;
}
```

The C++ version is much cleaner. You can glance through the code and feel the cout and cin objects receiving and sending data values and strings.

As with `scanf()`, `cin >>` can get only strings that contain no white space (spaces, newlines, or tabs).

The direction of the `<<` and `>>` operators, and the names `cin` and `cout`, tell you whether input or output is being performed. You also can input several values at once using a single line of code. The following line inputs three values from the standard input device (the keyboard):

```
cin >> num1 >> num2 >> num3;   // Gets three values
```

The user has to type only a space, tab, or newline between each value entered to fill `num1`, `num2`, and `num3` with values.

As with most of the input functions you are familiar with, `cin >>` has no control over what the user actually types. If you ask for an integer and the user types a double floating-point value, the resulting value is bad because a double does not fit in an integer. Make sure that the user understands, through ample output messages before each input, what the program expects.

`<<` and `>>` indicate the direction data flows. You can see the direction of the data, either to the output device (specified by the `cout` object) or from the input device (the `cin` object).

Displaying Errors

Use the `cerr` object for error messages. (As discussed earlier in this chapter, the buffered version of `cerr`, named `clog`, rarely is used by today's programmers. `cerr` is much quicker to respond and is more reliable with extreme errors.) If the user reroutes the standard input and output to other devices, you want your program's errors to still appear on the user's screen (called the *console* in this context).

For instance, the user might want to read values from a data file and send them to the printer. As you know from C, you can redirect standard input and output at the operating system level. PCs and UNIX-based computer programmers use the operating system's `<` and `>` redirection symbols, and mainframe programmers use JCL to accomplish device redirection. Sending errors to `cerr` ensures that the messages get to the user's screen instead of going to the datafile along with the other standard output by mistake.

To send an error message to the cerr object (the screen), you only have to replace cout with cerr, like this:

```
cerr << "Danger! That file has no backup!\n";
```

Formatting with Manipulators

Even though C++ I/O does not require format characters to describe the data types, you might want to control the way data values are printed. To format I/O data, select from any of the several *manipulators* offered by C++. Table 3.2 shows some of the more common C++ manipulators.

Table 3.2. C++ I/O manipulators.

Manipulator	Description
Numeric Base Manipulators	
dec	Decimal output (base 10)
hex	Hexadecimal conversion of output (base 16)
oct	Octal conversion of output (base 8)
Character Control Manipulators	
endl	Sends a newline and flushes the buffer
ends	Inserts a null character (\0) into the stream
flush	Flushes the buffer
Format Control Manipulators	
resetiosflags(*long*)	Resets effect of setiosflags(*long*)

continues

Table 3.2. continued

Manipulator	Description
setprecision(*int*)	Specifies the digits of floating-point precision
setiosflags(*format flag*)	Sets the output format to the *format flag*'s value (See Table 3.3 for a listing of available *format flag*s)
setw(*int*)	Sets field widths to a specific value

To use these manipulators, you must insert them within the I/O stream. Most are used almost exclusively for controlling output. The following sections describe the three sets of manipulators and how to use them.

Some C++ compilers, such as Borland C++ and Microsoft C++, support several more manipulators. Check your compiler's documentation for compiler-specific manipulators that might be available on your system.

Numeric Base Manipulators

With the base manipulators, you can print integer and character values in their decimal, hexadecimal, or octal representations. Because the default is decimal, you only have to specify dec if you used another base and want to revert to decimal.

To print the value of 192 in three bases, you only have to insert the manipulators inside the output stream, like this:

```
cout << 192 << '\n';          // Default is decimal

cout << hex << 192 << '\n';   // Prints the value in hex

cout << oct << 192 << '\n';   // Prints the value in octal

cout << dec << 192 << '\n';   // Reverts to decimal
```

These lines produce the following output:

192

c0

300

192

The base you set remains active for all future couts until you send a different base through the output stream. The following section of code prints three hexadecimal numbers, even though hex is specified on the first one only:

```
cout << hex << 192 << '\n';
cout << 192 << '\n';
cout << 192 << '\n';
```

Manipulators usually remain in effect until you specify another one.

Even if you print with cout in different functions, C++ remembers the previous manipulator. Unlike the printf()'s %x format code, the hex manipulator remains in effect until another appears in the program or until the program ends. In the next program, a hexadecimal 192 (c0) prints five times. The function pr_it() is aware that main() sets the output hexadecimal manipulator.

MANIP1.CPP. Demonstrates the long-term effect of conversion manipulators.

```
// Filename: MANIP1.CPP
// Demonstrates the long-term effect of conversion manipulators.

#include <iostream.h>
void pr_it(); // Prototype

void main()
{
 cout << hex << 192 << '\n';  // Sets the manipulator once
 cout << 192 << '\n';  // Still prints in hex
 pr_it();
 cout << 192 << '\n';  // Still prints in hex
}

void pr_it()
{
 cout << 192 << '\n';  // Still prints in hex
}
```

Base Manipulators with Input

If you need to receive input in hex or octal, you can insert a base conversion manipulator in the input stream like this:

```
cin >> oct >> var;   // Expects an octal value
```

This line expects an octal number. If the user types a valid octal number, that number is stored in var. If the user types an invalid octal number, such as 882, var does not change. If the user types an octal number followed by something that is not octal, such as 23&, C++ puts only the octal value up to the bad character into var.

Character Control Manipulators

The character control manipulators work on the output stream to control behavior of the output. endl and ends send a newline and a null character, respectively, to the buffer. endl also flushes the buffer. Although some output streams, such as a line printer's output buffer, are automatically flushed when you send a newline, a newline does not always guarantee a flush. Therefore, use endl and not '\n' whenever you need to ensure a flush of the output buffer after a newline. The following line prints a message, a newline, and flushes the buffer:

```
cout << "Learning C++ is fun!" << endl;
```

The flush manipulator flushes the output buffer. When the standard output is directed to a line printer, flush helps ensure that the output is sent right away and is not buffered with successive output. Programmers use flush to flush an output stream to which a newline character has not yet been sent. The following two sections of a program are equivalent:

```
cout << "Learning C++ is fun!" << endl;
```

and

```
cout << "Learning C++ is fun!" << '\n';
```

```
cout << flush;
```

Use ends when you want to send a null character to an output stream. Because strings always end with null terminating characters, you do not normally need to send null characters to screens and printers. However, for output streams routed to a disk or a modem, you might have need for the ends. (ends is exactly the same as sending '\0' to an output device.) The following line of code sends some numbers, separated with a null

character, to the output stream:

```
cout << 12.4 << ends << 25.9 << ends << 100 << ends << endl;
```

Format Control Manipulators

The remaining manipulators from Table 3.2 require an additional header file included at the top of each C++ program. Therefore, most C++ programs that perform I/O contain the following two directives:

```
#include <iostream.h>
#include <iomanip.h>
```

The setw() and setprecision() manipulators control the width and precision of printed data. setw() determines how wide a field the data prints in. For example, without setw(), the following output statements print three numbers next to each other.

```
cout << 50;
```

```
cout << 60;
```

```
cout << 70;
```

The output appears below.

```
506070
```

Without a setw() manipulator, C++ supplies only as much width for each value as the output requires. The following section of code ensures that each value prints within a width of 10 spaces on the screen (eight spaces apart from each other).

```
cout << setw(10);  // Sets the width of the next data item
```

```
cout << 50;
```

```
cout << setw(10);
```

```
cout << 60;
```

```
cout << setw(10);
```

```
cout << 70;
```

The only problem with setw() is that C++ resets the width of each field after each one. setw() is the only manipulator that does not "remember" its former state. The next section of code produces the same results as the last. Notice that even though all the values print using the same cout object, three setw(10)s are required to ensure that each value prints within fields of 10 spaces.

setw() is the only manipulator that resets after each value input or output.

49

```
cout << setw(10) << 50 << setw(10) << 60 << setw(10) << 70;
```

setw() is a good way to print columns of data. Because each field of data prints within a fixed number of spaces, with blanks used as padding in the remaining spaces, the data prints in evenly-spaced columns. (Many C++ compilers have ways to change the pad character from a space to something else.) C compilers require that *each* printf() format character contains the width specifier. To print three values in a 10-character field width in C, you have to code this:

```
printf("%10f %10f %10f", x, y, z);
```

If the value is larger than the width you supply, C++ ignores the setw() setting. The following line prints 1234 even though setw() is set for a width of 2.

```
cout << setw(2) << 1234;   // Correctly prints 1234
```

By default, numeric values are right-justified within the setw() field and character data is left-justified. Even though the following setw()s specify widths of 10 spaces each, the numeric and character values are justified differently within each field of 10 spaces.

```
cout << setw(10) << 45 << endl;
```

```
cout << setw(10) << "ab" << endl;
```

These two lines produce the following output:

```
        45
```

```
ab
```

setprecision() determines how many digits of precision print. setprecision() is especially useful for floating-point values to limit the number of decimal places printed. Consider the following two lines of code:

```
cout << 3.14159 << endl;
cout << setprecision(3) << 3.14159 << endl;
```

The output appears as the following:

```
3.14159
```

```
3.142
```

Use setprecision() to round the output to the number of decimal places you specify in the parentheses.

Precision Default

If you do not specify a precision with setprecision(), C++ prints six decimal digits to the right of a decimal point. (This is the same default for the %f format character in C as well.) If the number contains more than six decimal places, the seventh digit is rounded up to make the six positional digits.

If you have changed the precision with setprecision() and you want to revert the precision to its default number of places, you can use either of the following statements:

```
cout << setprecision(0);  // Resets to the default  six
                          //  places
```

and

```
cout << setprecision(6); // Sets to the default  six
                         //  places
```

The remaining two manipulators mentioned in Table 3.2, setiosflags() and resetiosflags(), each perform one of several possible I/O manipulations, depending on the arguments you place within their parentheses. The arguments are called *format flags*. Table 3.3 shows the commonly used arguments for these manipulators. The names of the format flags look strange, and they all contain the scope resolution operator ::. For now, just look at their descriptions; you do not have to understand their relationship to the scope resolution operator. As you learn more about OOP concepts, the meaning of the format flags' contents will become clearer.

Table 3.3. C++ format flags for iostream.h.

Format Flag Name	Description
ios::left	Left-justifies output within the width set with setw()
ios::right	Right-justifies output within the width set with setw()
ios::scientific	Formats numbers in scientific notation
ios::fixed	Formats numbers in regular decimal format
ios::dec	Formats numbers in base 10

continues

Table 3.3. continued

Format Flag Name	Description
ios::hex	Formats numbers in base 16
ios::oct	Formats numbers in base 8
ios::uppercase	Formats all characters in hexadecimal and scientific notation numbers (such as 93.E+04) in uppercase
ios::showbase	Forces output of numbers to include a base prefix (0x for hexadecimal and 0 for octal numbers)
ios::showpos	Outputs a positive sign, +, when printing positive numbers

You can use any of the format flags in the setiosflags() to activate them, or use them in the resetiosflags() to cancel them. Some are alternatives to the other manipulators you saw earlier. The following program uses each of the format flags to illustrate their use. You can do even more with manipulators and format flags as soon as you learn about OOP.

FLAGS.CPP. Uses each of the format flags.

```cpp
// Filename: FLAGS.CPP
// Uses each of the format flags.
#include <iostream.h>
#include <iomanip.h>
void main()
{
 int i = 193;
 float x = 75.92;

 // Left-justifies numbers within a field
 cout << setw(10) << setiosflags(ios::left) << i << '\n';
 // Right-justifies numbers within a field
 cout << setw(10) << setiosflags(ios::right) << i << '\n';

 // Prints number in scientific notation
 // (right-justification is still active)
 cout << setiosflags(ios::scientific) << x << '\n';
 // Reverts to regular fixed-decimal format
 cout << setiosflags(ios::fixed) << x << '\n';

 // Prints in hexadecimal, octal, and decimal
 cout << setiosflags(ios::hex) << i << '\n';
 cout << setiosflags(ios::oct) << i << '\n';
```

```
cout << setiosflags(ios::dec) << i << '\n';

// Prints hex and scientific numbers with uppercase letters
cout << setiosflags(ios::hex);
cout << setiosflags(ios::uppercase);
cout << setiosflags(ios::scientific) << x << '\n';
cout << i << '\n';
// Resets the scientific to fixed
cout << resetiosflags(ios::fixed);

// Shows the base of the number
cout << setiosflags(ios::showbase) << i << '\n';
// Resets hex to decimal
cout << resetiosflags(ios::hex);

// Displays positive sign
cout << setiosflags(ios::showpos) << i << ' ' << x << '\n';
}
```

The program's output follows. Study the output as you trace through the program to make sure you understand the results of the various format flags.

```
193
        193
7.592e+01
75.919998
c1
301
193
7.592E+01
C1
0XC1
+193 +75.919998
```

As soon as you set a format flag with setiosflags(), you can reset it by either issuing a resetiosflags() with the same format flag or setting the opposite condition with setiosflags(). For example, suppose that you change the output base to hexadecimal for some output, but then decide that you want to see decimal again. Both of the following statements revert the output stream to decimal:

```
cout << setiosflags(dec);  // Back to decimal
```

and

```
cout << resetiosflags(hex);  // Back to decimal
```

Combining Format Flags

Writing so many setiosflags() on so many lines in FLAGS.CPP gets cumbersome in programs with lots of output. Each of the format flags has an associated value that enables you to combine two or more flags with the ¦ operator (the bitwise OR operator).

For example, suppose that you want to set output for uppercase hexadecimal left-justification. You can use all three flags in three separate setiosflags(), like this:

```
cout << setiosflags(ios::uppercase);
cout << setiosflags(ios::hex);
cout << setiosflags(ios::left);
```

Or you can combine them in a single setiosflags(), like this:

```
cout << setiosflags(ios::uppercase ¦ ios::hex ¦ ios::left);
```

You also can reset several format flags at once by combining them with ¦ inside a resetiosflags() manipulator.

Summary

The C++ style of I/O is no more difficult than C's printf() and other I/O functions. They are, however, very different and take a little getting used to. Although each compiler comes with its own set of extended manipulators, the ones presented in this chapter are the most common and the most helpful for the first-time C++ programmer.

The rest of this book uses the I/O features you read about in this chapter. Throughout this book, you will see the I/O extended even further. There is much more you can do with the I/O objects, << and >> operators, and manipulators. As you will soon see, not only can C++ output built-in data types, but cout << and cin >> can output and input your own data types as well, including complete structures that you define.

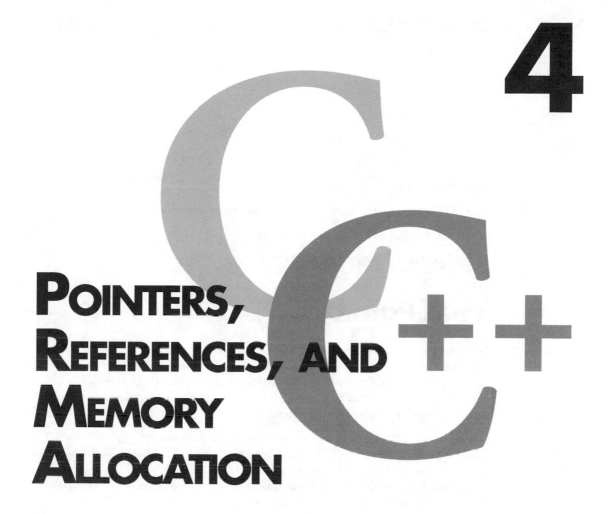

POINTERS, REFERENCES, AND MEMORY ALLOCATION

"You have a point."

C++ handles pointers and dynamic memory allocation in several ways that are different from regular C. Although C outshines other programming languages with its ease of pointer manipulation, C++ takes this ease one step further—it adds power *and* simplicity to pointers and dynamic memory allocation.

Several pointer and memory techniques you use in C are merely "workarounds." For example, to pass an integer by address, you have to precede the variable with an ampersand (&) everywhere it appears in the receiving function. To dynamically allocate memory for data, you have to call a built-in function, such as `malloc()`, typecasting values and supplying extra arguments. C++ offers extended memory features that better implement the usage of some pointers and memory allocation.

In this chapter, you will learn about:

- void pointer usage

- How to declare reference pointers

- Alias names for data

- References, pointers, and constants

- Declaring structures and enumerated data types

- The new and delete memory operators

- Exception handling of allocation errors

void Pointers

Although current ANSI C supports the use of void pointers, you may not be very familiar with them. void pointers were not implemented in early versions of C, but they have been around for a few years. void pointers play an important role in C++, even more important than in C. Just to refresh your memory before moving on to the C++ pointer specifics, this section presents a review of void pointers.

A void pointer is a pointer variable that can point to any data type.

Some novice C programmers mistakenly believe that a void pointer is a pointer to nothing, or to a zero or null value. void pointers can point to any value, but more important, they can point to data of any data type. When you declare a void pointer variable, that variable can point to integers, floating-points, or any of the other built-in data types. void pointers can point to your own data types as well, such as structure variables you create.

To declare a void pointer variable, precede the variable name with void *. You can declare global or local void pointers, depending on where you declare them. Here are three declarations for void pointers named ptr1, ptr2, and ptr3:

```
void* ptr1;  // Declares three void pointers
void * ptr2;
void *ptr3;
```

Notice that the location of spaces does not matter. Some programmers feel that the third style is not as clear as the first because it appears that the asterisk might be part of the variable name, and an asterisk cannot appear in a variable name. Perhaps even more important, the first two styles work in function prototypes, as in the following:

```
int  fun1(char *);
float fun2(float *, int *);
```

The location of the asterisk is a style issue, so use whatever form you feel most comfortable with.

You cannot declare a regular pointer and then make it point to a variable of a different type unless the pointer is a `void` pointer. For example, the following statement declares an integer variable and a floating-point pointer:

```
int  ivar=58;  // Defines an integer variable
float * point; // Defines a floating-point pointer
```

The floating-point pointer variable can point *only to floating-point values.* You could never do the following:

```
point = &ivar;  // INVALID
```

The compiler would keep this program from running because a pointer of one type cannot point to a variable of another type.

The rules change, however, when you make a `void` pointer point to a variable. Because `void` pointers can point to any data type, you are free to assign them to any variable's address. The following shows a `void` pointer being assigned the address of an integer variable, and a `void` pointer being assigned the address of a floating-point variable.

```
int  ivar=58;
float fvar = 12.34;

void * ptr1;  // Declares two void pointers
void * ptr2;

ptr1 = &ivar;  // No problem
ptr2 = &fvar;  // No problem
```

You also can assign pointers of specific data types to `void` pointers, as shown here:

```
int  ivar = 58;  // Defines an integer variable
int * iptr = &ivar;  // Makes the integer pointer point to ivar
void * vptr = ivar;  // The void pointer also points to ivar
```

You can assign the value of any pointer to a `void` pointer, but you cannot assign the value of a `void` pointer to a typed pointer. In other words, the following is not allowed:

```
iptr = vptr;  // INVALID
```

unless you typecast the `void` pointer first, like this:

```
iptr = int(vptr);  // Okay
```

References

References are new kinds of C++ variables. They act like pointers in some respects, but references take the concept of pointers even further than C did. You may already be familiar with the & operator; & is the "address of" operator and the bitwise AND operator. The & is overloaded further in C++ so that it can designate reference variables. To create a reference variable, put an & before its name when you declare it.

You must initialize all reference variables when you declare them. From then on, the reference variable acts like the value references. Because of the & before the reference name, you do not have to precede the variable being referenced with an &. Here is an example of a reference variable, ref1, being defined:

```
int ivar = 58;

int & ref1 = ivar;  // Notice that ivar needs no & here
```

References are aliases for other variables.

References are alternative names for values and variables. In the preceding lines of code, ref1 points to the contents of ivar, in effect making ref1 an *alias* for ivar. Figure 4.1 shows ref1 in memory. As soon as it is defined, changing ivar changes ref1, and vice versa. The address of ref1 is the same address as ivar's.

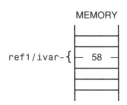

Figure 4.1. The variable names ref1 *and* ivar *refer to the very same memory location.*

The next program shows the relationship between a reference alias and its associated variable:

REF1.CPP. Shows similarities between references and variables.

```
// Filename: REF1.CPP
// Shows similarities between references and variables.
#include <iostream.h>
void main()
```

```
{
  int ivar = 10;  // Simple integer variable
  int & iref = ivar;  // Reference to ivar

  ivar++;
  cout << "ivar is now " << ivar << "\n";
  cout << "iref is now " << iref << "\n\n";  // Don't use &

  ivar++;  // Increments both again
  cout << "ivar is now " << ivar << "\n";
  cout << "iref is now " << iref << "\n\n";  // Don't use &
}
```

Here is the output from this program:

```
ivar is now 11
iref is now 11

ivar is now 12
iref is now 12
```

Both the reference variable iref and the regular integer variable ivar refer to the same memory location. iref is not a constant pointer because you can change its value. However, you cannot make iref point to *any value other than* ivar. The next program is similar to the last one, except that it contains an additional integer variable, ivar2. As the output shows, assigning iref to the value of the second variable is the same as assigning ivar1 the value as well.

REF2.CPP. Shows similarities between references and variables.

```
// Filename: REF2.CPP
// Shows similarities between references and variables.
#include <iostream.h>
void main()
{
  int ivar1 = 10;  // Simple integer variables
  int ivar2 = 20;
  int & iref = ivar1;  // Reference to ivar

  cout << "ivar1 is " << ivar1 << "\n";
  cout << "ivar2 is " << ivar2 << "\n";
  cout << "iref is " << iref << "\n\n";
```

continues

REF2.CPP. continued

```
ivar1++;
cout << "After ivar1++: \n";
cout << "ivar1 is now " << ivar1 << "\n";
cout << "iref is now " << iref << "\n\n";  // Don't use &

iref=ivar2;  // iref and ivar1 BOTH contain value of ivar2

cout << "After iref=ivar2: \n";
cout << "ivar1 is now " << ivar1 << "\n";
cout << "iref is now " << iref << "\n\n";  // Don't use &
}
```

The output from this program further shows the close relationship between ivar1 and its reference.

```
ivar1 is 10
ivar2 is 20
iref is 10

After ivar1++:
ivar1 is now 11
iref is now 11

After iref=ivar2:
ivar1 is now 20
iref is now 20
```

Unlike with pointer variables, you cannot dereference a reference variable. Nowhere in the previous program could you use *iref, and you do not have to. iref is the value of ivar1. You would have to precede iref with an asterisk if it were an ordinary pointer variable and you wanted the value to which it pointed.

Reference variables are not exactly the same as pointer variables. With pointer variables, you have a distinct variable that holds the address of another variable. You can change the address in the pointer variable (making the pointer point elsewhere) or change the value to which the pointer variable points. Figure 4.2 shows the difference between a reference variable and a pointer variable and illustrates how the following data resides in memory:

```
int dataval = 65;       // Regular variable
int * ptr = &dataval;   // Pointer variable to dataval
int & ref = dataval;    // Reference to dataval
```

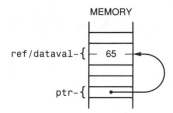

Figure 4.2. The pointer variable ptr *points to* dataval, *which holds 65. The reference variable* ref *is an alias to* dataval.

You can reference numeric values as well as variables. The next program creates a reference to the value 10. The reference is a pointer to the value 10 until the program changes iref.

REF3.CPP. References a value.

```
// Filename: REF3.CPP
// References a value.
#include <iostream.h>
void main()
{
  int & iref = 10;   // Reference to a value

  cout << "iref is " << iref << "\n\n";

  iref++;   // Changes the value of the reference

  cout << "After iref++: \n";
  cout << "iref is " << iref << "\n";
}
```

Here is the output:

```
iref is 10

After iref++:
iref is 11
```

References eliminate the need for complicated pointers to pointers. You can now create a reference to a pointer instead of using the cumbersome notation that pointers to pointers caused you in C.

Constants and Pointers

You can apply the `const` keyword to pointers, turning those pointers into pointer constants. Bringing constants into the picture, however, adds a few subtleties of which you should be aware.

For example, as soon as you declare a constant value, you cannot change that constant. This is nothing new. After the definition

```
const float normal_temp = 98.6;
```

you cannot assign `normal_temp` a different value by trying this:

```
normal_temp = 100.0;  // INVALID
```

Although it is not as obvious, you cannot change a constant with an indirect pointer variable either. The C++ compiler knows that constants cannot be changed, so it does not enable you to take the address of a constant, as the following code attempts to do:

```
const float normal_temp = 98.6;  // Okay so far
float * fp;  // Declares a floating-point variable

fp = &normal_temp;  // INVALID! C++ will not allow it
```

If C++ enabled you to declare a pointer to a constant value, you could change the constant by dereferencing the pointer, like this:

```
*fp = 50.0;  // Causes havoc if allowed; can't change constants
```

Clarifying Pointers, References, and Constants

Constants and pointers add a layer of complexity that you might not notice at first. You might hear the words *constants, pointers, references, constant pointers, pointer constants,* and *references to constants* thrown around casually, but each refers to a specific type. Four possibilities can result from constants, references, and pointers:

- Pointers to constants

- Constant pointers

- Constant pointers to constant values

- References to constants

The following is a pointer to a constant named val:

```
const float * val;
```

You can change the address stored in val because val is a pointer variable. There is nothing wrong with

```
val = &a_float;
```

but you cannot do this:

```
*val = 125.0;   // INVALID
```

because C++ knows that val points only to constant values.

The following is an example of a constant pointer:

```
float a_float = 85.12;
float * const val = &a_float;   // You cannot change val
```

You can change the value where val points, as in

```
*val = 100.0;
```

but you cannot change the value in val because val is a constant:

```
val = &another_float;   // INVALID
```

Here is an example of a constant pointer to a constant value:

```
const float a_float = 55.55;   // Now assigns the constant ptr
const float const * val = &a_float;   // to the constant
```

val is a constant pointer to a constant value named a_float. You can neither change the constant like this:

```
a_float = 100.0;   // INVALID
```

nor dereference the constant pointer's value like this:

```
*val = 123.45;   // INVALID
```

There is a way to declare a read-only reference alias and still allow the variable referenced to be changed. Consider the following code:

A reference to a constant is a read-only alias.

```
float value = 85.25;   // Regular floating-point variable
const float & ref = value;   // Reference is a constant
```

value is a regular floating-point variable. The program could change value like this:

```
value = 12.3 * .04;   // Okay
```

but you could not change ref, even though they both refer to the same memory location. ref is a read-only alias, or a reference to a constant. This is not allowed:

```
ref = 12.3 * .04;   // INVALID
```

Avoid Aliases

Do not insert lots of aliases to variables in your code. Aliases add complexity and detract from a program's readability. It is too easy to think that the alias is a variable separate from its reference. Confusion builds when you have two or more names for the same data value, scattered throughout code with lots of other variable names.

References have extremely useful purposes, especially in function argument lists. This chapter seeks to describe references and their relationships to pointers and other variables. It is easy to understand reference variables when you see them acting as aliases for other variables, but aliases are not their primary purpose. Now that you understand references, you are ready to tackle their use in the more advanced C++ programs starting in the next chapter.

Structures and Enumerated Data Types

In C, you can declare a structure with the following statement:

```
struct nameadr {
  char name[30];
  int age;
  float salary;
};
```

To define a structure variable, you must list the `struct` keyword, along with the structure tag `nameadr`, as follows:

```
struct nameadr person;   /* A single struct variable */
struct nameadr people[100];   /* An array of 100 struct variables */
```

`nameadr` is a user-defined data type. `nameadr` is not an integer, nor is it a character variable, nor even an aggregate data type such as an array. `nameadr` is a data type that looks like a character array followed by an integer followed by a floating-point value. Because C has no built-in data type `nameadr`, the user must define one—hence the term *user-defined data type*.

Having to repeat the `struct` keyword adds redundancy. C programmers often resort to the `typedef` keyword to define the new data type to the compiler. Here is the way `typedef` helps eliminate the repeated `struct` keyword:

```
typedef struct {
  char name[30];
  int age;
  float salary;
} nameadr;
```

Once you define the type to C, you can define the structure variables without `struct`:

```
nameadr person;   /* A single struct variable */
nameadr people[100];   /* An array of 100 struct variables */
```

C++ supports the definitions of `person` and `people` as defined with or without the `typedef` usage. However, C++ goes one step further than regular C. (It seems as if C++ earns its title: Because ++ is the increment operator, C++ is an incremental step ahead of C.) C++ recognizes user-defined data types. As soon as you declare a special data type such as a structure (or a union or an enumerated data type), C++ remembers that data type. You never need the `struct` keyword again if you define variables of a structure declared earlier. For example, to declare the `person` and `people` variables in C++, you do only this:

```
struct nameadr {
  char name[30];
  int age;
  float salary;
};

nameadr person;   // A single struct variable
nameadr people[100];   // An array of 100 struct variables
```

In C++ terminology, these statements create *instances* of the structure variables without the need for `struct`. C++ recognizes enumerated constant definitions and unions just as easily. Here are two C-style enum and union definitions:

```
enum color {   /* Declares the enumerated constant */
  black, blue, green, red, yellow, white
};

enum color light1, light2, light3;   /* Variables that take
                                         on the enum values */

union bitflags {   /* Declares the union data type */
  int i1;
  int i2;
  float f1;
};

union bitflags memory1, memory2;   /* Defines two union variables */
```

Of course, you rarely define structure variables, enumerated constants, and union variables so close to the data type's declaration. Typically, `struct`, `enum`, and `union` appear

globally at the top of the source file, and their associated definitions (with variables) appear locally in functions that follow. Even more common in data processing organizations, header files contain all the data type declarations, and they are included in the source code that needs them.

Because C++ does not need the repeated occurrence of enum and union, the following code is the C++ style of defining the enum and union definitions just shown:

```
enum color {  // Declares the enumerated constant
  black, blue, green, red, yellow, white
};

color light1, light2, light3;  // Variables that take
                               // on the enum values

union bitflags {  // Declares the union data type
  int i1;
  int i2;
  float f1;
};

bitflags memory1, memory2;  // Defines two union variables
```

C++ *enum* Extra

Unlike C, C++ issues a warning whenever you assign an integer to an enum variable. This is C++'s attempt to ensure that you store only proper values in variables you declare.

Although the following code works and compiles, C++ issues a warning on the 11th line because the constant value 3 is not a valid enum value.

ENUM.CPP. Potential problem with enum.

```
// Filename: ENUM.CPP
// Potential problem with enum
#include <iostream.h>
enum Days {
  SUN, MON, TUE, WED, THU, FRI, SAT
};
```

```
void main()
{
  Days birthday;  // Notice that enum is not required
  birthday = 3;  // ** Warning issued here **
  cout << birthday << "\n";
  birthday = WED;  // No warning here
  cout << birthday << "\n";
}
```

Allocating Memory in C and C++

If you have allocated memory dynamically, you have used C's `malloc()` and `free()` functions. `malloc()` and `free()` allocate and free memory from the *heap,* an unused area of memory. The advantage of allocating memory dynamically (as your program executes), as opposed to declaring all your data at compile time using variable declarations, is that you use only the memory you need at any one time.

Although this book's assumption is that you already understand `malloc()` and `free()`, a little background into these functions might ease the transition to the C++ way of allocating memory.

Suppose that you were writing an inventory program for a new hardware store. There are currently 250 items in the store's inventory, but the owner predicts a tremendous growth and tells you to make room for as many as 1,000 parts. A structure is the perfect place to store the inventory data. Such a structure might look like this:

```
struct inventory {
  char partno[8];
  char partname[30];
  int quantity;
  float cost;
  float price;
}
```

As soon as you declare the inventory items, you can then declare an array of 1,000 structure variables, like this:

```
inventory parts[1000];  // No struct keyword needed
```

67

The computer must have lots of memory to hold an array of structure variables such as parts. In addition, thousands of those bytes of storage sit unused until the store's inventory grows to 1,000 parts. Most of the inventory will stay in a disk file, but this array of structures can hold all the inventory items at one time to speed sorting and searching when needed.

Instead of allocating 1,000 structure variables, many of which will not be filled for a long time, the inventory justifies the use of dynamically allocated structure variables. Instead of setting aside 1,000 structure variables, allocate only as many as there are inventory parts. If the inventory has only 250 parts right now, allocate only 250 structure variables. As the inventory grows, allocate new structure variables. A good data structure would be an array of pointers to the structures. Here is how you could reserve the array of pointers:

```
inventory * parts[1000];   // Array of structure pointers
```

Although 1,000 pointers are reserved, you allocate the structure variables with malloc(), pointing the next structure pointer to the newly allocated structure variable. (If you set up a linked list, you don't even need the array of 1,000 pointers.) Here is the malloc() function call that allocates a new structure variable, "hooking up" the 25th array pointer to it:

```
parts[26] = (inventory *)malloc(sizeof(inventory));
```

C would need the struct keyword before each inventory in this line, but other than struct, both C and C++ support this kind of dynamically allocated memory. You reserve only pointers to memory, pointing them to newly allocated memory on-the-fly as you need it. When you are done with the allocated memory, free() sends that memory back to the memory heap for use later.

C does not really need the function typecast. malloc() returns a void pointer to the newly allocated memory. C++, with its stronger type checking, will not promote a void pointer to the correct data type. C++ requires the (inventory *) typecast. Even in regular C, you should always typecast void pointers to show your original intent.

Allocating with *new* and *delete*

new and delete *allocate and free memory.*

malloc() and free() require either the alloc.h or stdlib.h header files. The extra type-casting and sizeof() make malloc() a cumbersome function. C++ supports malloc() and free(), but C++ offers a much better way of allocating and freeing memory. There are two operators in C++ that allocate and free memory—new and delete. new is the C++ improvement over malloc() and delete is the replacement for the free() function. Because new and delete are operators and not functions, they do not require typecasting

or `sizeof()` to know the correct size of the memory to allocate. The following code allocates a new structure for the inventory array described in the preceding section:

```
parts[26] = new inventory;  // Allocates a new inventory item
```

`new` returns a pointer to the newly allocated memory. The free memory being allocated is called the *memory store* or *heap* in C++ terminology.

`new` makes it easy to dynamically allocate any data you need. The following section of code allocates a character, integer, and floating-point variable.

```
char *cvar = new char;    // Allocates a new character
int *ivar = new int;      // Allocates a new integer
float *fvar = new float;  // Allocates a new floating-point
```

If you want to allocate an array of pointers to memory, you can do so. Again, the new operator makes allocating an array of data almost as easy as defining it at compile time. Here is code that initializes a floating-point pointer to point to an array of 50 floating-point values:

```
float * fara = new float [50];
```

`fara` is now a floating-point pointer variable that points to the beginning of the 50 floating-point values. C++ does not initialize the memory (neither did `malloc()`), but the memory is now available for use. If you want to initialize the allocated memory with a value, you can do so by putting the initial value in parentheses after the new operation. The 50 floating-point values are allocated and initialized to 0.0 in the following line:

```
float * fara = new float [50] (0.0);  // Allocates and zeroes
```

The zero initial value looks strange, but C++ requires this parentheses notation if you want the memory allocated.

---

new fails if there is not enough memory to satisfy the request. new returns a null pointer if it fails.

`delete` returns the allocated memory to the free store. `delete` is an intelligent operator. However many bytes the corresponding new allocated, `delete` deallocates them. Consider the following code:

```
int *iptr = new int [100] (0);  // Allocates and zeroes memory
if (iptr == 0) {  // Checks for error
  error_function();
  exit(1); }
```

```
//
// Body of program goes here
//   :
//

delete[] iptr;   // Frees all 100 integers
```

The `delete` knows that `iptr` points to 100 integers, so it frees all that memory automatically.

You can put 100 inside the brackets in the last line of the preceding program, like this:

```
delete [100] iptr;   //Frees all 100 integers
```

but C++ does not require it. If you allocate an array with `new`, be sure to deallocate the array with `delete[]` so that C++ knows that it is to deallocate the entire array and not just the pointer to the array.

> Never mix `new` and `delete` with `malloc()` and `free()` functions (and related C-style allocation functions such as `calloc()`). Because the `new` and `delete` operators do not work well with the C allocation functions, you should stick with `new` and `delete`. As you learn more about C++, you will see that `new` and `delete` do more work behind the scenes than `malloc()` and `free()`.

Handling Allocation Errors

The designers of C++ know that every attempt to allocate free memory might result in an error. Depending on the system resources, there might not be enough memory to allocate the requested amount. As discussed and shown in the preceding section, you can check the return value of `new` to see whether it worked or failed.

Because of its ease of use, `new` is a very common operation. Allocating memory on-the-fly is easy. As more and more personal computers become networked to other computers, and as more and more personal computers begin *multitasking* (running several programs in memory at the same time), dynamic memory allocation becomes even more important. You do not want to take memory away from other processes that might need it until you are ready to use that memory.

Instead of checking for a null return pointer from new, you can eliminate tedious memory-error checking by taking advantage of a C++ feature called *exception handling*. You can supply a function that you want C++ to execute every time a memory allocation error occurs. Because the assumption is that the allocation will work most of the time, the function executes only when exceptions to the standard occur—that is, when new cannot find enough memory to satisfy your allocation request.

new errors are easy to trap in C++.

C++ calls the function set_new_handler() every time a new fails. As soon as you set up set_new_handler(), you no longer have to check for a zero return value after each new operation. You can forget about checking for errors because C++ does that for you. C++ invokes the set_new_handler() function only if an error occurs. The following program demonstrates the exception handler's use. Notice that you must include the prototype file named new.h if you want to invoke the exception handler.

EXCEPT.CPP. Shows the exception handler function in action.

```
// Filename: EXCEPT.CPP
// Shows the exception handler function in action.
#include <iostream.h>
#include <stdlib.h>
#include <new.h>

extern void (*set_new_handler(void (*memory_err)()))();
            // Declares a pointer to a function in new.h
            // that takes a function pointer as its argument

void memory_err()  // Your function goes here
{
  cout << "A memory allocation error occurred. \n";
  exit(1);  // Quits program
}

void main()
{
  set_new_handler(memory_err);  // Sets up exception handler
  // Successfully allocates memory
  float *fp1 = new float [10];  // No problem here
  cout << "First allocation worked. \n";

  // Allocates too much memory
  float *fp2 = new float [999999999999999999999];  // No way
  cout << "Second allocation worked. \n";
  delete fp1;
  delete fp2;
}
```

Here is the output from this program:

```
First allocation worked.
A memory allocation error occurred.
```

The second new requested far too much memory, so the exception handling function, memory_err(), executed. set_new_handler()'s argument is a pointer to your own function that takes care of the error condition. If you are unfamiliar with pointers to functions, notice that you only have to supply your own error function, include new.h, insert your function's name in the extern declaration of the set_new_handler(), and set up the exception handling by calling set_new_handler() when main() first begins. Follow the pattern of the program you just saw and you can leave the memory allocation error checking to the compiler.

> If possible, your exception handling function should attempt to free some memory and return. If it does, the new continues to work, this time successfully. Often, however, it is impossible to free memory. Most exception handling functions inform the user of the problem and exit.

Summary

This chapter reviewed a few C concepts and introduced new C++ material. void pointers and reference variables are vital to C++, especially when you begin programming with objects. You do not have to use OOP to take advantage of reference variables, though. As you see in the next chapter, "C++ Function Advantages," references make passing parameters by address much easier than in regular C.

C++ allocates and frees heap memory much more elegantly than C, while handling memory allocation errors with ease. Simple allocation of memory means added flexibility later when you learn to allocate OOP objects.

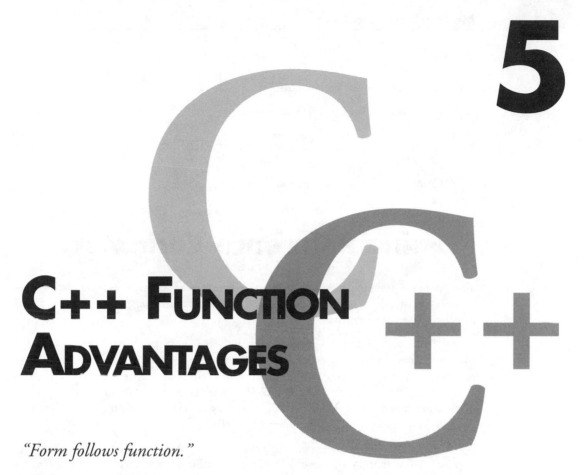

C++ Function Advantages

5

"Form follows function."

One of the most important non-OOP advantages C++ has over regular C is its intelligent function maintenance. Through function overloading and default argument lists, you can write cleaner code that executes more accurately and that is easier to maintain. C++ also cleans up C's job of passing data by address. C++ enables you to pass reference variables to functions, eliminating the need to precede received address parameters with & as in C.

You do not have to send values to all functions that receive arguments. C++ enables you to specify default argument lists. You can write functions that assume argument values even if you do not pass them any arguments.

C++ also enables you to write more than one function with the same function name. This is called *overloading functions*. As long as their argument lists differ, C++ takes care of determining which function your code calls.

In this chapter, you will learn about:

- How to pass reference variables by address

- How to declare default argument values

- The advantages of function overloading

- Combining C and C++ functions in the same program

Passing Reference Variables

Unlike C, C++ enables you to pass by reference as well as by value and by address.

There are three ways to pass values from one function to another in C++. C++ shares two of these three methods with C. Both C and C++ pass values *by value* and *by address*. C++ can also pass values *by reference*.

By default, both C and C++ pass arguments from one function to another by value (sometimes called *by copy*). That is, a copy of the value in the calling function is sent to the receiving function. When the receiving function modifies the value, it modifies only a copy, so the calling function's value is left intact. When arrays are passed, a copy of the address of the argument is passed. Therefore, when an array is changed in the receiving function, the array is changed in the calling function as well.

The following program reviews passing by value. `main()` passes an integer to the receiving function, called `fun()`. `fun()` modifies and prints the integer, and then returns to `main()`. Because only a copy of the integer was sent from `main()`, it is left unchanged in `main()`, as the output demonstrates.

BYVAL.CPP. Passes a variable by value.

```
// Filename: BYVAL.CPP
// Passes a variable by value.
#include <iostream.h>
void fun(int val);
void main()
{
  int val = 15;
  cout << "Before the function call, val is " << val << "\n";
  fun(val);  // Passes val by value
  cout << "After the function returns, val is " << val << "\n";
}
```

```
void fun(int val)  // Receives val by value
{
  val += 15;  // Adds 15 to the value
  cout << "Inside fun(), val is " << val << "\n";
}
```

The program's output appears as follows:

```
Before the function call, val is 15
Inside fun(), val is 30
After the function returns, val is 15
```

Passing data by value protects that data's original contents. Because a copy of the data is passed, the receiving function works only on a copy of the value. This insulates the calling function's variables, but sometimes causes memory problems. Because C and C++ make a copy of the variable passed, even if it is a very large structure there could be instances where not enough memory exists to make the copy. When this happens, you get a stack overflow message from the compiler. If you are dealing with small structures and only a handful of variables, the stack overflow problem should not occur.

Passing by value takes extra memory and time.

Another drawback to passing data by value is the time overhead needed to make a copy of the data. Some programmers, to save critical processing time, might forgo the advantage of data protection and pass by address so that the compiler will not take the memory and time to make copies of passed data.

When you pass a pointer from one function to another, or precede the argument with the address of operator (&), you pass the address of the argument instead of a copy of the argument's value. The following program is similar to the last, except that it passes val by address. Notice that when fun() changes val, val also changes in main() because it is the same variable in both functions.

BYADR1.CPP. Passes a variable by address.

```
// Filename: BYADR1.CPP
// Passes a variable by address.
#include <iostream.h>
void fun(int *val);
void main()
{
  int val = 15;
  cout << "Before the function call, val is " << val << "\n";
  fun(&val);  // Passes val by address
```

continues

75

BYADR1.CPP. continued

```
  cout << "After the function returns, val is " << val << "\n";
}
void fun(int *val)  // Receives val by address
{
  *val += 15;  // Adds 15 to the value
  cout << "Inside fun(), val is " << *val << "\n";
}
```

Here is the output from this program, showing that fun() changed main()'s val.

```
Before the function call, val is 15
Inside fun(), val is 30
After the function returns, val is 30
```

Non-array data types (such as integers and floating-point variables, as opposed to arrays) are called *scalar* variables. The drawback of passing scalar variables by address is the notation needed to do so. Having to dereference each occurrence of val in the receiving function with * is messy and does not lend itself to clean, easy-to-read code. Nevertheless, in C and C++, the extra notation is a must if you want to pass scalar variables by address.

Luckily, you do not need the dereference notation when passing arrays by address. Because array names are actually just addresses where the arrays begin in memory, you pass arrays by address without the need for the & and * operators. The following program passes an array by address to a receiving function. After the function changes the array, notice that main()'s array changes, too.

BYADR2.CPP. Passes an array by address.

```
// Filename: BYADR2.CPP
// Passes an array by address.
#include <iostream.h>
#include <string.h>
void fun(char ara[]);
void main()
{
  char ara[] = "C++ is fun!";
  cout << "Before the function call, ara is " << ara << "\n";
  fun(ara);  // Passes ara by address; no & needed
  cout << "After the function returns, ara is " << ara << "\n";
}
```

```
void fun(char ara[])  // Receives ara automatically by address
{
  strcpy(ara, "C++ program");  // Changes ara
  cout << "Inside fun(), ara is " << ara << "\n";
}
```

Here is the output to show you that the array is changed both in main() and in fun() when fun() changes it:

```
Before the function call, ara is C++ is fun!
Inside fun(), ara is C++ program
After the function returns, ara is C++ program
```

So far, this section should have been review for you. As a C programmer, you should be comfortable with these topics before proceeding. The next method of passing arguments, *by reference,* is new in C++ and as yet is not supported by ANSI C compilers. Passing by reference gives you advantages of passing scalar arguments by address without the messy & and * notation. When you pass a reference variable (introduced in Chapter 4, "Pointers, References, and Memory Allocation"), you pass an alias to the variable.

As you know from your study of reference variables, a reference variable is a special type of pointer. It contains the same memory location as the variable to which it points. Loosely speaking, when you pass a reference variable, you pass not only the address, but the value itself. When you pass a variable by reference, the receiving function gets an alias of the calling function's variable, which is actually the same value in every respect, with a different name. There is no need for extra &s and *s, as there is when you pass by address.

The easiest way to learn about passing references is to see an example. In the following program, a variable named age is declared in main(). main() then passes age to get_age(), where the user types his or her age into age. When control returns to main(), main() knows the new value of age that the user typed.

AGEREF.CPP. Passes a variable by reference.

```
// Filename: AGEREF.CPP
// Passes a variable by reference.
#include <iostream.h>
void get_age(int &age);
void main()
{
  int age;
  get_age(age);  // Passes age by reference
```

continues

AGEREF.CPP. continued

```
  cout << "Are you really " << age << " years old?\n";
}

void get_age(int &age)  // age is a reference to main()'s age
{
  cout << "How old are you? ";
  cin >> age;
}
```

Here is the output. Notice that age is the very same variable in both functions due to the reference.

```
How old are you? 30
Are you really 30 years old?
```

Use references with care.

Although passing by reference is cleaner than passing by address, it is easier to forget that the calling variable can be modified. Unless you pay attention to the prototype of the function, you might not realize by looking at the function call that the value was passed by reference (unless the variable is an array, which always passes by address). Therefore, C++ programmers reserve passing references to the following situations:

- When they want to save time and memory and do not want to make a copy of the receiving variable.

- When they pass a value that is not going to change in the receiving function. They then use the const keyword to ensure that the value is passed.

These conditions make the preceding program, AGEREF.CPP, suspect. AGEREF.CPP violates the second rule. Therefore, AGEREF.CPP is a better candidate for passing by address, even though the programmer has to change get_age() to look like this:

```
void get_age(int *age)  // age is an address of main()'s age
{
  cout << "How old are you? ";
  cin >> *age;  // Must continue to dereference notation
}
```

This is an example of when maintainability is more important than coding ease. Passing age by address makes it clear that get_age() can change age, whereas passing age by reference is not so clear.

As long as you do not need to change any of their members' data, you should pass structures by reference. You do not have to use the structure pointer (->) to access the

members. Include the const qualifier when receiving a value passed by reference to ensure that the receiving function cannot change the value. Consider the following function:

```
void disp_inv(const inventory & item) // Receiving an inventory
{               // structure variable by reference
  cout << "Part Listing for item #" << item.partno << "\n";
  cout << "Name:\t\t" << item.name << "\n";
  cout << "Quantity:\t" << item.quantity << "\n";
  cout << "Cost:\t\t" << item.code << "\n";
  cout << "Retail:\t" << item.retail << "\n";
}
```

This function receives a structure variable by reference. The function does not modify the variable, so the variable's value is protected in the calling function. To guard against accidental modification, the programmer added const to this function's prototype, making the reference a very safe pass.

> As with pointer variables, you can return a reference from a function, but make sure that it references only global variables. If you return references to automatic local variables, those variables' values disappear when the function ends, and the reference will be lost.

Default Argument Lists

Suppose that you are writing a program that needs to print a message on-screen and ring the terminal's bell. For instance, you could pass it an error message stored in a character array, and the function would print the error message and sound the warning.

The prototype for such a function might be this:

```
void er_msg(char note[]);
```

Therefore, to request that er_msg() print Turn printer on, you call it this way:

```
er_msg("Turn printer on");  // Passes a message to be printed
```

This prints the message Turn printer on and rings the bell by sending '\a' to the terminal. To request that er_msg() print Press a key to continue..., you would call it this way:

```
er_msg("Press a key to continue...");  // Passes a message
```

As you write more of the program, you begin to realize that you are printing one message—for instance, the `Turn printer on` message—more often than any other message. It seems as if the `er_msg()` function is getting that message five or six times more often than any other message. This might be the case if you're writing a program that sends many reports to the printer. You want to use `er_msg()` for other messages, but the printer is the most-used.

Instead of calling the function over and over, typing the same message each time, you can set up the prototype for `er_msg()` so that it *defaults* to `Turn printer on` in this way:

List default argument values in the prototype.

```
void er_msg(char note[]="Turn printer on");  // Prototype
```

After you prototype `er_msg()` with the default argument list, C++ assumes that you want to pass `Turn printer on` to the function *unless you pass something else to it*. For instance, in `main()`, you could call `er_msg()` this way:

```
pr_msg();  // C++ assumes that you mean "Turn printer on"
```

This makes your programming job easier. Because most of the time you want `er_msg()` to print `Turn printer on`, the default argument list takes care of the message, and you do not have to pass the message when you call the function. During those few times when you want to pass something else, however, go ahead and pass a different message. To make `er_msg()` print `Incorrect value`, type the following:

```
er_msg("Incorrect value");  // Passes a new message
```

> **TIP**
>
> Whenever you call a function several times and find yourself passing that function the same parameters most of the time, consider using a default argument list. The C++ compiler does more of your work than C compilers do.

Multiple Default Arguments

You can specify more than one default argument in the prototype list. Here is a prototype for a function with three default arguments:

```
float funct1(int i=10, float x=7.5, char c='A');
```

There are several ways you can call this function. Here are some samples:

`funct1();`	All default values are assumed.
`funct1(25);`	25 is sent to the integer argument, and the default values are assumed for the rest.
`funct1(25, 31.25);`	25 is sent to the integer argument, 31.25 is sent to the floating-point argument, and the default value of 'A' is assumed for the character argument.

> **NOTE**
>
> If only some of a function's arguments are default arguments, those default arguments must appear to the far *left* of the argument list. No default arguments can appear to the left of those not specified as default.
>
> This is an *invalid* default argument prototype:
>
> ```
> float func2(int i=10, float x, char c, double n=10.232);
> ```
>
> This is invalid because a default argument appears to the left of a nondefault argument. To fix this, you would have to move the two default arguments to the far right (the end) of the argument list. Therefore, when you rearrange the prototype (and the resulting function calls) as follows, C++ enables you to accomplish the same objective that the preceding line attempted:
>
> ```
> float func2(float x, char c, int i=10, double n=10.232);
> ```

The following program illustrates the use of defaulting several arguments. `main()` calls the function `de_fun()` five times, sending `de_fun()` five sets of arguments. The `de_fun()` function prints five different things, depending on `main()`'s argument list.

DEFARG.CPP. Demonstrates default argument list with several parameters.

```
// Filename: DEFARG.CPP
// Demonstrates default argument list with several parameters.
#include <iostream.h>
#include <iomanip.h>

void de_fun(int i=5, long j=40034, float x=10.25,
     char ch='Z', double d=4.3234);  // Prototype
```

continues

DEFARG.CPP. continued

```
void main()
{
  de_fun();  // All defaults used
  de_fun(2);  // First default overridden
  de_fun(2, 75037);  // First and second default overridden
  de_fun(2, 75037, 35.88);  // First, second, and third
  de_fun(2, 75037, 35.88, 'G');  // First, second, third, and fourth
  de_fun(2, 75037, 35.88, 'G', .0023);  // No defaulting
}

void de_fun(int i, long j, float x, char ch, double d)
{
  cout << setprecision(4) << "i: " << i << "  " << "j: " << j;
  cout << "  x: " << x << "  " << "ch: " << ch;
  cout << "  d: " << d << "\n";
  return;
}
```

Here is the output from this program:

```
i: 5  j: 40034  x: 10.25  ch: Z  d: 4.3234
i: 2  j: 40034  x: 10.25  ch: Z  d: 4.3234
i: 2  j: 75037  x: 10.25  ch: Z  d: 4.3234
i: 2  j: 75037  x: 35.88  ch: Z  d: 4.3234
i: 2  j: 75037  x: 35.88  ch: G  d: 4.3234
i: 2  j: 75037  x: 35.88  ch: G  d: 0.0023
```

Notice that each call to de_fun() produces a different output because main() sends a different set of parameters each time it calls de_fun().

Overloaded Functions

Unlike regular C, C++ enables you to have more than one function with the same name. That is, you can have three functions called abs() in the same program. Functions with the same names are called *overloaded functions*. C++ requires that each overloaded function differ in its argument list. Overloaded functions enable you to have similar functions that work on different types of data.

For example, suppose that you wrote a function that returned the absolute value of whatever number you passed to it. The absolute value of a number is its positive equivalent. For instance, the absolute value of 10.25 is 10.25, and the absolute value of –10.25 is 10.25.

Absolute values are used in distance, temperature, and weight calculations. The difference in the weights of two children is always positive. If Joe weighs 65 pounds and Mary weighs 55 pounds, their difference is a positive 10 pounds. You can subtract 65 from 55 (getting –10) or 55 from 65 (getting +10) and the weight difference is always the absolute value of the result.

Suppose that you needed to write an absolute value function for integers and an absolute value function for floating-point numbers. Without function overloading, you would need these two functions:

```
int iabs(int i)  // Returns absolute value of an integer
{
  if (i < 0)
  { return (i * -1); }  // Makes positive
  else
  { return (i); }  // Already positive
}

float fabs(float x)  // Returns absolute value of a float
{
  if (x < 0.0)
  { return (x * -1.0); }  // Makes positive
  else
  { return (x); }  // Already positive
}
```

Without overloading, if you had a floating-point variable for which you needed the absolute value, you would pass it to the fabs() function, as in:

```
ans = fabs(weight);
```

If you needed the absolute value of an integer variable, you would pass it to the iabs() function, as in:

```
ians = iabs(age);
```

Because the code for these two functions differs only in their parameter lists, they make perfect candidates for overloaded functions. Call both functions abs(), prototype both of them with different parameter lists, and code each of them separately in your program. After overloading the two functions—each of which works on two different types of parameters despite having the same name—you pass your floating-point or integer value to abs(). The C++ compiler figures out which one you really want to call.

If two or more functions differ only in their return types, C++ cannot overload them. Two or more functions that differ only in their return types must have different names and cannot be overloaded.

Overloading functions simplifies your programming considerably. Instead of having to remember several different function names, you have to remember only one function name. C++ takes care of passing the arguments to the proper function. Overloaded functions are similar to overloaded operators such as >>. Recall that >> is both a bitwise right-shift operator and the input extractor operator. C++ enables you to overload operators as well as functions so that the operators work on your own user-defined data types. Imagine being able to add two sets of structure variable members together with the + operator instead of having to call a function to do the work. Chapter 12, "Operator Overloading," shows you how to overload operators to make them work the way you need them to.

As you write more C++ programs, you will see many uses for overloaded functions. The following program is a demonstration program showing how you can build your own output functions to suit your needs. main() calls three functions named output(). Each time one is called, main() passes a different value to the function.

When main() passes output() a string, output() prints the string, formatted to a width (using the setw() manipulator) of 20. When main() passes output() an integer, output() prints the integer with a width of 5. When main() passes output() a floating-point value, output() prints the value to two decimal places. This generalizes output of different types of data. You do not have to worry about formatting your own data. output() takes care of the proper formatting, and you have to remember only one function name that outputs all three types of data.

OVF.CPP. Outputs three different types of data with the same function name.

```
// Filename: OVF.CPP
// Outputs three different types of
// data with same function name.
#include <iostream.h>
#include <iomanip.h>
void output(char []);   // Prototypes for overloaded functions
void output(int i);
void output(float x);
```

84

```
void main()
{
  char name[] = "Overloading makes C++ easy!";
  int ivalue = 2543;
  float fvalue = 39.4321;

  output(name);  // C++ chooses the appropriate function
  output(ivalue);
  output(fvalue);

return;
}

void output(char name[])
{
  cout << setw(30) << name << "\n";
  // The width truncates string if it is longer than 30
  return;
}

void output(int ivalue)
{
  cout << setw(5) << ivalue << "\n";
  // Just printed integer within a width of five places
  return;
}

void output(float fvalue)
{
  cout << setprecision(2) << fvalue << "\n";
  // Limited the floating-point value to two decimal places
  return;
}
```

Here is the output from this program:

```
Overloading makes C++ easy!
 2543
39.43
```

All three lines, each containing a different type of data, print with the same function call.

Name-Mangling

C++ uses *name-mangling* to overload functions. Generally, you do not care how C++ performs this technique, but understanding it will help you as you become more of an advanced C++ programmer.

C++ uses name-mangling to keep straight the names of overloaded functions.

When C++ compiles a function, C++ changes the name of the function and adds letters that match the parameters to the end of the function name. Different C++ compilers do this in different ways. To get an idea of what the compiler is doing, take the absolute value function described earlier. C++ might change the integer absolute value function name to `absi()` and the floating-point absolute value function name to `absf()`.

When you call the function with the function call

```
ians = abs(age);
```

C++ looks at the integer parameter and knows that you really want to call the `absi()` function. As far as you know, C++ is not mangling the names; you never see the name differences in your program's source code. However, the compiler performs the name-mangling so that it can keep track of overloaded functions that appear to have the same name.

Running C and C++ Together

Over the years, you might have written many useful C functions. Rarely do people have time to rewrite code. As you move to C++, your programs will need routines already written in C, and you might not have time to rewrite those routines in C++. Luckily, you do not have to. C++ offers a way to call C functions from within a C++ program.

If your C++ program calls a C function to which you will later link, you must ensure that C++ does *not* name-mangle the C function call. Even if your program contains no overloaded functions, C++ mangles the function names, as described in the preceding section. Because C++ has no idea that you might be calling C functions, you must add a C *linkage specification* that looks like this:

```
extern "C" {
  float salary_calc(float rate, int hours);
  void disp_msg(void);
}
```

This code tells C++ *not* to mangle any function call that calls `salary_cal()` or `disp_msg()` when it compiles this program. Therefore, when this program is linked to the C code that contains `salary_calc()` and `disp_msg()`, those functions are matched to their calling code. (C does not perform name-mangling; only C++ does.)

Summary

This chapter concludes the straight, non-OOP concepts of C++. So far in this book, you have seen straight comparisons and contrasts between C and C++. You have also seen how C++ implements several improvements over C, such as overloaded functions, default argument lists, and passing values by reference.

If C++ contained only the improvements described so far, it would still stand apart from C. However, C++ doesn't stop here. Now that you know the basics, you are ready to begin tackling the object-oriented topics. Actually, most of the concepts you have learned so far were not designed just to improve on the C language. Almost every C++ concept you now know lays groundwork for the things you can do with OOP.

Take time to review this first section before venturing into OOP. As soon as you are comfortable with the main topics, turn to Chapter 6, "Hiding Data from Code," and begin your journey toward mastering object-oriented programming with C++.

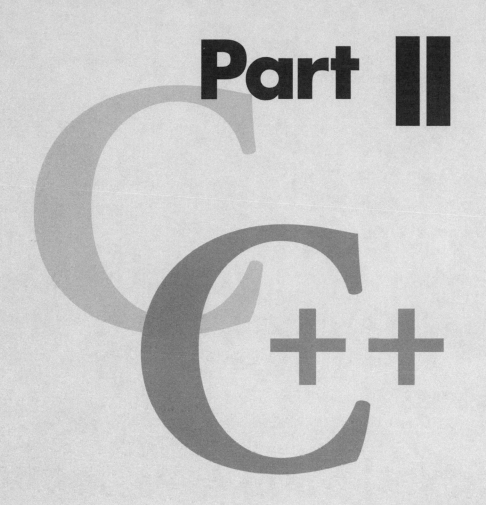

Part II

C C++

OBJECTS AND CLASSES

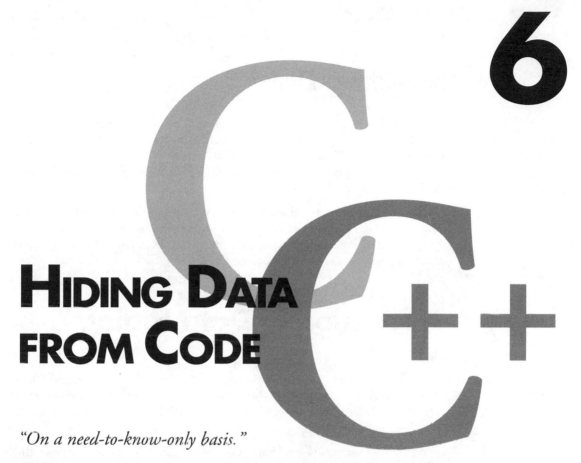

HIDING DATA FROM CODE

6

"On a need-to-know-only basis."

One of the most important concepts behind object-oriented programming is keeping data away from functions and procedures that do not need the data. You already understand C's method of hiding data from functions; you have worked with local variables that are visible only within the functions that need to access those variables.

The OOP method of hiding data goes far beyond that of local variables. The foundation of OOP lies in hiding data, and this chapter attempts to ease you into OOP by reviewing many concepts you already know. You should find this short chapter extremely simple, and that is its purpose. Too many people attempt to learn OOP without reviewing these vital concepts.

In this chapter, you will learn:

- The importance of local variables

- How C and other non-OOP programming methods increase program maintenance problems

- The C++ concept of abstract data types (sometimes called user-defined data types)

Protecting Data

There is good reason to hide data from various parts of a program. Not all functions need access to all the data in the program. At first glance, making certain data invisible to certain functions might seem like programming overkill; after all, *you* write the programs, *you* know which data should be visible to which functions, so shouldn't *you* be able to keep the correct data visible to the correct functions?

The answer is not simple. You do not use local variables just to protect yourself from your own programming mistakes. The concept of local variables does not exist just to keep programmers from modifying variables in the wrong place. Local variables give you programming advantages you would not have otherwise.

Introduction to Data Hiding

If you have looked at a C++ reference manual, you might have seen the term *data hiding* as well as other new words such as *encapsulation* and *polymorphism*. It seems as though programmers rarely use a small word when a big one will do nicely (and confuse more people!). Understanding these terms, as well as most of the C++ and OOP concepts, begins with the hiding of data.

Hiding data can be nothing more than using local variables.

The biggest C++ advantage is data hiding. Data hiding is nothing more than protecting data. Only those functions that should change the data *can* change the data. As explained in the preceding section, you will already understand the concepts of data hiding if you understand local variables. A variable is local to a function (or, more specifically, to the block) in which it is defined. Functions cannot change another function's local variables without strict access via the passing of those local variables. Global variables let too many functions change variables they should not be able to change.

Consider the following program. This short C++ program reviews the concept of local and global variables.

LOCGLO.CPP. Reviews the concept of local and global variables.

```
// Filename: LOCGLO.CPP
#include <iostream.h>
#include <iomanip.h>
float calc_tax(const float total_sales);  // Prototype
float profit_margin = .40;  // Global variable

void main()
{
   float total_sales = 12.51;  // Local variables
   float tax, profit;

   cout << setprecision(2);  // Prints with two decimal places
   cout << "Your total sales are $" << total_sales << "\n";
   tax = calc_tax(total_sales);  // Calculates and prints tax

   profit = profit_margin * (total_sales - tax);
   cout << "Your sales tax is $" << tax << "\n";
   cout << "The profit is $" << profit << "\n";
}

float calc_tax(const float total_sales)
{
   float tax_rate = .075;  // Tax rate is 7.5%
   return (tax_rate * total_sales);  // Return tax amount
}
```

Here is the output from this program:

```
Your total sales are $12.51
Your sales tax is $0.94
The profit is $4.63
```

The variable total_sales is local to the main() function. There is no way that calc_tax() can change total_sales. calc_tax() borrows a copy of total_sales only when main() passes it. In effect, total_sales is hidden from the calc_tax() function; calc_tax() can use it, but not change it. The variable profit_margin is global, so any function can change it (although no function does in this program).

C++ takes the concept of variable protection even further. You control which functions can change certain variables. You still write the functions that change data. However, instead of functions owning variables, the variables own the functions! You make the variables themselves control which functions modify them in the program.

User-Defined Data Types

Here is the definition of a C++ structure:

```
struct date {
   int day;
   int month;
   int year;
};
```

This structure has three members—day, month, and year. Often, you put such a structure definition in a header file and include it at the top of all programs that use the structure. No variables are reserved with this structure definition. If you want to declare a structure variable that has the structure's format, you would do this:

```
date today;  // Declares a single structure variable
```

Structure definitions are called abstract data types or user-defined data types.

You might recall from Chapter 4, "Pointers, References, and Memory Allocation," that C++ (as opposed to C) does not require the struct keyword when declaring structure variables. This struct statement declares a variable called today that has the format of the structure tagged date. Because there is no built-in data type that looks like date, one had to be defined. In C, you defined a structure variable called date. C++ programmers, however, prefer to say that you are defining an abstract data type, or ADT for short. *Abstract data type* is a fancy name for data types that you define, as opposed to the built-in data types such as int, float, and so on.

The term *abstract data type* is somewhat unfortunate. There is very little that is abstract about abstract data types. They are not built-in data types (like int), but as soon as you define them, C++ treats them almost as though they were built-in data types. Therefore, the term *user-defined data type* may be more appropriate than *abstract data type* when referring to struct and similar definitions. C++ is *extensible,* which means that you can extend the actual language capabilities. You add your own data types to the compiler's repertoire by declaring a new aggregate data type such as a structure.

Structures make data hiding even more important because so much data is local or global at any time; it would be too easy to accidentally modify a large structure if it were global. The concept of a structure is much more important to C++ than to C. The designers of C++ created another abstract data type (called a *class*) that you will read about in the next chapter. Be sure that you understand structures before tackling the next chapter.

Keeping structure data local can be critical.

So far, all these code concepts should be review. Here is a program that uses the date structure:

ADT.CPP. Using the date ADT (structure).

```
// Filename: ADT.CPP
// Using the date ADT (structure)
#include <iostream.h>
struct date {
   int day;
   int month;
   int year;
} today;  // Global definition for the date structure

void main()
{
   // Assigns the today structure members some values
   today.day = 14;
   today.month = 3;
   today.year = 1993;

   // Prints the date's values
   cout << "Today's date is ";
   cout << today.month << "/" << today.day;
   cout << "/" << today.year << "\n";
}
```

At this point, you should already be able to predict the output of this program. The dot operator is used to access each member of the structure variable called today. If you were to run this program, you would get the following output:

```
Today's date is 3/14/1993
```

Back to Data Hiding

This chapter's title is not "C++ Structures," but structures were a good place to begin. As a C programmer, you probably have used structures a lot. C++ programmers also use structures a lot. As a matter of fact, structures (and their related data types) provide the foundation for almost every object-oriented concept in C++.

There is much danger involved with the C structures you are used to. There is nothing to keep the programmer from assigning invalid data to structure variables. For instance, in the preceding program, the programmer could do this if he or she wanted to:

```
today.month = 610;   // Assigns a very invalid month
```

Because the programmer is you, and because you are very conscientious, you might not see the importance of being so careful. After all, why would you assign such a silly number to a month? Maybe you would never assign a month a value such as 610, but what if you assign date values that are based on the user's input? What if you were asking for a user's birthday and the user accidentally typed 610 instead of 10 for October? The bad number would go straight to the month member of the today structure variable. To ensure that a bad date does not get into the program, you will have to add extensive error checking.

Programs rarely perform adequate error checking.

Many programmers fail to provide a large amount of error checking. Error checking code takes a lot of time to write, it detours programmers from their primary goal of the application, and anyway, users ought to know how to enter correct data!

As much as programmers would like to pass the blame for accurate data to the users, programmers are the ones responsible for the users' mistakes. Programmers must think ahead and add error checking to code and protect variables, not only from user data-entry mistakes but from their own programming actions as well. That is why good C programmers emphasize the use of local variables. Functions not in the scope of local variables have no access to those variables and cannot inadvertently change their values.

Error Checking

Sometimes the error-checking routines in programs are the biggest time-consuming components of the programming process. The time needed to provide accurate error checking is not always available to programmers with a backlog of work. More often than not, the data's format changes in the middle of a programming project and the error-checking routines are left unchanged or do not get fully converted to the new data's format.

Local variables help limit the actions a program can take, but localizing variables does not alleviate the tedious burden of protecting data completely. As you will see as you progress through the next few chapters, C++ makes the former maintenance nightmare of changing code after it is already written and implemented much simpler. When the data changes, you rarely have to change a C++ program that uses that data. Only a handful of specialized functions will see your C++ variables, and the other parts of the program will work through these specialized functions.

If you program in a group programming environment on projects written and maintained by several programmers, there is virtually no control over variables. A programmer can decide to insert a global variable into the middle of a program "for a quick fix that I'll change later" that might conflict with other global or local variables already being used. The danger increases even more when several programmers produce separate source files that will be linked into a single program. C++ provides an extremely flexible framework in which large groups of programmers can work together without the usual data clashes.

Summary

If you are asking yourself "When will we get to the new stuff?", we already have. This book attempts to make you fully aware of problems with current standard programming methods. Although local variables help protect variables from functions that have no need to access them, local variables do not help at all with validating user input. Worse yet, given the methods programmers have used for years to write code, even when they employed good structured programming techniques, the maintenance of code in this rapidly changing world creates a programming bottleneck that will not soon disappear until other programming methods are adopted.

C++ is an attempt to offer another method of programming. The object-oriented method extends the advantages of local variables much further than non-OOP procedural programming languages. C++ treats structure data as intelligent, active parts of the program, not as just passive entities that code moves around. These intelligent data structures include not only data members, but code as well.

With this introduction, you now are ready to read Chapter 7, "C++ Classes," which explains how C++ takes the concept of local structures further, turning them into more powerful data elements than you have ever seen in other programming languages.

C++ CLASSES

"You may now move to the head of the class."

C++ provides a new way of storing data, called the *class*. The class is the most important new concept in C++—so much so that the original name of C++ was *C with classes*. Class data extends the structure capabilities of C++ and forms the foundation of object-oriented programming.

In this chapter, you will learn about:

- The similarities and differences between the class and struct
- How to declare class variables
- More OOP terminology: *instance of a class*
- private and public access specifiers

Introduction to C++ Classes

When learning about classes for the first time, many C programmers seem to get bogged down in many new concepts and descriptions. Confusion does not have to be the end result. At this point, if you understand only one new concept in this chapter, it should be that

Classes and structures are very similar.

classes and structures are almost equivalent in C++. We can take the `date` structure you saw in the last chapter and turn it into a class by substituting the word `class` for `struct`, like this:

```
class Date {
    int month;
    int day;
    int time;
};
```

After this `class` declaration, you could declare new `class` variables, just as you declared new structure variables:

```
Date today, tomorrow;  // Defines two new class variables
```

The `class` variables each contain three members—`day`, `month`, and `year`—just as though they were structure members.

More Class Terminology

C programmers often use the term *structure variable* to refer to an occurrence of a structure. Because a `class` is so similar to a `struct`, you might think that the same terminology holds true for `class` variables.

C++ programmers do not use the term `class` *variable* very often. Instead, they like to call a variable that is defined as a class an *instance of the class*. Therefore, in the preceding discussion, `today` and `tomorrow` are two instances of the `class date`. To keep you moving through this book smoothly, I use both descriptions for a while. Calling them "class variables" and "instances of the class" often piles another unneeded layer of semantics on the beginning C++ programmer.

The term *object* also is very important, as you can guess from the acronym OOP. Objects are nothing more than variables, which are nothing more than instances of a class. Therefore, here is a class:

```
class Customer {
   char name[30];
   char num;
};
```

and this is an object, and a variable, and an instance of the class called `Customer`:

```
Customer bigspender;   // bigspender is an object, a class
                       // variable, and an instance of the
                       // class called Customer
```

Figure 7.1 shows the relationship between classes and objects.

Class	Object
Description of what an object looks like.	Simply a variable, a defined region in memory, and an instance of the class.
Example:	Example:

`class Payroll {`
`   char name[30];`
`   float salary;`
`};`
	`Payroll employee;`

	(`employee` is an object.)
(`Payroll` is a class.)	

Figure 7.1. Objects are examples of classes.

Public and Private Members

There is one more difference between a C++ class and a C++ structure besides the words class and struct. This difference is simple, but very important. Without it, there would be no reason for you to change from structures to classes. The difference determines what code has access to the class data members.

Consider the new class date defined earlier. To make this a more concrete example, here is the first part of a program that might use such a class:

```
#include <iostream.h>

class Date {
   int day;
   int month;
   int year;
};

main()
{
   Date today, tomorrow;  // Defines two new class variables
      // :
      // Rest of program follows
```

How would you assign values to the members of today? Until this point, you might attempt this in main():

```
today.day = 12;
today.month = 5;
today.year = 1992;
```

However, *this will not work*. main() has no access rights to the members of the variables today and tomorrow! This might go against the grain of all you know about structures in C, but it provides the data protection needed in C++.

A program's code cannot change private data members.

All members of a class are said to be *private*, whereas all members of a structure are said to be *public*. There are two new keywords in C++, private and public. private and public are called *access specifiers* in C++. (A third access keyword, protected, appears in Chapter 15, "Inheritance Issues.") When a member is private, no function in the program can read, change, or erase that member. When a member is public, any function can read, change, or erase that data member.

102

If you add the `public` keyword to the `date` class, you can access the members, as the three previous assignments attempted to do. For example, if the class were declared like this:

Making members public gives the rest of the program access to the data.

```
class Date {
public:
   int day;
   int month;
   int year;
};
```

then `main()` could use and change the members after it declared `class` variables. All members after the keyword `public` are `public` to the whole program. Always put a colon (:) after the `public` and `private` access specifiers.

> Unless you declare them `public`, all `class` members will be `private` by default.

If you declare all members `public`, there is no difference between a `class` and a `struct`. The following two definitions are *exactly the same*. Without the `public` keyword, however, they would be very different because no function in the program could access the `class` data members.

```
class Date {
public:
   int day;
   int month;
   int year;
};
```

This has the very same effect as this `struct` declaration:

```
struct date {
   int day;
   int month;
   int year;
};
```

You can use the `private` keyword to make structure members `private` (instead of the `public` access that structures default to). The following two declarations are exactly the same:

```
class Date {
   int day;
   int month;
   int year;
};
```

103

This has the very same effect as this `struct` declaration:

```
struct date {
private:
   int day;
   int month;
   int year;
};
```

`public` and `private` do not have to go immediately after the `class` keyword. You can put either of these access specifiers throughout a class, even using them more than once within the same class. For example, here is a class with six data members. The members alternate; half are `public` and half are `private`:

```
class Store {  // A "busy" class
public:
   char name[25];  // public store name
private:
   int s_num;
public:
   char address[30];
private:
   double sales;
public:
   long int sq_feet;
private:
   float pr_margin;
};
```

Don't overdo
public and
private.

For obvious reasons, do not flood a `class` declaration with all those access specifiers! The switching is cumbersome, error-prone, and difficult to follow. Nevertheless, this example shows the freedom C++ allows with the access specifiers. As soon as you use an access specifier, `private` or `public`, it stays in effect until the `class` declaration ends, or until another access specifier replaces the one in effect.

Most C++ programmers put the `private` members first, followed by the `public` members. There is no technical reason to do this, other than the fact that `private` is the default, so you do not need to specify `private` if the `private` members appear first in the class. Here is an improved, clearer version of the six-member `Store` class:

```
class Store {  // A much better Store class
   int s_num;     // private by default and
   double sales;  // remains private until changed
   float pr_margin;
public:
   char name[25];  // public members follow
```

```
    char address[30];
    long int sq_feet;
};
```

Figure 7.2 shows what this class looks like to the rest of the program. C++ puts an imaginary fence around the `private` members so that the rest of the program cannot use them and does not even know they exist. The program can, however, use any of the public members.

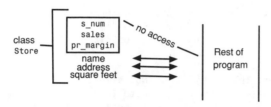

Figure 7.2. The program has no access rights to the private `Store` *class members.*

Just to give you another perspective, here is a short program that uses this `Store` class. Notice that two objects (variables or `class` instances) are created, one called `big_store` and one called `little_store`. Neither `main()` nor any other function that `main()` might call can do anything with the `private` members. The `private` members really are hidden from the program!

PRIPUB.CPP. Shows private and public member access.

```
// Filename: PRIPUB.CPP
// Shows private and public member access.
#include <iostream.h>
#include <string.h>

class Store {  // A much better Store class
   int s_num;  // private by default
   double sales;  // All private until changed
   float pr_margin;
public:
   char name[25];  // public members follow
   char address[30];
   long int sq_feet;
};
void main()
{
```

continues

PRIPUB.CPP. continued

```
    Store big_store;  // Defines a class variable
    Store little_store;  // These two lines could be combined

    strcpy(big_store.name, "SaveAll");  // Fills one of the objects
    strcpy(big_store.address, "1023 E. 23rd");
    big_store.sq_feet = 9894;

    // Now fills the other's accessible members
    strcpy(little_store.name, "Mom's Foods");
    strcpy(little_store.address, "83 N. Oak");
    little_store.sq_feet = 1213;

    // **Important: The following is NOT allowed:
    // big_store.sales = 84543.43;   Both INVALID because their
    // little_store.snum = 934;      members are private

    // Print the available data members
    cout << "Store: " << big_store.name << "\n";
    cout << "at " << big_store.address << "\n";
    cout << "has " << big_store.sq_feet << " feet.\n\n";

    cout << "Store: " << little_store.name << "\n";
    cout << "at " << little_store.address << "\n";
    cout << "has " << little_store.sq_feet << " feet\n";
}
```

Here is the program's output:

```
Store: SaveAll
at 1023 E. 23rd
has 9894 feet.

Store: Mom's Foods
at 83 N. Oak
has 1213 feet.
```

Because private members are protected, and because they offer greater protection than even local variables, declare all your structure-like data as classes in the future. All class data defaults to being private.

> `private` members are hidden from the program's code. This is what *data hiding* is really all about.

Any data that works as a structure works as a class as well. Suppose that a company's payroll department wanted the programmers to write a program to keep track of retirement money. The company has a pool of money that it adds to as an employee works, the company takes money out after the employee reaches retirement, and the money sits in a solid money-market mutual fund earning a fixed rate of return. A good candidate for a class would look like this:

```
class Retirement {
    double balance;  // Customer's retirement balance
    float rate;
};
```

Can you spot anything wrong with this short `class` declaration? It is very small and obviously incomplete, but something else should bother you about the `Retirement` class. It is all `private` and no function, and the program that follows it could use the class for anything. The solution is not to make all of the `class` members `public` because that defeats the purpose of a class. The solution lies in the next chapter.

Summary

The primary focus of this chapter was on the `class`, a new keyword and aggregate data type in C++. C++ classes and structures are identical in every way except for their access rights. A `class` is a `struct` with all its members `private` by default, and a `struct` is a `class` with all its members `public` by default. The bottom line is that `private` `class` members cannot be seen by the rest of the program and that `public` `class` members can be seen (and used) by the rest of the program.

At this point, you should have some questions, such as "If all my data is `private`, and if even my `main()` function can't access that data, what good is this `class` and C++ stuff, anyway?" Another question might be "How can I get to the `private` data?" These questions are answered in Chapter 8, "Member Functions."

MEMBER FUNCTIONS

8

"You must be a member to join this class!"

The preceding chapter, "C++ Classes," introduced classes and explained the relationship between the class and the struct. The only difference between the two is in their default access rights. C++ programmers use classes much more often than structures. They feel that the private access keeps data hidden very well from code that should not have access to those members. C++ promotes the idea of data protection much more strongly than C does, so the class seems to fit the C++ style much better.

This chapter answers your unanswered question from the last chapter: "How can I get to the private data?" This chapter teaches you about *member functions* (a new term). Member functions are easy to understand, but they have no corresponding concept in C or in any other procedural non-OOP language.

In this chapter, you will learn:

- The need for member functions
- Advantages of inline member functions

- Better data protection
- `Private` member functions

Member Functions

Put member functions with data members in classes and structures.

A member function is just that: a function that is a member of a class. Until now, you have seen structures and classes that hold data members only. All structures you worked with in C contained data members. With the introduction of C++, structures (and therefore classes) also can contain functions as members—hence the term *member functions*.

Look at the following `class` declaration to help ease the transition of learning member functions:

```
class Date {
   int day;  // Private data members
   int month;
   int year;
public:
   int bonus_flag;  // Public bonus date flag
   int get_month(void);  // Public member functions follow
   int get_day(void);
   int get_year(void);
   void set(const int d, const int m, const int y);
};

Date today, tomorrow;  // Defines two instances (two objects)
```

This is a declaration of a class called `Date`, with both member data and member functions. Two `class` variables are defined—`today` and `tomorrow`. Assuming that `main()` appears after this definition, `today` and `tomorrow` will be global variables. Although global variables are not as safe as local ones, globally defining these variables shortens the example for this discussion.

Three of the data members—`day`, `month`, and `year`—are `private`. Neither `main()` nor any other function that `main()` calls can see those variables. One data member, `bonus_flag`, is public. `main()` knows about that data member. Figure 8.1 shows the concept behind the `Date` class.

The `Date` class also contains declarations for four functions. This is the most important divergence of C++ from C: Every object is capable of manipulating itself. Instead of data's being a passive entity that you must write code to manage, each data variable contains all

the code to do the work it needs to do. These two Date variables contain more than some data values; they also know how to do something with those values.

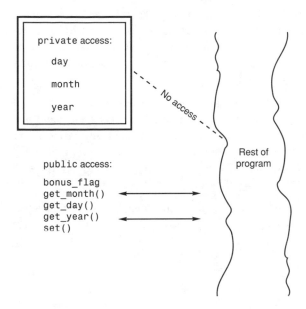

Figure 8.1. *The program's access differences between* private *and* public class *members.*

The member functions shown here are not yet complete. Obviously, this example, Date class, contains only prototypes for the member functions. The actual function code can be either inline within the class or defined later. For now, do not worry about the member functions' actual code. Try to get used to the fact that class data contains normal data as well as commands (member functions) that act on that data.

> In reality, each class variable does not contain copies of the member function's code. The member function's code exists only once in the program. Nevertheless, conceptually you should think of the class variables as holding both data and functions that operate on that data.

Combining member functions and data is where C++ mirrors the real world so much better than standard C. Real-world objects "know" how to behave. A child's block is more than just a six-sided piece of wood. A building block cannot roll, but it will come to rest

C++ models the real world much more closely than C.

111

on one of its sides after you throw it. A ball is more than just a smooth sphere. It "knows" it can roll, and it will do so if you throw it.

Member functions give your class (and struct) data active capabilities. With both data and member functions, you can begin to model real-world objects and give them both data and functional capabilities. In C++ terminology, class objects have *properties* (data members) and *behaviors* (member functions). The ball might be round and blue (two properties) and it rolls and bounces (two behaviors).

With C and the other non-OOP languages, you can model data values (properties) only. For instance, suppose that you worked for a rental car agency and needed to write a C program to handle rental car records. You would have many passive structure variables that tracked all the car's rental statistics; then you would write a lot of code that worked with that data. If the data changed, you would have to change the entire program because C code and data are not closely linked as they are in C++.

With C++, your car rental program would represent the cars as instances of a class. Each car variable would have packed with it not only the rental data, but also functions that acted on that data, such as if_rented(), check_damage(), and clean_car(). Because your data is now active, it behaves more like the real-world cars themselves. You will automatically produce faster code because the code more closely overlays the real-world objects it represents.

Before exploring member functions in more detail, think for a moment about the placement of the four member functions in the Date class. Why are they public? They must be public, for if they were not, no other function could call them. The public member functions are the avenues through which you access the private data members. The member functions have access to the private data, and only they have access. (There are exceptions that you will see when you read further into this book, but for now, accept the fact that private data members can be accessed only by member functions of the same class.) Figure 8.2 shows how the rest of the program can access only public members, and how the private members are accessible only through the public members. In other words, the public members are the tools needed to access the private ones.

The Need for Member Functions

Member functions can access private member data values. A member function can change, erase, and print private members in the class. For now, member functions are the only way to work with private data. Putting the member functions and member data together makes the data active and more cohesive. The object's (the class variable's) data and members work as a team, and no other part of the program can interfere (and mess things up).

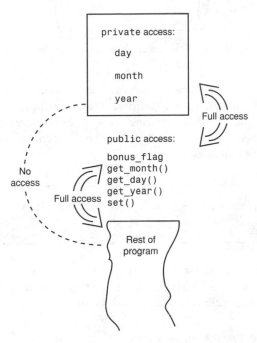

Figure 8.2. The program accesses private class *members through the* public *members.*

If you have ever programmed using an API (Application Program Interface) such as the Windows API, you are familiar with the concept of private and public access. You gain access to the internal workings of the system through generalized functions that manipulate that internal data. Figure 8.3 shows still another view of the member functions and how they aid the rest of the program. Member functions are the "go-between" for the private members and the rest of the program.

In C++ terminology, member functions are sometimes called *methods*. Instead of adding another layer of complexity, this book keeps referring to them as member functions (functions that are members of a class or a struct).

113

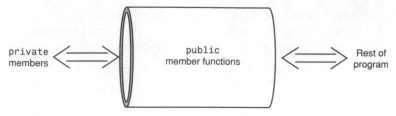

Figure 8.3. public *members help the rest of the program use the* private *members.*

The earlier code listing that contained both data members and member functions was not a complete class definition. It served its purpose for introducing the placement of member functions. The next listing contains the same class with the member function's code as well. These functions are very small—so small, in fact, that each function's code makes a perfect candidate for inline functions.

 The inline keyword is not needed when you define member function code inside the class declaration.

This listing is the complete class definition. It is "complete" because you can see the member data as well as the complete code for the member functions. You could add much more to this class, but it makes a good introduction for understanding member functions.

```
class Date {
    int day;  // Private data members
    int month;
    int year;
public:
    int bonus_flag;  // Public bonus date flag
    int get_day(void)  // Public member functions
        { return (day); }  // inline functions
    int get_month(void)
        { return (month); }  // No inline keyword needed
    int get_year(void)
        { return (year); }
    void set(const int d, const int m, const int y)
        { day=d;     // Assigns each of the data members
          month=m;   // the passed arguments
          year=y;
          return; }
};  // End classes with semicolons

Date today, tomorrow;  // Defines two instances (two objects)
```

The Date class certainly seems much busier than the C structures you are used to working with. The keywords public and private, as well as the member functions, extend the concept of a data structure. As you will see as you progress through this book, these extended classes do not add to program complexity. In fact, they do just the opposite—they decrease program complexity.

Think about the following: Until these last two chapters, all structures you worked with contained only data. All of a sudden, you have to get used to seeing data and functions in your class (and structs). The code for your member functions will be code that normally went in the body of a C program. The code and data were not tied together in C, and too many functions had too much access to the data. C++ program bodies are much smaller than corresponding C programs. The data now contains member functions that work on that data (accessing, printing, changing the data, and so on). The body of a C++ program gets much smaller because the code is taken out of the general pool of code and placed with its data. You therefore compartmentalize your code into easy-to-maintain segments (objects) to decrease programming time and bugs.

Review the program example just shown, and remember the following three important concepts about the program:

1. private data can be accessed only by member functions such as get_day().

2. No inline keyword is needed when you put the class function code inside the class declaration.

3. main() (and any other functions in the body of the program that go below the class) can access only the five public members called bonus_flag, get_day(), get_month(), get_year(), and set().

Encapsulation is the combination of member data and member functions in an object.

C++ programmers and reference manuals call this binding of struct and class member data and member functions *encapsulation*. The data and functions that work on that data are combined into their own "capsule" in the program. *Encapsulation* is an unfortunate word, because its length and sound scare away more would-be C++ programmers than they should. Now that you see the need for encapsulation, you should not be too worried about the term. You can see that *encapsulation* fairly well describes the binding of data and functions into a capsule-like form.

Class Scope: Accessing *private* Members

The member function set() is the only function in the entire program that can change the data members day, month, and year. Why? These three data members are private and only member functions of the same class can do anything with the private data. Two instances of the Date class were defined in this code's fragment—today and tomorrow. Because these two objects are variables of the Date class, do you think that these objects are visible to main() (assuming that main() appears after the class code in the program)? The answer is yes. main() can use these variables because today and tomorrow are global. Any function from the global definition to the end of the source code can see these two class variables because they are visible throughout the rest of the source file, as all global variables are.

private class members have class scope.

Even though main() can access the global class variables today and tomorrow, main() does not have access to every piece of those variables. C++ has an additional scope that does not exist in C. It is known as *class scope*. The private data members have class scope (they are visible within the class) but not global or even local scope.

You probably are wondering when this chapter will get around to discussing using the member functions. There are four member functions in the Date class—get_day(), get_month(), get_year(), and set(). The only purpose of the first three functions is to tell the outside program what values are in the private data members. Almost every class has functions that return private data members' values. These types of functions are called *access functions*. They access private data for the rest of the program. The rest of the program can use the public member functions, so when the program needs to know the value of a private data member, the program can call one of the access functions for that particular class. There is nothing magical about the names of the access functions; you can name them whatever you like. Not all classes need access functions, although most have some in one form or another.

How Far Does This Go?

The access functions return private data values in a very controlled way. If you write a class and do not want a program to know that private data's values, you control the access by not supplying any access functions such as get_year().

Can you think of any way for the programmer to get at that private data if he or she really wants to? The only thing the programmer has to do is insert the public keyword at the top of the class. At that point, all bets are off. Any function can access any member of that class (as long as the class variable is within the scope of the function).

Data hiding is not a bulletproof mechanism. Programmers have full access to the `class` declaration and can change it according to their whims. Nevertheless, changing `class` access modes violates the spirit of data hiding and, ultimately, of object-oriented programming. Think twice about modifying a `class` declaration, because data-hiding is meant to help you program more strictly and accurately, using the C++ regulations set up by the programmer.

Going back to the Date class program, suppose that you want to set the value of the `bonus_flag` member in the `today` variable. Keeping in mind that a class is just like a `struct`, here is how your program would access the `today` variable's `bonus_flag`:

```
today.bonus_flag = 1;  // Sets today's bonus flag to true
```

This prints `today`'s `bonus_flag` variable:

```
cout << today.bonus_flag << endl;
```

As you might expect, you can access and change both `today`'s and `tomorrow`'s `bonus_flag` values all you want because those members are `public` to the rest of the program. However, you could never try any of these:

```
today.day = 13;        // INVALID  These
tomorrow.month = 2;    // INVALID      are
today.year - 1993;     // INVALID        all
tomorrow.year = 1993;  // INVALID          private!
```

Not only can you not initialize these `private` data members of either `class` variable, but you cannot print them either. This, too, is not valid:

```
cout << "Today is " << today.day << "\n";        // INVALID
cout << "Tomorrow is " << tomorrow.day << "\n";  // INVALID
```

To print any of the `private` Date `class` members, you must call the access functions from `main()` or from any other function in the body of the program. Because the dot operator can go between a `class` variable and its member, you call member functions like this:

```
avar = tomorrow.get_day();
```

Do not get bogged down in syntax. This is nothing more than a function call. It begins to show some insight in C++. Look at the `get_day()` member function. `avar` is assigned the return value of `get_day()`. Nowhere in `get_day()`'s argument list do you see the variable `tomorrow`. Therefore, how does C++ know which object, `today` or `tomorrow`, to get? Obviously, C++ tells `get_day()` to use the `tomorrow` object. C++ secretly passes a pointer to `tomorrow` into the member function's argument list. This secret pointer is not a big deal at this time, but remember that C++ does a lot behind the scenes.

> As with `struct` and `class` data members, you can call a member function with the `->` operator as well. The `->` requires a pointer on the left side and a member on the right (just as with regular C `struct` data members). If you defined a pointer to a `class` object like this:
>
> ```
> Date * dateptr = today;  // Defines a pointer to today
>                          // object
> ```
>
> you could call the `get_day()` member function like this:
>
> ```
> dateptr->get_day();  // Calls today's get_day()
>                      // function
> ```

Of course, before assigning or printing the `Date` members, you must initialize them. Because `main()` cannot assign values to the hidden data members of `today` and `tomorrow`, the `Date` class programmer supplied a `public` member function that could be called to pass values to the `private` data. This line of code assigns values to the `tomorrow` variable's `day`, `month`, and `year`:

```
tomorrow.set(21, 8, 1993);  // Calls the member function
                            // and sets three private values
```

In C++ terminology, you are not calling a function; you are *sending a message to an object*. The message is "Set `tomorrow`'s members to these three values: 21, 8, and 1993." In other words, the object knows how to do several things from its member functions. The programmer just has to tell the object what to do. The message-passing analogy becomes more intuitive the more you see of C++.

A Complete Program Using the *Date* Class

Finally, here is a complete program that uses the `Date` class. This program declares two local `Date` class variables, `date1` and `date2`; sets the first date to 7/4/1993 and the second to 12/31/1993; and prints them with appropriate holiday messages to the screen. As with `struct` data, just because the members appear in *day-month-year* order does not mean that you have to initialize or print them in any order.

DATE1.CPP. Uses the Date class.

```cpp
// Filename: DATE1.CPP
// Uses the Date class.
#include <iostream.h>
class Date {
   int day;  // Private data members
   int month;
   int year;
public:
   int bonus_flag;  // Public bonus date flag
   int get_day(void)  // Public member functions
      { return (day); }  // inline functions
   int get_month(void)
      { return (month); }  // No inline keyword needed
   int get_year(void)
      { return (year); }
   void set(const int d, const int m, const int y)
      { day=d;    // Assigns each of the data members
        month=m;  // the passed arguments
        year=y;
        return; }
};  // End classes with semicolons
void main()
{
   Date date1, date2;      // Defines two class variables
   date1.set(4,7,1993);    // Sets the first variable's members
   date2.set(31,12,1993);  // Sets the second variable's members

   // Prints the dates using the access functions
   cout << "Celebrate Independence Day on this ";
   cout << date1.get_month() << "/" << date1.get_day();
   cout << "/" << date1.get_year() << "\n";
   cout << "Happy New Year on this ";
   cout << date2.get_month() << "/" << date2.get_day();
   cout << "/" << date1.get_year() << "\n";
}
```

Here is the output from this program:

```
Celebrate Independence Day on this 7/4/1993
Happy New Year on this 12/31/1993
```

Member functions give the rest of the program all the access needed to use the private members safely.

Notice that main() does not need access to the private data; the public member functions give main() a pathway to the private data. main() can use the values of the private data with the get_...() access functions, and main() can change the private data with the set() function. Even though main() can both read and write the private data,

119

access to the private data is *fully controlled through member functions*. (At this point, the Date class has no error-checking to make the control complete, but it will soon enough.) When developing a class, include all the functions the rest of the program needs to access the private data. If the rest of the program is not supposed to change data, do not write public member functions that allow the program to change the data.

Despite the controlled access, the Date class program is far from complete. There is no error-checking in the set() function, but there should be. The class member functions should ensure that none of their data members get bad values. Therefore, C++ objects can be self-protecting. As the program now stands, the programmer can set the Date variables to any value, effectively rendering the controlled access useless. Here is an improved version that traps incorrect Date values. The error-checking is kept extremely simple. The only checking is keeping the days less than or equal to 31, the month less than or equal to 12, and the year greater than 1990. The programmer could never set the date like this:

```
set(99, 125, 0);  // Testing functions will not allow
```

Despite the primitive error-checking (negative values and correct months of 28, 29, and 30 days are not checked), the class is becoming more complete. As you are beginning to see, the more work your objects do, the less work the programmer that uses those objects has to do. Study the revised program. Now that a little (very little) error-checking is added, the access is more controlled. This program asks the user for valid date values and sets the date accordingly as long as the date falls within the checked ranges.

While looking at the program, see if you can determine why the three set...() testing functions are the private section.

DATE2.CPP. Adds some error-checking to the Date class.

```
// Filename: DATE2.CPP
// Adds some error-checking to the Date class.
#include <iostream.h>
class Date {
    int day;  // Private data members
    int month;
    int year;
    int test_day(const int d)   // Private member functions
        { return (d>31) ? 0: 1; }
    int test_month(const int m)
        { return (m>12) ? 0 : 1; }
    int test_year(const int y)
        { return (y<1990) ? 0 : 1; }
public:
```

```
   int bonus_flag;  // Public bonus date flag
   int get_day(void)  // Public member functions
      { return (day); }  // inline functions
   int get_month(void)
      { return (month); }  // No inline keyword needed
   int get_year(void)
      { return (year);  }
   int set(const int d, const int m, const int y)
      { if (test_day(d) && test_month(m) && test_year(y))
         { day=d;     // Assigns each of the data members
           month=m;  // the passed arguments
           year=y;
           return (1);
         }
        else return(0); }  // Bad date
};  // End classes with semicolons

void main()
{
   Date today;  // Defines a class variable
   int m, d, y;  // Holds user's input values

   cout << "What is today's day, month, and year (i.e., 18 3 1993)? ";
   cin >> d >> m >> y;

   // Sets the date class values, printing them if correct
   if (today.set(d, m, y)) {  // Returns 1 if date okay
      cout << "The date is set to " << today.get_month();
      cout << "/" << today.get_day() << "/" ;
      cout << today.get_year() << "\n";
   }
   else {
      cout << "You did not enter a correct date."; }
}
```

Have you determined why the test functions are private? As with data members, only public members can call private functions within the class. main() has no need for the testing functions; the functions are called from set(). Because set() is a member function of the class, it has full access to the testing functions. Any time you need a class function that is called only from another member function, declare it private to keep it away from the rest of the program that should not have access to it.

> In the preceding program, notice the functions that do not change their parameters. These functions' parameter lists include the const keyword before many parameters. Although it is not required, const ensures that the functions will not attempt to damage the contents of the parameters.

Doing It the C Way

In C, the same date program would have no controlled access to the data. As an OOP programmer, you should write complete objects that other programmers (and you) can use in their programs. Try to predict all the operations ever needed on the class data and include member functions that perform the work. Then, to use the objects, you and other programmers only have to use the member functions instead of re-inventing the wheel by writing functions that access the data. If you foresee all the class needs, your classes will be stand-alone, fully operational objects that a programmer can use, just like ready-made parts that the programmer can pick off a shelf.

DATE.C. C's version of the date program.

```
/* Filename: DATE.C */
/* C's version of the date program */
#include <stdio.h>
struct Date {
   int day;
   int month;
   int year;
   int bonus_flag;   /* Unused so far */
};
int test_day(const int);   /* Prototypes */
int test_month(const int);
int test_year(const int);
int set(struct Date *, int, int, int);

void main()
{
   struct Date today;   /* Defines a structure variable */
   int m, d, y;   /* Will hold user's input */

   printf("What is today's day, month, and year (i.e., 18, 3, 1993)? ");
```

```
   scanf(" %d, %d, %d", &d, &m, &y);

   /* Sets the date class values, printing them if correct */
   if (set(&today, d, m, y)) {  /* Must pass today by address */
      printf("The date is set to %d/%d/%d", today.day,
             today.month, today.year); }
   else printf("You did not enter a correct date.");
}

int set(struct Date *today, int d, int m, int y)
{
   /* Dereferences today so that it's changed in main() too */
   if (test_day(d) && test_month(m) && test_year(y)) {
      today->day=d;     /* Assigns each of the members the */
      today->month=m;   /* passed arguments */
      today->year=y;
      return (1);
   }
   else return(0);   /* Bad date */
}

int test_day(const int d)  /* These are called from set() */
{
   return ((d > 31)? 0: 1);
}

int test_month(const int m)
{
   return ((m > 31)? 0: 1);
}

int test_year(const int y)
{
   return ((y < 1990)? 0: 1);
}
```

For these short examples, the length of the C and C++ program versions are not much different. However, as your programs grow, the C++ versions should be much shorter than their C counterparts would be. Of course, a shorter program does not always mean a better program, but shorter C++ programs are usually much easier to maintain than C equivalents.

The C version is not necessarily more difficult to understand, but its primary drawback is the passing of today by address. By preceding a function call with its class variable, C++ takes care of letting the function have a pointer to the proper object. This eliminates the need for you to dereference the object. Another drawback that you probably can predict by now is that the program has total access to the individual structure members. Because there

123

is no way to privatize the members, the programmer does not have to use the set()
function. He or she can go right ahead and bypass the function by directly assigning the
values, such as this:

```
today.day = d;
today.month = m;
today.year = y;
```

C++ eliminates this possible error-causing directness.

Summary

Even after seeing the controlled access of data hiding (encapsulation), you might still be
wondering what this OOP fuss is all about. At this point, you might think that member
functions have only added an extra layer of complexity. In reality, a layer of complexity is
taken away by member functions! They relieve the program of having to worry about data
manipulation. The main() program and its functions become controlling statements that
send objects messages, and the objects themselves go off and perform the action requested
by the message.

With the body of your programs getting smaller, the programs become much more
manageable. The objects become pieces that you put together, and because of their isolated
nature, you never have to worry about the code within each object. You also never have to
worry about overwriting a value by accident, because C++ does not enable you to change
private data.

The housing industry would never be as efficient as it is today without modular parts. A
builder can build a house in only a few days (with help) because a builder does not really
build the entire house. Rather, the builder buys prebuilt windows, prehung doors, existing
A-frames, dishwashers, cabinets, and lots of other already-built parts. The builder only has
to assemble those pieces into a house.

Some day, if the OOP purists have their way (thankfully, it looks as if they *are* getting
their way), programs of the future will be written by piecing together prewritten objects.
As more and more C++ programmers are trained, you will see (and write) many class
libraries. Unlike with C libraries, you don't have to know anything about the internal
workings of C++ classes to use them effectively. Even more powerful abilities will come your
way as you read through the rest of this book, learning more about OOP and C++.

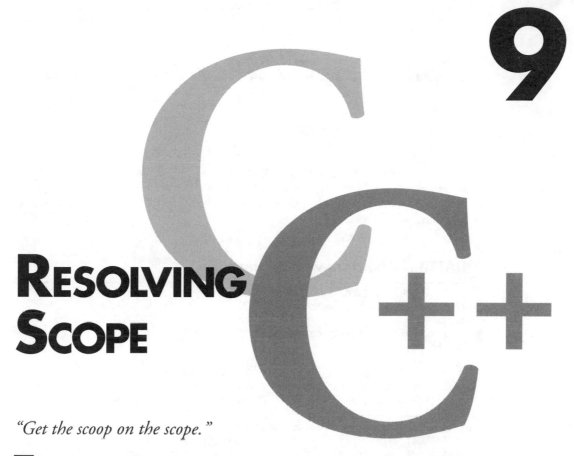

RESOLVING SCOPE

"Get the scoop on the scope."

This chapter continues the discussion of member functions by showing you how to code non-inline member functions. When a member function's code gets too lengthy, the class becomes too "busy" if you put the code inline. Not only that, the C++ compiler rarely respects your inline request when the function gets too long.

In this chapter, you will learn about:

- Non-inline member functions

- Using the scope resolution operator with classes

- Default arguments with member functions

- The advantages of separating class code from source files

- The this pointer

Non-*inline* Function Members

You should now begin to see that objects are very self-contained pieces of active information. You can get to the object's private members, whether data or functions, only through the very strict public member functions listed in the class.

Despite their self-containment, you do not have to put all the object's code inside the class declaration. In the preceding chapter's Date class example, all the class code was included in the class. Here is the same class without the code. Only the data and member functions' prototypes are in the class.

DATE3.H. The class without the code.

```
// Filename: DATE3.H
// The class without the code
class Date {
   int day;  // Private data members
   int month;
   int year;
   int test_day(const int d);    // Private member functions
   int test_month(const int m);  // that test each data member
   int test_year(const int y);   // to see if within good range
public:
   int bonus_flag; // Public bonus date flag
   int get_day(void);    // Public member functions that
   int get_month(void);  // return the private data to the
   int get_year(void);   // calling code
   int set(const int d, const int m, const int y);  // Sets the
                     // private data if it's within valid range
};  // End classes with semicolons
```

This class declaration is much cleaner than that at the end of the preceding chapter because it contains no member function code. The function code has to follow the class (or be linked to the class code). When the member function code falls below the class declaration, it looks like this:

```
int Date::test_day(const int d)  // Defines the Date class functions
   { return (d>31) ? 0: 1; }

int Date::test_month(const int m)
   { return (m>12) ? 0 : 1; }
```

```
int Date::test_year(const int y)
   { return (y<1990) ? 0 : 1; }

int Date::get_day(void)  // Public member functions
   { return (day); }  // inline functions

int Date::get_month(void)
   { return (month); }  // No inline keyword needed

int Date::get_year(void)
   { return (year);  }

int Date::set(const int d, const int m, const int y)
   { if (test_day(d) && test_month(m) && test_year(y))
       { day=d;    // Assigns each of the data members
         month=m;  // the passed arguments
         year=y;
         return (1);
     }
     else return(0); }  // Bad date
```

By removing the code from its `inline` state to the regular function listing, you remove the clutter from your objects.

Your classes are cleaner without lots of inline code.

You might have noticed the additional use of the scope resolution operator, `::`. In Chapter 2, "C++ Data and Program Basics," you saw the `::` used to access global variables when a local variable had the same name. The `::` is much more practical when you use it for `class` functions. When you write member function code that is *not* `inline`, always precede the function name with its `class` name and the `::`. The reasons are twofold.

First, you can have as many classes in your program as you need. Two or more classes can have member functions with the same name. For example, you might have a customer class, an employee class, and a supplier class, each with a `disp()` member function. When you move the `disp()` code away from the `class` declarations, you must tell C++ which `disp()` member function belongs to which class. That is, you must resolve the scope of the function—hence the term *scope resolution operator*. Here is a skeleton of such a series of `disp()` member functions:

```
//  :
// The class declaration must appear earlier
Customer::disp()     // The scope resolution operator
{                    // tells C++ that this disp()
// : Code goes here  // function goes with the Customer
}                    // class

Employee::disp()
{
```

127

```
// : Code goes here
}

Supplier::disp()
{
// Code goes here
}
```

You might imagine the conflict if you did not resolve the class scope. C++ would have no way of knowing which disp() to execute without the proper class before the function name.

The scope resolution operator also helps you (and the compiler) differentiate the class member function from the regular functions.

The other reason for resolving the scope is to let C++ know that certain functions are class functions. C++ therefore will not treat them as regular functions that require prototypes (outside of a class). Also, C++ would enable you to call the function with an object. In other words, you would not be able to do this:

```
cust.disp();  // INVALID if disp() had no resolved scope
              // because C++ could not find disp() in a class listing
```

You do not have to define every function in the date program outside the class. As a matter of fact, many functions, such as the one-line access functions such as get_year(), are much better left inline. The overhead needed for the function call is too great to warrant separate non-inline functions.

Here is the complete date program from Chapter 8, "Member Functions," with much of its member function code moved outside the class:

DATE3.CPP. Moves the longer functions to the program's body.

```
// Filename: DATE3.CPP
// Moves the longer functions to the program's body.
#include <iostream.h>
class Date {
   int day;  // Private data members
   int month;
   int year;
   int test_day(const int d);  // Private function prototypes
   int test_month(const int m);
```

```
    int test_year(const int y);
public:
    int bonus_flag;   // Public bonus date flag
    int get_day(void)   // inline public member functions
        { return (day); }
    int get_month(void)
        { return (month); }  // No inline keyword needed
    int get_year(void)
        { return (year);  }
    int set(int d, int m, int y);
};  // End classes with semicolons

int Date::test_day(const int d)   // Non-inline functions
{ return (d>31) ? 0: 1; }

int Date::test_month(const int m)
{ return (m>12) ? 0 : 1; }

int Date::test_year(const int y)
{ return (y<1990) ? 0 : 1; }

int Date::set(const int d, const int m, const int y)
{ if (test_day(d) && test_month(m) && test_year(y))
    { day=d;      // Assign each of the data members
      month=m;   // the passed arguments
      year=y;
      return (1);
    }
  else return(0);   // Bad date
}
void main()
{
    Date today;  // Defines a class variable
    int m, d, y;  // Holds user's input values

    cout << "What is today's day, month, and year (i.e., 18 3 1993)? ";
    cin >> d >> m >> y;

    // Sets the date class values, printing them if correct
    if (today.set(d, m, y)) {  // Returns 1 if date okay
        cout << "The date is set to " << today.get_month();
        cout << "/" << today.get_day() << "/" ;
        cout << today.get_year() << "\n";
    }
    else {
        cout << "You did not enter a correct date."; }
}
```

This program is exactly the same code as you saw in the preceding chapter, except for the member function code's being moved outside the Date class. The code for get_day(), get_month(), and get_year() is inline because their code resides in the class, but the rest of the member functions are regular non-inline class functions. Keep in mind that C++ might not respect an inline request. It might treat get_day(), get_month(), and get_year() as non-inline member functions, but these functions are so short that C++ probably will inline them.

If the functions are short enough, you can request that the member function code defined outside the class be inline. To let C++ know about the inline request, put inline before the member function name. Here is test_day() as an inline member function defined outside the class:

```
inline int Date::test_day(int d)   // Inline function
{ return (d>31) ? 0: 1; }
```

Another Class Example

The concept of class variables containing both code and data is still new to you. Before you go any further, it would help you to see another sample program. To give you a different angle on classes, a payroll-savings account class program follows.

The Date class program you have been seeing is far from complete. For the Date class to be more usable, it needs much more error-checking, month-name print capabilities, date-arithmetic member functions, and so on. You can imagine that a complete Date class requires much more than is shown in these programs to be ready for general-purpose use. You also can imagine that the more your class contains, the less that code needs to do to use the class. As programmers write additional classes, the more general-purpose objects the rest of the programming community can use. It is this reusability of objects that should begin to shorten data processing backlogs over the next few years.

The following program might be used by a payroll department to track an employee benefit savings plan. The payroll savings account is a good candidate for a class. The class is called PaySave in the program. The program tracks data for employee accounts, tracking interest rates and employer deposits. The program also requires that the account balance be printed and that each month the account's interest be credited. These are perfect jobs for member functions. As with the Date class program, much more could be done to make the PaySave class more complete, but this is a good first shot at it.

PAYSAV1.CPP. Payroll savings account program.

```cpp
// Filename: PAYSAV1.CPP
// Payroll savings account program
#include <iostream.h>
#include <iomanip.h>

class PaySave {
   float rate;  // Rate savings plan currently earns
   float mnth_cmpny;  // Monthly amount company contributes
   float balance;  // Balance for this employee
public:
   float get_rate(void) {
      return (rate); }  // Accesses rate (read-only)
   float get_mnth_cmpny(void) {  // Accesses company amount
      return (mnth_cmpny); }
   float get_balance(void) {  // Accesses balance in account
      return (balance); }
   void set_rate(const float r);  // Sets the rate
   void set_cmpny(const float m);  // Sets company's contribution
   void set_balance(const float b);  // Sets beginning balance
   void emp_deposit(const float emp_amt);  // Adds deposit
   double emp_with(const float emp_amt);  // Subtracts withdrawal
   void month_end(void);  // Updates balance with interest rate
};

// Code for member functions follows
void PaySave::set_rate(const float r) {  // Sets the rate
   rate = (r > 0.0) ? r : 0.0;  // Ensures against negative rate
}

void PaySave::set_cmpny(const float m) {  // Sets company month-
   mnth_cmpny = (m > 0.0) ? m : 0.0;       // end contribution
}

void PaySave::set_balance(const float b) {  // Sets initial balance
   balance = b;
}

void PaySave::month_end(void) {  // Updates balance with
   balance += ((rate * balance) + mnth_cmpny);  // month-end
}                                                // figures

void main()
{
   PaySave boss, worker;  // Defines two class variables
   boss.set_rate(.003);  // Sets up Boss's initial data
```

continues

131

PAYSAV1.CPP. continued

```
        boss.set_cmpny(250.00);
        boss.set_balance(0.0);   // Initializes balance first time

        worker.set_rate(.002);
        worker.set_cmpny(100.00);
        worker.set_balance(0.0);   // Initializes balance first time

        cout << setprecision(2);   // Sets output for two decimals
        cout << "The boss's payroll investment balance information: \n";
        cout << "Balance: $" << boss.get_balance() << "\n";
        cout << "Monthly Rate: %" << (boss.get_rate()*100.0) << "\n\n";

        cout << "The worker's payroll investment balance information: \n";
        cout << "Balance: $" << worker.get_balance() << "\n";
        cout << "Monthly Rate: %" << (worker.get_rate()*100.0) << "\n\n";

        // Update for end-of-month values
        boss.month_end();
        worker.month_end();

        cout << "At the end of the 1st month, the boss's balance is $";
        cout << boss.get_balance() << "\n";
        cout << "At the end of the 1st month, the worker's balance is $";
        cout << worker.get_balance() << "\n";

        // Update for second end-of-month values
        boss.month_end();
        worker.month_end();

        cout << "At the end of the 2nd month, the boss's balance is $";
        cout << boss.get_balance() << "\n";
        cout << "At the end of the 2nd month, the worker's balance is $";
        cout << worker.get_balance() << "\n";
}
```

Here is the program's output:

```
The boss's payroll investment balance information:
Balance: $0
Monthly Rate: %0.3

The worker's payroll investment balance information:
Balance: $0
Monthly Rate: %0.2
```

```
At the end of the 1st month, the boss's balance is $250
At the end of the 1st month, the worker's balance is $100
At the end of the 2nd month, the boss's balance is $500.75
At the end of the 2nd month, the worker's balance is $200.2
```

TIP

The beginning balance set function, `set_balance()`, is a good candidate for a C++ default argument. If the prototype looks like this:

```
void set_balance(const float b=0.0);  // Sets beginning
                                       // balance
```

the default 0.0 argument makes more sense than leaving it blank. Most of the time, an employee's beginning balance will be zero, and because `set_balance()` is useful only for initializing the `balance` member, the 0.0 default argument enables you to initialize `balance` like this:

```
set_balance();  // Argument unneeded; balance defaults to
                // 0.0
```

Actually, C++ has a better mechanism than default arguments for initializing `class` data members. The next chapter, "Constructor and Destructor Functions," shows you improved (and easier) ways to initialize data than calling specific code to do it.

Throughout your C++ programming career, you might wonder which data makes good `class` candidates and which does not. Generally, any time your program tracks several occurrences of anything, you have found good `class` candidates. In the preceding program, the company would have several employees (although this program tracks only two of them, the boss and a worker). The multiple employees are good `class` objects. If the program were expanded to become a general-purpose employee tracking and payroll program, a variable such as the company's federal tax ID number would not go in a class because it is a stand-alone variable, not linked to any one employee.

NOTE

There might be two C++ alternatives to the federal tax ID number and similar stand-alone variables. The federal ID might be part of a larger company class that tracks and modifies company statistics and identification data. Depending on how the program accessed the company information, it might be well-suited to a class, especially if you want to protect the data members' integrity from other functions. Also, Chapter 13, "`static class` Members," explains *static members*. Stand-alone variables such as the federal ID number sometimes work well as static data members.

Here is the same employee savings account program in regular C. Again, in C there is no capability to hide data from functions that should not access the data. Although data-hiding is an important feature of C++, it is not the most important. Soon you will see more reasons why the C++ code is far superior to the C version. For now, analyze the different placement of the work functions in C. If you change the `class` data structure, such as adding a bonus member, the C++ `main()` program does not have to change much; you would change only the member functions or add new functions. In the C program, you would have to trace through the program, making sure that the changes do not affect other parts of the program.

PAYSAV1.C. C's version of the payroll savings plan.

```c
/* Filename: PAYSAV1.C */
/* C version of the payroll savings plan */
#include <stdio.h>

struct PaySave {
    float rate;   /* Rate savings plan currently earns */
    float mnth_cmpny;  /* Monthly amount company contributes */
    float balance;  /* Balance for this employee */
};

/* Prototypes */
float get_rate(const struct PaySave emp);
float get_mnth_cmpny(const struct PaySave emp);   /* Accesses amount */
float get_balance(const struct PaySave emp);  /* Accesses balance */
void set_rate(struct PaySave *, const float r);   /* Sets the rate */
void set_cmpny(struct PaySave *, const float m);  /* Company adds */
void set_balance(struct PaySave *, const float b);  /* Sets balance */
void month_end(struct PaySave *);  /* Updates balance with */
                                   /* interest rate */

void main()
{
    struct PaySave boss, worker;  /* Two struct variables */

    /* Passes structure variables by address to change them */
    set_rate(&boss, .003);  /* Sets up Boss's initial data */
    set_cmpny(&boss, 250.00);
    set_balance(&boss, 0.0);  /* Initializes balance first time */

    set_rate(&worker, .002);
    set_cmpny(&worker, 100.00);
    set_balance(&worker, 0.0);  /* Initializes balance */
    printf("The boss's payroll investment balance information: \n");
    printf("Balance: $%.2f \n", get_balance(boss));
```

```
      printf("Monthly Rate: %%%.2f \n\n", (get_rate(boss)*100.0));
      printf("The worker's payroll investment balance information: \n");
      printf("Balance: $%.2f \n", get_balance(worker) );
      printf("Monthly Rate: %%%.2f \n\n", (get_rate(worker)*100.0));

      /* Update for end-of-month values */
      month_end(&boss);
      month_end(&worker);

      printf("At the end of the month, the boss's balance is $");
      printf("%.2f \n", get_balance(boss));

      printf("At the end of the month, the worker's balance is $");
      printf("%.2f \n", get_balance(worker));
}

float get_rate(const struct PaySave emp) { /* Read-only access functions */
   return (emp.rate); }              /* are not really needed because all */
                                     /* C's struct members are public */

float get_mnth_cmpny(const struct PaySave emp) {
   return (emp.mnth_cmpny);
}

float get_balance(const struct PaySave emp) {
   return (emp.balance);
}

void set_rate(struct PaySave * emp, const float r)  /* Sets rate */
{
   (*emp).rate = (r > 0.0) ? r : 0.0;  /* Ensures against */
}                                      /* negative rate */

void set_cmpny(struct PaySave * emp, const float m)  /* Sets company */
{                                         /* month-end contribution */
   (*emp).mnth_cmpny = (m > 0.0) ? m : 0.0;
}

void set_balance(struct PaySave * emp, const float b)  /* Balance */
{
   (*emp).balance = b;
}

void month_end(struct PaySave * emp)  /* Updates balance with rate */
{                                     /* payment and contribution */
   (*emp).balance+=(((*emp).rate*((*emp).balance))+(*emp).mnth_cmpny);
}
```

It takes a lot of wrestling to get such a program working in C. It is difficult to pass and receive addresses of structures (unneeded in the OOP version), and you must make sure that parentheses enclose the structure dereference before the dot operator. (In other words, `(*emp).balance` refers to the balance, but `*emp.balance` does not.) Because C does not offer a hidden pointer to the structures you pass, you have to pass the structure address to every function that modifies the structure. Obviously, C leaves a lot to be desired when put side-by-side with C++. Even the familiar standby, `printf()`, seems archaic (with the three `%s` just to get one `%` printed to the screen) compared to `cout`.

Separating the *class* Code from Your Program

The `Date` class and the `PaySave` class programs both are great starts toward C++ class usage. These classes are simple. They have very little error-checking, so you can concentrate on the placement of object-oriented member functions. So far, you have learned the following about classes:

- The difference between `struct` and `class`

- The `private` member access by `public` member functions

- How to call member functions from the program

- Reasons for moving the member function code out of the `class` definition using the scope resolution operator

The last item, moving function code into the body of the program, enables you to keep the class as concise as possible, leaving only the data, the member function prototypes, and the short `inline` member functions. There is an additional way to clean up C++ programs. Most C++ programmers take the `class` member functions completely out of the source code that uses them.

The `class` description often is called the *class header*. For instance, here is the `PaySave` class header:

```
class PaySave {
    float rate;  // Rate savings plan currently earns
    float mnth_cmpny;  // Monthly amount company contributes
    float balance;  // Balance for this employee
public:
    float get_rate(void) {
```

```
      return (rate); }  // Accesses rate (read-only)
   float get_mnth_cmpny(void) {  // Accesses company amount
      return (mnth_cmpny); }
   float get_balance(void) {  // Accesses balance in account
      return (balance); }
   void set_rate(const float r);  // Sets the rate
   void set_cmpny(const float m);  // Sets company's contribution
   void set_balance(const float b);  // Sets beginning balance
   void emp_deposit(const float emp_amt);  // Adds employee's deposit
   double emp_with(const float emp_amt);  // Subtracts employee withdrawal
   void month_end(void);  // Updates balance with interest rate
};
```

As you probably can guess from the name *class header,* you should put this code in a separate header file. A good name for the file would be paysave.h, and you would include it at the top of the C++ program that uses it with this line:

```
#include <paysave.h>
```

Programmers who use the paysave.h file have to know the class member function names, or they cannot use the class. Because header files are text files (as opposed to compiled code), programmers could print the class to see the names of its data and functions. Commercial classes, of which there are more available all the time, come with class header files much larger than paysave.h. These class headers usually come with ample documentation that describes in detail the class and how to use it.

Compile member functions separately from the source code.

You also should separate the member function code from the program that uses it. Unlike with the class header, most C++ programmers supply member function code *already compiled* in object code form. Commercial C++ class writers rarely supply the source code for their class functions, and programmers who use the classes do not need the source code. There is no reason why programmers using classes should see the member function source code. Actually, the less you know about the internal workings of a class, the more likely you are to concentrate on your own application, use the class as it was intended to be used, and stay away from tweaking the class and bringing bugs into it.

 Distributing the compiled object code instead of the source code also protects your programming work if you sell `class` libraries to others. Because the class's implementation code does not appear in its source format (you keep that), you retain full control over it, not letting someone else use pieces of the code in other software.

Figure 9.1 shows how you would put together the `PaySave` class program. Programmers always need the `class` header source code because they have to know the internal names of the `class` members. The programmer needs only the actual `class` code in compiled object format.

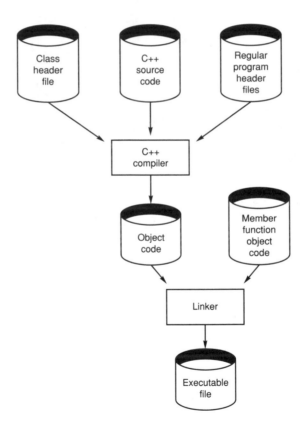

Figure 9.1. The parts of a typical C++ program.

Most of the programs in this book include all `class` code as well as the member function listings so that you can see how the program interacts with the class.

General-Purpose Classes

A C++ program is a lot like a component stereo system you put together. With the stereo, you might buy a CD player from one store, a receiver from another, and a tape deck and speakers from a third. All the components might be made by different companies, but they were designed to be used together to form a single stereo system.

You need only a little knowledge of the stereo to connect the parts. You do not have to know anything about how the CD laser beam works, how the receiver amplifies the radio signals, or how the tape deck produces stereo sound. All you need to know (and all the instruction manual tells you) is how to connect the components and how to use them. An instruction manual would be useless to the majority of stereo users if it described the electronics inside the equipment.

The stereo analogy is perfect for C++ `class` libraries. When you use a class, whether you purchase it from a software vendor or write it yourself, blind yourself to the actual inner-working `class` code. You need to know only how to use the class, such as the member function arguments, the return values, and the names of the `public` data members (if there are any). The class becomes a collection of parts, like the stereo parts, that you piece together and use in your programs. The objects know how to behave, so you do not need to understand their code to use it.

Same Function, Different Objects

In the payroll savings plan program, two different objects, `boss` and `worker`, use the same member functions, such as `get_rate()` and `month_end()`. More accurately, the program sends those functions messages. In these two statements:

```
boss.month_end();
```

and

```
worker.month_end();
```

the program sends the `month_end()` function a message to perform the `month_end()` code on the `boss` and `worker` data members, respectively.

The same function acts on two different objects, `boss` and `worker`. In the program shown earlier, these objects had the same format. Not all objects look the same (just as all structures in C programs do not look the same). Through the power of C++, you can perform the same functions on objects that are different. As this book progresses through the more advanced stages of C++ programming, you will see how to apply the same member functions to different types of objects.

For now, just get used to the fact that this is possible. The concept of the same member function working on different objects is similar to the way overloaded functions work (as explained in Chapter 5, "C++ Function Advantages"). You can give the same function name to functions with different argument lists, letting C++ figure out the correct code to execute.

In real life, you use the same instructions for different objects all the time. For instance, you open a box and you open a door. Both open very differently, but when you hear the word *open,* you have no problem acting out the operation because you know how to open both. You sit on a chair, you sit on a couch, and you sit on the floor. You (the "object" in this case) accomplish these three things differently, yet the verb "sit" poses no problem for you because you know how to accomplish the three related, but different, tasks.

Polymorphism: When the same function works on different types of objects.

When writing C++ programs, you can apply the same function to different types of objects. C++ programmers have a name for this feature: *polymorphism.* Polymorphism is a word that sounds much more frightening than it is, but it has been in use for a long time and it looks as if it is here to stay. Polymorphism means "many different forms." In other words, the same function can work on different types of objects.

When you can apply the same function to different objects, you shorten your program development time. Polymorphism is one reason why C++ programmers can write programs faster than C programmers (and programmers of other non-OOP languages). Suppose that you have two different objects, a customer record and an employee record. Even though some of the data members are similar (such as first name, last name, address, and so on), many of the data members look very different (such as annual salary and exemptions for the employees and year-to-date purchases and customer pricing codes for the customers).

In the program, you would need to print both the employee and the customer data. Instead of a different print function for both objects, you can use the same print function

to print the two objects, even though both of the object's formats are very different. You do not need to keep track of a different function name that prints customers, a different function name that prints employees, and a different function to print all the other objects in the program. You could print the various objects with the same function name, such as this:

```
employee.print();  // Prints the employee objects
customer.print();  // Prints the customer object
```

Polymorphism, using the same function name for different types of objects, keeps the clutter out of your code. Again, C++ attempts to model the real world better than other programming languages do. In the real world, you apply the same word to different actions (such as *ride* a motorcycle and *ride* a bike). As you progress through this book, you will read a more complete discussion of polymorphism, and you also will see its true power.

Throughout the last couple of chapters, this book has made references to a hidden pointer that C++ keeps track of. C++ sends to every member function a hidden argument that you do not see in the argument list. (Even if your argument list specifies void arguments, C++ passes a hidden pointer.) C++ must do this work behind the scenes before polymorphism works. The secret pointer C++ passes is called the this pointer.

Looking at *this*

When the PaySave class program calls a member function like this:

```
boss.set_rate(.07);
```

and

```
worker.set_cmpny(100.00);
```

C++ actually sends to set_rate() and set_cmpny() the following function calls:

```
set_rate(&boss, .07);
```

and

```
set_cmpny(&worker, 100.00);
```

There is nothing magical about how C++ figures out which object to send. C++ is just doing a little work for you. When you call a member function, preceding the function name with the object name, C++ takes the address of that object and passes it to the member function. The receiving member function's parameter list does not look the way it does in the class listing either. There has to be an extra parameter to receive the address to the

object. Here are the true prototypes for `set_rate()` and `set_cmpny()`:

```
void set_rate(PaySave * this, const float r);
```

and

```
void set_cmpny(PaySave * this, const double m);
```

C++ calls the hidden object pointer `this` and precedes all your data members with a reference to `this`. The `set_rate()` function looks like the following:

```
void PaySave::set_rate(const float r) {  // Sets rate
   rate = (r > 0.0) ? r : 0.0;  // Ensures against negative rate
}
```

   Internally, C++ changes it to this:

```
void PaySave::set_rate(PaySave *this, const float r) {  // Sets rate
   this->rate = (r > 0.0) ? r : 0.0;  // Ensures against negative rate
}
```

   Now you can see how C++ knows which class's data to really work on. You do not have to bother with the extra argument. As long as you call the function with the correct object, C++ does the rest of the work.

   There are times when knowing about the `this` pointer enables you to take a shortcut. You can access the object, inside the member function, by using `*this`. You will not always have a need to know about `*this`, but the true C++ programmer always remembers it is there and uses it when it would be helpful. One of the few times you might need `this` is for returning the object from a function. You might need to return the object that a member function was passed. This code does that:

```
return (*this); // Returns the same object that was passed to this function
```

   When writing member function source code, you do not know, because of polymorphism, exactly which object will be passed to the function. Nevertheless, whatever object is passed, you can get to it by indirectly referencing `this`.

> `*this` is a constant, so do not try to modify it.

Summary

This chapter delved fairly deeply into classes, member functions, the scope resolution operator, `inline` functions, and the secret `this` pointer. Make sure that you understand the concepts from this chapter before reading further. This chapter marks a turning point in many new C++ programmers' training. With this chapter, you are beginning to see how a C++ programmer thinks and how he or she implements object-oriented programming with data hiding and polymorphism (the ability to apply the same function name to different objects).

These OOP concepts are very new to you if you have never used an OOP language. Putting code inside data just isn't the way you did things before. Seeing the compiler insert hidden pointers in argument lists might not sit well with you either, but that is exactly what C++ does. In the long run, you will see that the C++ way is a much better way of programming. Objects should more closely model the real world they represent, and C++ lets program data do just that.

If this chapter is still fuzzy, read over it one more time. If you understand the concepts, take a deserved rest. As soon as you have mastered this chapter, the rest of C++ flows smoothly. Although there is still much material to cover, you will have little problem tackling the rest of C++ as soon as this chapter's foundation becomes rooted in your understanding.

The next chapter, "Constructor and Destructor Functions," shows you the C++ way of initializing objects. C++ supplies a mechanism called a *constructor* which ensures that your data will always have good values and a *destructor* that cleans up data when your program is done with it. With constructors and destructors, your data takes on even more responsibility, eliminating more work from your programs that use `class` data.

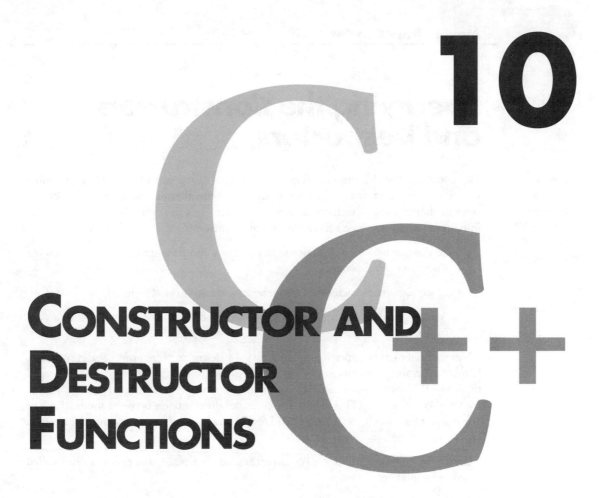

CONSTRUCTOR AND DESTRUCTOR FUNCTIONS

"Objects, objects everywhere."

C++ provides *constructor functions* and *destructor functions* (usually called *constructors* and *destructors*). Almost every C++ class contains constructors and destructors. They are member functions that initialize and clean up `class` objects. Constructors give you a way to ensure that objects are defined with initial values without violating the constraints of data hiding. Destructors become important when you need to free object memory that you allocated with the constructor.

Constructors and destructors are member functions.

In this chapter, you will learn:

- How to specify constructors

- How to specify destructors

- When constructors and destructors get called

Specifying the Constructors and Destructors

A class can have one or more constructors and one destructor.

List constructor and destructor functions along with the rest of your `class` member functions. Constructors and destructors are always member functions, and most classes contain them. A class can have as many constructors as necessary (because objects are initialized in different ways) and a maximum of one destructor.

Unlike the other member functions, constructors and destructors have strict naming rules. They are the following:

- Always give constructor functions the *same* name as the class itself.

- Always give destructor functions the same name as the class, preceded with a tilde (~).

Never specify return types for constructor and destructor functions (not even `void`). Constructors always return an initialized object of the class, so the return type is not needed or allowed. Constructors can have arguments, however. The arguments enable you to overload constructors. (This is how the compiler differentiates between more than one constructor function if you supply one.) Destructors have neither arguments nor a return type.

Given these naming rules, the constructor and destructor names for a class called customer would be

```
customer();  // Constructor
```

and

```
~customer();  // Destructor
```

The payroll savings `class` header file you saw introduced in the last chapter would look like this after adding some constructor and destructor functions:

```
class PaySave {
   float rate;  // Rate savings plan currently earns
   float mnth_cmpny;  // Monthly amount company contributes
   float balance;  // Balance for this employee
public:
   PaySave();  // Three constructor functions
   PaySave(r=0.05, m=100.0);
   PaySave(r=0.05, m=100.0, b=0.0);
   ~PaySave();  // Destructor function
   float get_rate(void) {
```

146

```
      return (rate); }  // Accesses rate (read-only)
  float get_mnth_cmpny(void) {  // Accesses company amount
      return (mnth_cmpny); }
  float get_balance(void) {  // Accesses balance in account
      return (balance); }
  void set_rate(const float r);  // Sets the rate
  void set_cmpny(const float m);  // Sets company's contribution
  void set_balance(const float b);  // Sets beginning balance
  void emp_deposit(const float emp_amt);  // Adds deposit
  double emp_with(const float emp_amt);  // Subtracts withdrawal
  void month_end(void);  // Updates balance with interest rate
};
```

If you capitalized the first letter of the class name (as most C++ programmers do) or any letters inside the class name, be sure to retain the same capitalization of the constructor and destructor functions as well.

Unlike with other member functions, never call constructors or destructors explicitly. The C++ compiler does that for you, which explains the strict naming rules for constructors and destructors.

Using Constructor Functions

Perhaps the best way to introduce how constructors work is to relate them to something C and every other compiler does when it declares an instance of a variable. This book is getting into areas that are difficult to relate to the things you are used to in C. As you get more into OOP concepts, you will see that OOP offers many more elegant ways of accomplishing programming, and there are fewer and fewer possible analogies to non-OOP programming languages. Nevertheless, the C language uses constructors and destructors, but it does so without your knowing or caring. With C++, knowing about constructors and destructors becomes very important indeed.

Suppose that you define the following variables:

```
int   limit=100;
float weight=28.4;
```

C (and C++) does the following: It calls an internal constructor function to reserve two variable locations, one the size of an integer and one the size of a floating-point value. The compiler attaches the variable names limit and weight and puts 100 and 28.4 into them, respectively.

The memory was not allocated before the definition, and after the compiler reserves the variable's space, that space is reserved *until the variables go out of scope.* As soon as the variables go out of scope, the compiler releases the memory used by the variables by calling an internal destructor. The variables and their values disappear completely.

C and C++ have no problems calling their internal constructors and destructors for all the built-in data types. These data types are well-defined to the languages. Even when you do not initialize the values, C and C++ call internal constructors (and destructors when the variables go out of scope). For instance, two constructors are called here too:

```
int   limit;   // Variables are reserved, but
float weight;  // their values are unknown
```

The constructors reserve the space and attach the variable names to that space, but whatever values happened to be in that reserved memory are still there. Neither C nor C++ zeros the memory for you (with the minor exception of static variables, such as global variables, which you would and should use sparingly anyway), and it is your responsibility to initialize the variables.

The new problem introduced with C++ is the abstract data type, the `struct` and `class` variables that you define. C++ cannot read your mind and know what you want when you define a class. C++ does the best it can with the information it has for the new class, but things work out much better when you tell C++ how to define your `class` data with a constructor function. With a constructor, the C++ compiler properly declares, defines, and initializes your objects exactly the way you want them declared.

Don't Get Trapped by False Initialization

Beginning C++ programmers might try to initialize `class` members like this:

```
class AClass {
public:
   int a = 5;  // INVALID
   int b = 6;  // INVALID
   int c = 7;  // INVALID
};
```

You already should know that this is not allowed with a C `struct`. Because C++ classes are analogous to C structures (except that the class is `private` by default), this is no more allowed for a `class` than for a `struct`.

Until you define actual `class` variables (objects), C++ allocates no storage for your `class` data members. Because no storage is defined with a `class` declaration such as the one shown here, no memory is available in which to put initial values. It is only until you define an actual `class` variable like this:

```
main()
{
   AClass var1;  // Defines an actual class variable
   // Rest of program goes here
```

that you can initialize the members with values such as this:

```
var1.a = 5;  // Okay because there is now a variable to
var1.b = 6;  // initialize
var1.c = 7;
```

That is, this was the only way to initialize `class` data until the constructor function came along.

It is inside the constructor function that you tell C++ how to initialize the data. As soon as you write a constructor, you never have to worry about uninitialized data.

Never explicitly call constructor functions. The compiler calls the constructor for you when you define the object. The following program contains a class called `Sample`. `Sample` contains three private data members and two member functions, `print_it()` and the constructor function `Sample()`. Pay special attention to the `main()` function. It is very small, but the `class` data seems to be initialized and prints with no problems due to the constructor function.

C++ always calls constructor functions when you define an object.

SAMPLE1.CPP. Shows that C++ calls the constructor function without your intervention.

```
// Filename: SAMPLE1.CPP
// Shows that C++ calls the constructor
// function without your intervention.
#include <iostream.h>
#include <iomanip.h>
class Sample {
   char  c;
   int   i;
   float x;
```

continues

SAMPLE1.CPP. continued

```
public:
   Sample();  // A constructor function
   void print_it(void);
};

// The two member functions follow
Sample::Sample()  // Constructor code
{
   c = 'A';  // Initializes data members of the defined object
   i = 1;
   x = 2.0;
};

inline void Sample::print_it(void)
{
   cout << setprecision(1);  // For floating-point member
   cout << "In avar: c, i, x are " << c;
   cout << ", " << i << ", and " << x << endl;
}

void main()
{
   Sample avar;  // Defines the storage for avar AND calls constructor
   avar.print_it();  // Prints the data member values
};
```

Here is the output:

```
In avar: c, i, and x are A, 1, and 2.0
```

main() had to define only the class object called avar. The Sample class took care of the rest of the initializing job. C++ called the constructor function that initialized the members of avar when main() first defined avar.

In C, you would have to explicitly assign each of the structure members values when you defined the structure variable, such as this:

```
struct Sample avar = {'A', 1, 2.0};  /* The C method */
```

Variable initialization in C is error-prone at best.

The C approach is error-prone; you might forget to initialize one of the data members, or you might transpose one of the initial values. The error might not appear until many lines later when the values you thought were in the class are not actually there. If the structure has lots of members, you could call an initialization function after you've defined the structure, but again, you might forget to do this for every structure variable you define.

150

Constructors inside `class` definitions ensure that the end-programmer does not have to bother him- or herself with the initialization of the object.

C++ Cures Maintenance Migraines

In the program with the `Sample` class, the two-line `main()`'s only job is to let the objects take care of themselves, including initialization and printing. The `Sample` class is a simple one, but if the class were composed of hundreds of members, `main()` would be no different; it still would be two lines long. Here is the epitome of the power of C++ in action: Even if you greatly modified the `Sample` class, adding data members, changing the current data members, adding member functions that would not be used in this program but might be used by others, and changing the names of the internal data members, *you still would not have to make any changes to* `main()`.

Software must change in today's rapidly moving world. Software maintenance is the primary reason for the current tremendous backlog of programming projects. OOP enables you to compartmentalize each class, turning data into self-contained objects that do work (in effect, small programs within your larger programs). One of the biggest headaches of programming departments is changing the programs when the data changes. A "simple" change, such as adding an extra character to a customer code, can change hundreds or even thousands of lines of code with traditional non-OOP procedural languages because the code, maybe almost every single line in every single program, might be closely tied to the format of the data. With OOP, if the structure of the data changes, you change only the `class` member functions. The programs that use those classes require no change. All your maintenance is limited to a specific class that interfaces to the programs that use that class.

The Constructor's Timing

One overused but illustrative example in C++ tutorials is placing a `cout` inside the constructor function just to prove that the constructor is called by the compiler and that you do not explicitly do anything except define a `class` variable to trigger that constructor call. Suppose that you add a single `cout` statement to the constructor function in the program just shown (the code follows). The output shows that C++ called the constructor before anything else was done in `main()`.

SAMPLE2.CPP. Shows that C++ calls the constructor function without your intervention.

```
// Filename: SAMPLE2.CPP
// Shows that C++ calls the constructor
// function without your intervention.
#include <iostream.h>
#include <iomanip.h>
class Sample {
   char  c;
   int   i;
   float x;
public:
   Sample();  // A constructor function
   void print_it(void);
};

// The two member functions follow
Sample::Sample()  // Constructor code
{
   cout << "Constructor just called!\n";  // Added line
   c = 'A';  // Initializes data members of defined object
   i = 1;
   x = 2.0;
};

inline void Sample::print_it(void)
{
   cout << setprecision(1);  // For floating-point member
   cout << "In avar: c, i, x are " << c;
   cout << ", " << i << ", and " << x << endl;
}

void main()
{
   Sample avar;  // Defines the storage for avar AND calls constructor
   avar.print_it();  // Prints the data member values
};
```

Because C++ calls the constructor when avar gets defined, the cout in the constructor executes, resulting in the slightly modified output:

```
Constructor just called!
In avar: c, i, and x are A, 1, and 2.0
```

152

As a review, the following steps take place when you define an object (a class variable) and when a constructor member function exists:

1. C++ reserves memory for the object

2. C++ calls the constructor

See if you can guess the output if main() were slightly changed to the following:

```
void main()
{
   cout << "At the top of main()\n";
   Sample avar;  // Defines the storage for avar AND calls constructor
   cout << "In the middle of main()\n";
   avar.print_it();  // Prints the data member values
   cout << "At the end of main()\n";
};
```

main() has cout statements that execute before C++ calls the constructor, right after the constructor is called, and before the program terminates. Here is the output:

```
At the top of main()
Constructor just called!
In the middle of main()
In avar: c, i, and x are A, 1, and 2.0
At the end of main()
```

> Programmers rarely put constructor functions in the private part of a class. The class would be unusable to most code. If you tried to define an object, C++ could not call the constructor function because the constructor is private and main() has no access to private member functions or data. There are some advanced reasons for putting constructors in the private section, but for now, concentrate on letting your primary program define objects (and therefore, automatically call the constructors for those objects).

Constructor Arguments

The Sample constructor had no default arguments. It was left to the body of the constructor code to initialize the data members of the class. Because a constructor basically acts like any member function (except for the way it's called), you can supply an argument list, passing to the constructor values and using default argument lists.

For example, programmers frequently use constructors to zero out data. Such constructors make good candidates for default arguments; you can supply default zero arguments, but then override them if you need to for certain objects. Here is the Sample class program with a "zero everything" default argument list:

SAMPLE3.CPP. Shows that C++ calls the initializing constructor function without your intervention.

```
// Filename: SAMPLE3.CPP
// Shows that C++ calls the initializing constructor
// function without your intervention.
#include <iostream.h>
#include <iomanip.h>
class Sample {
    char  c;
    int   i;
    float x;
public:
    Sample(char, int, float);  // Constructor
    void print_it(void);
};

// The member functions follow
inline Sample::Sample(char p1='\0', int p2=0, float p3=0.0)
{
    c = p1;
    i = p2;
    x = p3;
}

inline void Sample::print_it(void)
{
    cout << setprecision(1);  // For floating-point member
    cout << "In avar: c, i, x are " << c;
    cout << ", " << i << ", and " << x << endl;
}

void main()
{
    Sample avar;  // Defines the storage for avar AND calls constructor
    avar.print_it();  // Prints the data member values
};
```

Because the function body is empty (the default argument list does all the work), the constructor resides inline with the `class` definition. Here is the output:

```
In avar: c, i, and x are , 0, and 0.0
```

> The value of c does not print because the default argument sets it to null zero. (Some compilers might print a special character for the value of c instead of the empty space before the comma.)

As with any default argument list, you can specify your own values when you define the `class` object, overriding the default values. The problem with overriding the defaults is that you do not explicitly call the constructor. So how do you indicate the overriding argument values?

The designers of C++ thought ahead enough to include a way to specify constructor arguments. All you need to do is place the overriding argument values in parentheses after the defined `class` variable. For example, if you want to override the zeroed-out argument list with the character Q and the integer 10, you can do so by defining the `Sample class` variable like this:

```
Sample avar('Q', 10);  // Overrides the first two default arguments
```

The floating-point member remains 0.0 because you did not override that default argument.

Here is a similar program that uses the `Sample` class, except that four objects are declared, each one using a different set of parameters:

SAMPLE4.CPP. Overriding the constructor's default arguments.

```
// Filename: SAMPLE4.CPP
// Overriding the constructor's default arguments
#include <iostream.h>
#include <iomanip.h>
class Sample {
   char  c;
   int   i;
   float x;
public:
   Sample(char, int, float);  // Constructor
```

continues

SAMPLE4.CPP. continued

```cpp
    void print_it(void);
};

// The member functions follow
inline Sample::Sample(char p1='\0', int p2=0, float p3=0.0)
{
    c = p1;   // Assigns the parameters to the data members
    i = p2;
    x = p3;
}

inline void Sample::print_it(void)
{
    cout << setprecision(1);   // For floating-point member
    cout << "\nIn avar: c, i, x are " << c;
    cout << ", " << i << ", and " << x << endl;
}

void main()
{
    Sample avar1;   // Defines the storage for avar AND calls constructor
    avar1.print_it();   // Prints the data member values

    Sample avar2('A');   // Defines storage and one default argument value
    avar2.print_it();

    Sample avar3('A', 25);   // Defines storage and two default argument
                             // values
    avar3.print_it();

    Sample avar4('A', 25, 100.0);   // Overrides all three default argument
                                    // values
    avar4.print_it();
};
```

The output, showing the different default arguments and their overriding values, appears as follows:

```
In avar: c, i, and x are , 0, and 0.0
In avar: c, i, and x are A, 0, and 0.0
In avar: c, i, and x are A, 25, and 0.0
In avar: c, i, and x are A, 25, and 100.0
```

Remember that in C++, you can define variables anywhere before you use them. This program defines four variables—avar1, avar2, avar3, and avar4—just before it prints each of them.

> **NOTE**
>
> If you want an object to receive its default arguments, never call the constructor with parentheses, like this:
>
> ```
> Sample avar();   // Not a proper way to construct with
>                  // default values
> ```
>
> The compiler would think that you were prototyping a function called avar() that took no arguments and returned a Sample object. Therefore, leave off the parentheses if you want all the default argument values used.

Other Constructor Forms

The preceding example showed one way to pass parameters to the constructor function. When you define a new object, you can place the arguments inside parentheses after the object, like this:

```
Sample avar4('A', 25, 100.0);   // Passes three values to the constructor
```

This method probably is the most common, but there are a few other forms that can come in handy at times. It was mentioned earlier in this chapter that you never explicitly call a constructor function. Although that is true because you never see a constructor call sitting on a line by itself, there is a way to call a constructor with arguments that appears to be an explicit function call. Here it is:

There are several ways to specify a constructor.

```
Sample avar4 = Sample('A', 25, 100.0);   // Passes three values to
                                          // the constructor
```

Because the constructor call, with three arguments, resides on the same line as the object definition, and because a constructor is always and only called when an object is defined, this last syntax is allowed. An object is always returned when a constructor is called, so the Sample() function's return object is assigned to the new object named avar4. To some, the call is clearer than the first one, because it shows the actual Sample() function. Nevertheless, there are a couple of reasons why many programmers do not use this method for single scalar (non-array) objects.

First of all, the assignment sign and repeated function name take extra keystrokes, which makes them more prone to errors than the more succinct version shown first. More importantly, different compilers handle this kind of constructor differently. One compiler might return a constructed object, directly placing that value into the new object. Other C++ compilers might call a special constructor called a *copy constructor* (that you will read more about in Chapter 12, "Operator Overloading") that creates a member-by-member copy of the new value to the object. At this point, the difference between these compiler-dependent methods means nothing, but keep in mind that different forms of constructors might do slightly different things.

The second form of the constructor call is very helpful when you want to dynamically allocate objects with the new operator. Because new returns a pointer to the object, you can declare and construct a new Sample object like this:

```
Sample *aptr = new Sample('A', 25, 100.0);
```

This line allocates a new Sample object from the heap, assigns the address of the object to aptr, and initializes the three data members to the arguments.

To sum all this up, using the Sample class shown in the last program, you would use the following to create an object using all the constructor's default arguments:

```
Sample avar;  // Defines the object, constructing it with default values
```

To use only some of the default arguments, you would define the object, like this:

```
Sample avar('A', 25);  // Only the third argument is defaulted
```

To override all the default arguments, explicitly specify all three arguments, like this:

```
Sample avar('A', 25, 123.4);  // Overrides all defaults
```

Another form, and an identical form as long as you define non-array values, is this:

```
Sample avar = Sample('A', 25, 123.4);  // Overrides all defaults
```

If you want to dynamically allocate objects and accept all the default arguments, create a pointer to the new object, like this:

```
Sample *avar = new Sample;  // Accepts all defaults
```

If you want to dynamically allocate an object and override one or more default arguments, do this:

```
Sample *avar = new Sample('A', 25, 123.45);  // Overrides all defaults
```

158

Default Constructors

Several of the preceding constructor examples were *default constructors*—that is, they either had no parameters, or none were required because default parameter values were specified. For example, given the `Sample` class, both of these constructor definitions are default constructors:

```
Sample::Sample(char p1='\0', int p2=0, float p3=0.0)
```

and

```
Sample::Sample()
```

The first is a default constructor because no arguments are required. The constructor can be called without any specified values. The second is a default constructor that relies on the body of the constructor (and not passed arguments) to determine the member values.

> Releases prior to AT&T 2.1 treated these two kinds of default constructors differently, but they have been the same for a few years now.

There are times when you must have default constructors and times when you do not have to have them. Sometimes, when you need to define several array objects, you need a default constructor. (The next section, "Constructors and Arrays," discusses constructors for arrays.)

You can even have too many default constructors. For example, suppose that both of the default constructors you just saw were in the same program. When you try to define an object such as this:

```
Sample an_obj;   // Tries to construct for you
```

C++ has no way of knowing which constructor to use. Because you specified no arguments, either of the constructors is a possible candidate. You have two ambiguous overloaded constructors. C++ would have to call a constructor, but either would work because neither requires arguments. Your compiler would issue a message similar to this:

```
Ambiguity between 'Sample::Sample(char,int,float)' and 'Sample::Sample
```

When you are first learning C++, it is easy to forget that C++ always calls a constructor when you define an object. One of four things is possible:

1. If you do not supply a constructor, C++ performs its own, generally by reserving space for the object, but not initializing it with anything.

2. If you supply a constructor, C++ uses it.

3. If you supply several constructor functions, thereby overloading constructors, C++ executes the one whose parameters match that of the arguments in your constructor call. As with any overloaded function, you must ensure that no two constructor functions match in their argument lists.

4. If you supply more than one default constructor, C++ will be confused because, in effect, you supplied two of the same overloaded function.

It is worth noting that the following two constructors are not ambiguous and would work together in the same class:

```
Sample::Sample(char p1, int p2, float p3)
```

and

```
Sample::Sample()
```

Unlike the two ambiguous constructors listed earlier, the first of these constructors has no default arguments; these two constructors represent valid overloaded constructors. The first one requires three arguments when called, and the second gets called only when *no* arguments are specified in the call (when C++ calls the constructor automatically).

Constructors and Arrays

Constructors are vital when you want to declare an array of objects and have a constructor called for *each* element in the array. For instance, if you did not supply a constructor, the following statement would define an array of 100 Sample class objects allocated from the heap:

```
Sample sp[100];
```

No constructor is needed (other than a simple internal constructor that C++ would call that simply gathers the memory for you). Each of the Sample objects is still uninitialized; more accurately, each of the Sample objects' data members contains garbage values until you call the code to put valid values into the 100 Sample object's data members.

The programmer should not have to worry about initializing data when constructors are so easy to write. In C, there is no way around writing the initialization code for each structure you define. The primary advantage of C++ constructor functions for arrays is that C++ calls the constructor *for every element in the array* automatically. Consider this modified Sample class program:

SAMPLE5.CPP. Shows that C++ calls the initializing constructor function for every array object.

```cpp
// Filename: SAMPLE5.CPP
// Shows that C++ calls the initializing constructor
// function for every array object.
#include <iostream.h>
#include <iomanip.h>
class Sample {
   char  c;  // Data members in each object
   int   i;
   float x;
public:
   Sample(char, int, float);  // Constructor
   void print_it(void);
};

// The member functions follow
inline Sample::Sample(char p1='A', int p2=25, float p3=123.45)
{
   c = p1;  // Assigns the default parameters
   i = p2;  // to the data members
   x = p3;
}

inline void Sample::print_it(void)
{
   cout << setprecision(1);  // For floating-point member
   cout << "In avar: c, i, x are " << c;
   cout << ", " << i << ", and " << x << endl;
}

void main()
{
   const count=5;  // Defaults to int

   // The next line reserves and initializes EVERY array element
   Sample sp[count];

   for (int i=0; i<count; i++) {  // Prints the array
     sp[i].print_it();
   }
};
```

Here is the program's output:

```
In avar: c, i, x are A, 25, and 123.4
In avar: c, i, x are A, 25, and 123.4
In avar: c, i, x are A, 25, and 123.4
In avar: c, i, x are A, 25, and 123.4
In avar: c, i, x are A, 25, and 123.4
```

C++ called the constructor for each of the objects in the array. The main() function stayed at a much higher level than a corresponding C program because it did not have to initialize each member in the array.

The reason for array constructors should seem obvious at this point. If you were to delete the constructor function from this program, C++ would still allocate an array of five objects, but it would not initialize them. You would get garbage in the output because each object's data members would have bad data.

Always supply constructors for objects, even if the constructor has an empty parameter list and an empty body of code. The world changes rapidly, and so do the needs of programs used today. By supplying a default constructor, albeit an empty one, you create a richer class that you can easily modify in the future. Actually, when supplying a default constructor, go ahead and initialize the values to some initial value. Zero is probably the best choice. Too many people who might later use the class could forget to initialize the data. The zeroes might not be the best initial values in all cases, but they are almost always safer than the garbage values that would be there otherwise.

If you do not supply a constructor, C++ uses an internal (and simple) one for scalar objects and arrays of objects. If you supply a constructor, but not a default constructor, C++ issues a compile error if you attempt to define an object without using arguments to trigger the constructor you supplied. For example, consider the following nondefault constructor:

```
Sample::Sample(const char p1, const int p2, const float p3)
{
  c = p1;   // Assigns the default parameters
  i = p2;   // to the data members
  x = p3;
}
```

If this were the only constructor in the program, C++ would issue a compiler error if you tried this in main():

```
Sample an_object[5];   // Error; C++ cannot find a default constructor
```

C++ refuses to use its internal simple constructor if you supply any constructor at all.

162

The new operator (introduced in Chapter 4, "Pointers, References, and Memory Allocation") easily allocates an array of values from the heap. Here is a program similar to the last one, except that the array is allocated dynamically (actually, the pointer to the heap memory acts like an array).

SAMPLE6.CPP. Shows that C++ calls the initializing constructor function for every allocated array object.

```
// Filename: SAMPLE6.CPP
// Shows that C++ calls the initializing constructor
// function for every allocated array object.
#include <iostream.h>
#include <iomanip.h>
class Sample {
   char  c;  // Data members in each object
   int   i;
   float x;
public:
   Sample();  // Constructor
   void print_it(void);
};

// The member functions follow
inline Sample::Sample()
{
   c = 'A';  // Assigns the default parameters
   i = 25;   // to the data members
   x = 123.45;
}

inline void Sample::print_it(void)
{
   cout << setprecision(1);  // For floating-point member
   cout << "In avar: c, i, x are " << c;
   cout << ", " << i << ", and " << x << endl;
}

void main()
{
   const count=5;  // Defaults to int

   // The next line allocates and initializes EVERY array element
   Sample *sp  = new Sample[count];
```

continues

SAMPLE6.CPP. continued

```
  for (int i=0; i<count; i++) {  // Prints the array
    sp[i].print_it();
  }
  delete [] sp;  // Makes sure delete works on all objects (count times)
};
```

Without the `delete`, C++ would free the memory of `sp` (the pointer) when it went out of scope, but not the heap memory pointed to by `sp`. (The operating system would be responsible for the clean-up, and the operating system should not have to do the programmer's work.) The brackets are required to let C++ know that an array, not just a single value, must be deleted.

Using Destructor Functions

A class can have at most one destructor.

As with constructors, destructor functions take care of the back end of cleaning up after your data. Often, more needs to be done than the variable's simply going out of scope and the memory's being released. For simple `class` members of built-in data types, you do not *always* need a destructor, because the data will go out of scope and the compiler will release its memory (although in C++, you should rarely have constructors without a destructor).

One very important, and obvious, need for clean-up is when a class contains a pointer to dynamically allocated memory. When the pointer goes out of scope, the compiler releases its memory space *but not the memory the pointer points to*. Instead of your program's having to worry about cleaning up after objects, why not have the objects clean up after themselves? Again, the more the objects do, the less the programs that use the class have to do, the less debugging time you expend, and the faster you produce working code.

C++ always calls the destructor function when an object goes out of scope.

Destructor functions take on the following properties:

1. The destructor name is always the same as the `class` name, preceded by a tilde (~).

2. They cannot have a return type.

3. They cannot have arguments.

4. Each class can have a maximum of one destructor.

5. The compiler automatically calls an object's destructor when the object goes out of scope.

Here is the preceding `Sample` class program with a destructor function. Not much happens in this destructor, except that a message prints showing that C++ calls the destructor for every array element. Make sure that you study the output to see what C++ does with the destructor.

SAMPLE7.CPP. Shows that C++ calls the initializing constructor function for every allocated array object.

```
// Filename: SAMPLE7.CPP
// Shows that C++ calls the initializing constructor
// function for every allocated array object and
// also calls the destructor when the objects leave scope.
// The destructor does nothing here except print a message.
#include <iostream.h>
#include <iomanip.h>
class Sample {
    char  c;  // Data members in each object
    int   i;
    float x;
public:
    Sample();  // Constructor
    ~Sample();  // Destructor
    void print_it(void);
};

// The member functions follow
inline Sample::Sample()
{
    c = 'A';  // Assigns the default parameters
    i = 25;   // to the data members
    x = 123.45;
}

inline Sample::~Sample()
{
    cout << "Destructor calling...\n";
}

inline void Sample::print_it(void)
{
    cout << setprecision(1);  // For floating-point member
    cout << "In avar: c, i, x are " << c;
```

continues

165

SAMPLE7.CPP. continued

```
   cout << ", " << i << ", and " << x << endl;
}

void main()
{
   const count=5;  // Defaults to int

   // The next line allocates and initializes EVERY array element
   Sample *sp  = new Sample[count];

   for (int i=0; i<count; i++) {  // Prints the array
     sp[i].print_it();
   }
   delete [] sp;  // Makes sure delete works on all objects (count times)
};
```

Here is the program's output:

```
In avar: c, i, x are A, 25, and 123.4
In avar: c, i, x are A, 25, and 123.4
In avar: c, i, x are A, 25, and 123.4
In avar: c, i, x are A, 25, and 123.4
In avar: c, i, x are A, 25, and 123.4
Destructor calling...
Destructor calling...
Destructor calling...
Destructor calling...
Destructor calling...
```

Destructors are especially important when your constructor allocates a chunk of memory. C++ ensures that the destructor, if you supply one, releases that memory back to the heap. This is the epitome of constructor and destructor power.

The next program shows a modified PaySave class program introduced in Chapter 9, "Resolving Scope." Instead of just calculating two employees' savings after the first month, this program also stores the employees' last names in an array of PaySave objects. The constructor allocates memory for the name, so each object contains a pointer to the allocated data. Figure 10.1 shows the data format set up in the PaySave class.

The main() function allocates the three objects. Each time the program defines one of the three objects, that object's constructor is called. The constructor then allocates additional memory for each object's employee name (as shown in Figure 10.1). Because main() allocated the three objects, main() must delete each object from the heap. As each is deleted, the destructor deallocates the memory for the employee name.

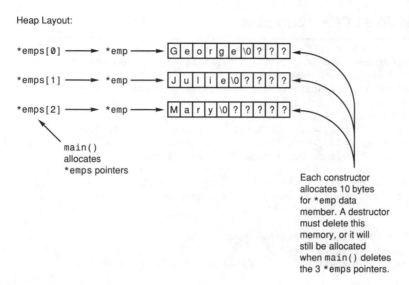

Heap Layout:

Each constructor allocates 10 bytes for *emp data member. A destructor must delete this memory, or it will still be allocated when main() deletes the 3 *emps pointers.

main() allocates *emps pointers

Figure 10.1. The format of each PaySave *object.*

This is a rather long listing. Study main() first to see how it uses the class member functions. Most of main() is simply initialization of the three employees' objects.

PAYSAV2.CPP. Payroll savings account program.

```
// Filename: PAYSAV2.CPP
// Payroll savings account program
#include <iostream.h>
#include <iomanip.h>
#include <string.h>

class PaySave {
   char * emp;  // Pointer to the employee name
   float rate;  // Rate savings plan currently earns
   float mnth_cmpny;  // Monthly amount company contributes
   float balance;  // Balance for this employee
public:
   PaySave();  // Constructor
   ~PaySave();  // Destructor
   char * get_name(void) {  // Accesses employee's name
      return (emp);  }
   float get_rate(void) {
```

continues

PAYSAV2.CPP. continued

```cpp
        return (rate); }   // Accesses rate (read-only)
    float get_mnth_cmpny(void) {  // Accesses company amount
        return (mnth_cmpny); }
    float get_balance(void) {  // Accesses balance in account
        return (balance); }
    void set_name(const char *);  // Initializes the name
    void set_rate(const float r);  // Initializes the rate
    void set_cmpny(const float m);  // Initializes company's contribution
    void set_balance(const float b);  // Initializes beginning balance
    void emp_deposit(const float emp_amt);  // Adds deposit
    double emp_with(const float emp_amt);  // Subtracts withdrawal
    void month_end(void);  // Updates balance with interest rate
};

// Code for member functions follows
PaySave::PaySave()    {
    emp = new char[10];   // 10-character maximum for the name
}

PaySave::~PaySave()  {
    delete [] emp;  // Deletes this object's name memory from the heap
}

void PaySave::set_name(const char * n) {  // Sets the rate
    strcpy(emp, n);  // Assigns passed name
}

void PaySave::set_rate(const float r) {  // Sets the rate
    rate = (r > 0.0) ? r : 0.0;  // Ensures against negative rate
}

void PaySave::set_cmpny(const float m) {  // Sets company month-
    mnth_cmpny = (m > 0.0) ? m : 0.0;       // end contribution
}

void PaySave::set_balance(const float b) {  // Sets initial balance
    balance = b;
}

void PaySave::month_end(void) {  // Updates balance with
    balance += ((rate * balance) + mnth_cmpny);  // month-end
}                                                // figures

void main()
{
```

168

```
PaySave *emps = new PaySave[3];  // Defines three class variables

emps[0].set_name("George");  // Sets this employee's name
emps[0].set_rate(.003);  // Sets up George's initial data
emps[0].set_cmpny(250.00);
emps[0].set_balance(0.0);  // Initializes balance first time
emps[1].set_name("Julie");
emps[1].set_rate(.002);
emps[1].set_cmpny(150.00);
emps[1].set_balance(0.0);
emps[2].set_name("Mary");
emps[2].set_rate(.004);
emps[2].set_cmpny(300.00);
emps[2].set_balance(0.0);

cout << "Before the first month:\n";
cout << setprecision(2);  // Sets output for two decimals
for (int i=0; i<3; i++)  {
   cout << emps[i].get_name() << "'s initial investment information: \n";
   cout << "Balance: $" << emps[i].get_balance() << "\n";
   cout << "Rate:    %" << (emps[i].get_rate()*100.0) << "\n";
}

// Updates for end-of-month values
cout << "At the end of the 1st month, the balances are\n";
for (i=0; i<3; i++)  {
   emps[i].month_end();
   cout << emps[i].get_name() << "\t" << emps[i].get_balance() << "\n";
}

// Updates for second end-of-month values
cout << "At the end of the 1st month, the balances are\n";
for (i=0; i<3; i++)  {
   emps[i].month_end();
   cout << emps[i].get_name() << "\t" << emps[i].get_balance() << "\n";
}

   delete [] emps;  // Calls destructor for EACH emps object
}
```

Here is the program's output. All the names you see were allocated and deallocated by the constructor and destructor calls.

```
Before the first month:
George's initial investment information:
Balance: $0.00
```

```
Rate:     %0.30
Julie's initial investment information:
Balance: $0.00
Rate:     %0.20
Mary's initial investment information:
Balance: $0.00
Rate:     %0.40
At the end of the 1st month, the balances are
George   250.00
Julie    150.00
Mary     300.00
At the end of the 1st month, the balances are
George   500.75
Julie    300.30
Mary     601.20
```

It is important that you understand that main()'s delete is not enough to deallocate all the heap memory. The delete in main() deallocates only the three pointers to the name data but not the name data itself. Figure 10.2 shows what would happen without the destructor's delete. You can see that in many cases, destructors are vital if you want to release all memory used by your program.

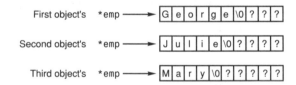

Heap layout:

Figure 10.2. Without the destructor, not all of the heap memory would be restored.

Constructors and destructors offer a strong case for using new and delete in place of malloc() and free(). Neither malloc() nor free() calls constructors or destructors, leaving the full initialization and clean-up burden to you.

Summary

The bottom line on constructors and destructors is that they give the compiler information about how to allocate, initialize, and release storage for your own abstract data types (classes). Both C and C++ already know how to allocate and initialize an integer, whether the integer is global or local. When a local integer goes out of scope, the compiler knows how to release its memory as well (although you do not get more heap memory when a variable goes out of scope). C++ has no way of knowing about data types you define unless you supply constructors and destructors. Because C++ automatically calls a constructor when you define an object, and the destructor when the object goes out of scope, you are in effect extending the compiler to work with your own abstract data types.

The more you program in C++, the more uses you will find for constructors and destructors. One nice thing about C++ is that it encourages you to program in ways you never thought of before, when the language you used was too restrictive. C++ continues to direct your attention to the application's needs and away from the petty details of coding. For example, suppose that you wrote a program that popped a help window onto the screen. A constructor is natural for the window, and a destructor would be a natural place to restore the screen to its pre-window state.

> You will learn about an important kind of constructor called the *copy constructor* in Chapter 12, "Operator Overloading." Although many C++ tutorials and books introduce copy constructors when they introduce constructors, you will be much better prepared for them after mastering friend functions, described in the next chapter.

This chapter concludes Part II of this book. You now have a fundamental understanding of classes, objects, member functions, constructors, and destructors. The next few chapters extend the concepts you now know to show you more power of C++. C++ takes a lot of the tedium from your programming responsibilities.

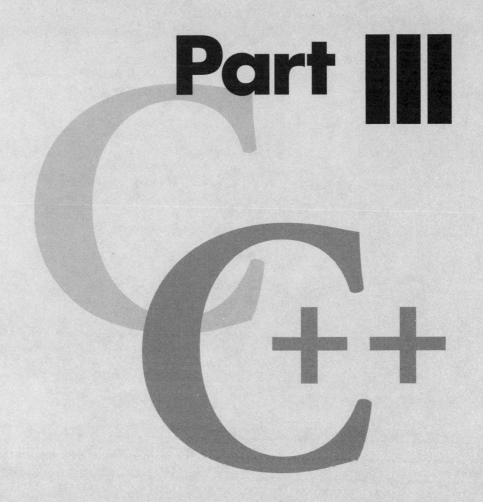

Part III

Operators and Friends

FRIEND FUNCTIONS AND CLASSES

"Who goes there—friend or foe?"

You are now ready to learn how to override hidden data. C++ offers a way for functions to access private members of a class *even if those functions are not members of the class.* "Wait a minute," you might say. "I've just read about a hundred pages that preached the virtues of hiding data. Why would overriding hidden data offer any advantages?"

private members should remain hidden from the rest of the application program; that much still holds true. Certain classes and functions, however, need access to other classes' private members because they work together so closely. When you need private data to be shared, you must follow certain C++ guidelines—namely, using friend functions and classes. friend functions can access private members of other classes. friend classes also can access private members of other classes. This chapter introduces friend functions and classes, explaining how to define and use them. As soon as you understand the fundamentals of friend functions, you will be ready for Chapter 12, "Operator Overloading," which describes the most common use of friend functions in C++.

In this chapter, you will learn:

- The advantages of `friend` functions and classes

- How to define `friend` functions and classes

- Uses of `friend` functions

Needing *friends*

Everybody needs friends, but not all classes need them. Rarely are there specific times when you *must* use `friend` functions. As you program more in C++, you will begin to recognize the need for `friend` functions and the need to use other C++ constructs instead of `friend` functions.

Both functions and classes can be friends with a class.

Not only can a function be a `friend` of another class, but an entire class can be a `friend` of another class as well. Two classes might be `friends` when they are closely related to each other. For example, you might have a class to hold Little League baseball statistics for all the teams. Another class might be a list manager that adds to, deletes from, and prints the team information. The list manager class would need access to the individual statistics of the team class.

The same function ordinarily cannot be a member of more than one class. Consider the following two `class` declarations:

```
class Customer  {
   char name[30];
   int  cnum;
   float ytd_balance;
public:
   Customer();  // Constructor
   void print_em();
};

class Account {
   char acctcode[5];
   float ac_balance;
public:
   Account();  // Constructor
   void print_em();
};
```

`print_em()` is not a member of both classes. Rather, each class has its own `print_em()` function. Therefore, if you define a variable for each class like this:

```
Customer person;   // Defines an object for each class
Account  ledger;
```

because each class contains its own print_em() member function, you can print each object by coding this in the body of the program:

```
person.print_em();   // Prints the person object
```

and this:

```
ledger.print_em();   // Prints the ledger object
```

And yet print_em() is not being called twice. Two different print_em() functions are being called. This should be a review by now. Figure 11.1 further illustrates the fact that print_em() occurs two different times in two different places and that both print_em()s are completely different functions.

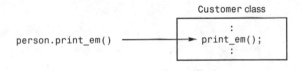

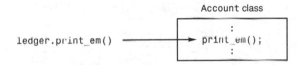

Figure 11.1. There are two different print_em() *functions.* C++ *resolves the proper scope of each one.*

Recall that class members have class scope. class scope is how the same program can have two different functions named print_em(), with each print_em() belonging to a different class.

Suppose that you want to write a print function that prints values from both objects. The data members of Customer are private to Customer and the data members of Account are private to Account. Without friend functions, you could not use a single function to print both classes' private members.

If you are already beginning to write C++ programs after reading the first ten chapters of this book (and the only way to really learn C++ is to write C++ programs), you might see many uses for `friend` functions and `friend` classes. Be warned, however, that there are more C++ building blocks to learn and that a `friend` function is not always the best answer when one class needs access to another class. Nevertheless, there are times when `friend` classes and functions make lots of sense. As you progress through this book, you will better learn the need for `friend` functions and `friend` classes, and you also will learn when to avoid them.

Defining *friend* Functions and Classes

friend functions have access to more than one class.

A `friend` function is exactly like any other function, with one exception: it can access `private` parts of a class as though it were a member of that class.

`friend` functions might or might not be member functions of another class. It is important to understand that a `friend` function differs from other functions (member functions or regular program functions) only in that it has access rights to `private` members of one or more classes.

Here is part of a program that uses a class and a `friend` function to access that class:

```
class Inventory {
   char partno[5];
   int quantity;
public:
   Inventory();   // Constructor
   ~Inventory();  // Destructor
   friend void reset(Inventory i, int val);
};

void reset(Inventory i, int const val) {
   i.quantity = val;
}
```

It does not matter to C++ whether you declare the `friend` function in the `private` or the `public` section of the class (or in the `protected` section that you will read about in Chapter 14, "The Need for Inheritance"). Put the `friend` function declarations

with the majority of other class functions (don't scatter them throughout the data members) because that is where you normally would look for them later if you wanted to modify the class.

reset() changes the value of one of the Inventory class's private members. reset() is not, however, a member function. reset() is simply a function that has access to Inventory's private members. Notice that you must pass the Inventory object to reset(). Because reset() is not a member function, it would have no way of accessing the object any other way. Therefore, if you were to define an Inventory object in main() like this:

```
Inventory item;  // Defines an Inventory object
```

you could later change the value of the item's quantity like this:

```
reset(item, 10);  // Sets the member to a value
                  // Must pass the item object
```

In this simple class, a member function that sets the quantity would be more appropriate than a separate friend function. For now, concentrate on the syntax and placement of friend functions and their uses.

As you can see, you must place the friend keyword before the function prototype in the class that allows the function to be a friend. Conceptually, a class lets another function have access to its private members.

Multiple Functions Sharing friends

Programmers might use friend functions so that a function could access members from two or more classes. Here is a Customer/Account print_em() program. This program uses a friend function to print data members from *two* classes:

FRNDACCU.CPP. Uses a `friend` function to print data members from two classes.

```cpp
// Filename: FRNDACCU.CPP
#include <iostream.h>
#include <iomanip.h>
#include <string.h>

class Account;   // Lets C++ know that Account exists

class Customer   {
   char name[30];
   int cnum;
   float ytd_balance;
public:
   Customer() { strcpy(name, "Joe"); cnum=10; ytd_balance=31.96;}
   friend void print_em(const Customer c, const Account a);
};                          // Declares a friend of this class

class Account   {
   char acctcode[5];
   float ac_balance;
public:
   Account() {strcpy(acctcode,"234"); ac_balance=43.22; }
   friend void print_em(const Customer c, const Account a);
};                          // Declares a friend of this class


void main()
{
   Customer c;   // Defines two class objects
   Account a;

   print_em(c, a);   // Calls the friend function
}

// Here is the function that befriended both Customer and Account classes.
// It prints private data from two different objects.
//
void print_em(const Customer c, const Account a) {
   cout << setprecision(2) << "Customer: " << c.name << ", Number: "
   cout << c.cnum << ", YTD Balance: " << c.ytd_balance << "\n";
   cout << "Account: " << a.acctcode;
   cout << ", Balance: " << a.ac_balance << "\n";
};
```

Here is the program's output:

```
Customer: Joe, Number: 10, YTD Balance: 31.96
Account: 234, Balance: 43.22
```

print_em() is a friend of both Account and Customer classes and therefore can access both classes' members. Figure 11.2 illustrates the way print_em() sees the data.

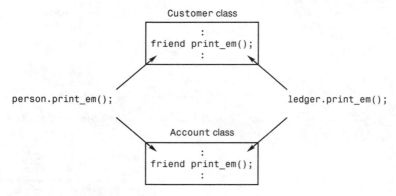

Figure 11.2. When you call a friend *function, the* friend *can access all data members from each class, in effect seemingly being a member of more than one class.*

One important element in this program fragment is the declaration of the Account class on the first line. You know from C that you should declare (prototype) functions before you use them. In C++ you *must* declare functions before you use them. You also must declare all classes before you use one inside another. In the Customer class, the prototype for the friend function print_em() includes the Account class argument. Because C++ would not have otherwise seen Account (it appears later), the first line must declare Account just to tell C++ that Account exists and that it will be defined later. Without the preliminary declaration of Account, C++ would issue an error when it saw the Customer class's print_em() prototype in the Account class.

C++ is being consistent when it requires the declaration. C++ is very strict and requires that you declare everything before you use it. There is an alternative method of referencing a class before you define it. The print_em() function call inside the Customer class could look like this:

```
    friend void print_em(const Customer c, const class Account a);
};                  // Declares a friend of this class
```

Because of the `class` keyword, you would not need the forward reference declaration (the first line in the program shown in the preceding section). Figure 11.3 graphically shows what these forward declarations actually declare.

```
class Account;
class Customer {
    char name [30];
    int cnum;
    float ytd_balance;
public:
    Customer() {strcpy(name,"Joe");
               cnum=10;
               ytd_balance=31.96;}
    friend void print_em (const Customer c, const Account a) {
```

Forward references the Account class

Figure 11.3. Because the friend *class is yet to be defined, you must declare the class, in effect letting C++ know that the definition is coming later.*

If a function changes a `private` data member of a single object, make it a member function. If a function accesses a member or modifies more than one `class` object, make it a `friend` function.

Nested *friend* Classes

You can make an entire class a `friend` of another. As with shared classes, you must declare the nested class before using it inside the other class. Here is an example of a nested `friend` class:

```
class Parttime;  // Declares the nested class
class Employee {
    char name[30];
    int enum;
public:
    friend class Parttime;  // Nesting the friend declaration
};

class Parttime {
    int hours;
```

```
   float rate;
public:
   void print();
};
```

The nested `friend` does not have to be `public`. Here is the `Parttime` class nested as a private member of `Employee`:

```
class Parttime;  // Declares the nested class
class Employee {
   char name[30];
   int enum;
   friend class Parttime;  // Friend class
};

class Parttime {
   int hours;
   float rate;
public:
   void print();
};
```

Of course, if you list the `nested friend class` before the enclosing one, you do not need the forward reference declaration on the first line because the `class` definition will be self-declaring, like this:

```
class Parttime {
   int hours;
   float rate;
public:
   void print();
};

class Employee {
   char name[30];
   int enum;
   friend class Parttime;  // Friend class
};
```

You might need a `friend` class inside another when all functions of the nested class need access to the others' members. Nesting the `friend class` definition keeps you from having to declare each function as a `friend` individually in the second class. You might want to make one class a `friend` of another when they share the same data at times but still need to remain separate. There are other (sometimes more elegant) ways to accomplish this dual sharing of data and functions, but the `friend` keyword is important to learn also. You want to protect your data from functions that do not need access to the data, but you might need to bend the rules at certain times when classes work together closely.

183

Do not expect a friend function to know what its friend's *this is. A friend function is no different from any other function, except that it can access private members of its friend class. Of course, if the friend function is a member function of a class, and not a stand-alone program function, it will have its own *this pointer for its own class, but not one for the class of which it is a friend.

friends of Each Other

There is no reverse relationship between friend classes unless you specifically designate that each is a friend of another. Just because you designate that class abc is a friend of class xyz does not make xyz a friend class of abc.

Also, if you designate class Apple to be a friend of Banana, and then designate class Banana to be a friend of class Cranberry, then it does not automatically hold that class Cranberry is a friend of Apple unless you explicitly specify that relationship. The designation of a friend class is a simple one. There is no inheritance, transitive, or reverse friend relationship.

Summary

This chapter introduced friend functions and classes. A friend is helpful when you have any of the following situations:

- Two classes relate closely to each other

- One class has a function that needs to print private data from another class

- A program's stand-alone function needs access to private members of a class

friend functions give functions access to private data, but otherwise they are exactly the same as any other function. friend functions override the data hiding mechanisms of private class data. Yet, despite the availability of friend functions, you should limit your use of them. As soon as you learn about inheritance (in Chapter 14, "The Need for Inheritance"), your need for friend functions might diminish. If you find yourself wanting to use a friend function too often, chances are good that you have two classes that

you should combine into a single class, or (more likely) you need to add more member functions to your existing classes.

Despite these caveats, this entire chapter devoted itself to friend functions for good reason. You will read about a very good use for friend functions in the next chapter. If you want C++ to amaze you with its extensibility, turn the page to read about operator overloading.

OPERATOR OVERLOADING

12

"Maybe a rose is a rose by any other name, but the same operator might do two entirely different things with each name."

Your venture into the world of C++ is about to pay off. Operator overloading takes the concepts you have learned to a new level of power. Although operator overloading is not in itself an object-oriented feature (non-OOP languages could just as easily implement operator overloading if they allowed overloaded functions), you can use it to extend what C++ does with its operators to work with your own data types. In a nutshell, operator overloading is the process whereby you tell C++ how to apply operators such as the addition sign, +, to your own abstract data types, such as class data.

You can overload any operator in C++ except ?:, sizeof, ::, ., and *. Although these operators cannot be overloaded, the rest can be, including typecasts, array subscripts, and logical and relational operators.

The overloaded operator works on your class (and therefore struct) data types the way you want it to. You can even overload the extractor (>>) and the insert (<<) operators.

Overloading these I/O operators is one of the most impressive features of C++. As you will see, as soon as you overload the I/O operators, you can input and output entire classes of data, in any format you like, with a single, simple command.

This is one of the longest chapters in this book, but its length does not portend difficulty. The length comes from the large number of operators there are to overload and the nuances involved in overloading many of them. The basic procedure for overloading operators is the same for almost all of C++'s operators.

In this chapter, you will learn:

- How to overload the math operators

- How to use `friend` functions to improve operator overloading effectiveness

- How to overload I/O operators

- How to overload postfix and prefix increment (++) and decrement (- -) operators

- How to overload relational operators

- How to overload subscripts

- How, why, and when to use a copy constructor

Overloading Math Operators

Throughout this book, you have seen (and will continue to see) the expression *extending C++*. C++'s *extensibility* is the means by which you add to the language features so that the language works the way you want it to in a certain situation. A language's extensibility can be a double-edged sword. Threaded languages such as Forth are so extensible that one Forth programmer's program might be unreadable by another Forth programmer, and yet both use Forth. C++'s extensibility does not extend far enough to make programs unreadable by other C++ programmers. For example, you cannot change the way the `for` command works.

C++ is a highly extensible language.

C++'s extensibility is governed by a set of strict rules to promote faster and more accurate coding while maintaining the entire flavor and command set of C++. You saw how to extend C++ a little when you learned about C++ classes and structures. No longer do you need to repeat the `struct` keyword as you did in C, because by declaring a `struct`, you literally add a new data type to C++. C++ is not magical, however (although it might appear to be at times). Even though you can add your own `class` and `struct` data types, C++ does

not automatically know how to add, subtract, multiply, and divide those new data types, as it does with `int`s and `float`s. Operator overloading comes to the rescue, however. You can teach C++ how to add or subtract your `class` and `struct` data types, and as soon as you do, C++ knows what you really want done when you add two `class` variables together.

Operating with Classes

What does it mean to add two `class` variables together? It means different things to different classes. Not all classes should be added together. For example, if you had an inventory class and an employee class, you probably would have no need to add or subtract them. However, if you had an hourly employee class and a salaried employee class, each with different members, you might need to know the total amount of your payroll. Although you would need to control exactly what got added together, you could do so with operator overloading.

As soon as you describe to C++ how to "add" these two different `class` variables together with operator overloading, you actually can perform the addition with a simple statement such as this:

```
total = hourly + salaried;  // Adds two different objects
```

This addition would work in C++, through the use of operator overloading, despite the fact that the `hourly` and `salaried` class contents look entirely different.

As soon as you define the way to manipulate various `class` objects with regular operators, abstract data types do not differ from built-in data types, except for the way you declare them. Your code automatically becomes clearer because you use familiar operators on your data types instead of resorting to using functions, as C programmers would have to do.

How C Would Do It

Suppose that you had the following C `struct`:

```
struct Employee  {
    char name[30];
    int empnum;
    float salary;
};
```

189

and suppose also that you had defined 100 employee struct variables, like this:

```
#define TOTAL 100
struct Employee personnel[TOTAL];
```

C does not know how to add together any of the personnel amounts. For instance, the array might be sorted in descending salary order, and you might want to compute how much your two highest-paid employees earn together. Such a total might be quite useful to the company's planners. Therefore, if you needed to add any two employee salaries together, you probably would write a function that looks like this:

```
double add_sal(struct Employee pay1, struct Employee pay2)
{
   double total_sal=0.0;
   total_sal = pay1.salary + pay2.salary;
   return (total_sal);
}
```

You could call this function when you were ready to compute the total with this statement:

```
total_sal = add_sal(personnel[0], personnel[1]);  /* Finds total */
```

This kind of programming is just not good enough for today's C++ language. There is nothing inherently wrong with the method of writing a function to "tell" C how to add together the two payroll array elements. Nevertheless, the calling mechanism is messy. Every time you want to add together two employee salaries, you must pass the employee structure records to the addition function. Even worse, what if you wanted to add three salaries, or four, or more? You would have to call several functions in succession, passing data and causing function overhead. Or you could write one function that added three salaries together, another that added four together, and so on.

The next section discusses how you can use the plus sign to add together such structures.

Overloading Regular Math Operators

C++ knows how to add integers together. If it sees something like this:

```
int a, b=3, c=4, d=5;  // Defines four integer variables
a = b + c + d;  // Adds three of them together
```

it knows to take the sum of b, c, and d and store the results in a. C++ also knows how to add floating-points, double floating-points, long integers, and all the other built-in data

types. Think for a moment about the internal code needed to add together different types of data. C++ must first "look" at the values on both sides of the plus sign. If C++ sees two integers, it performs integer addition. If it sees two floating-points, it performs floating-point addition. Floating-point addition is entirely different from integer addition, because C++ must deal with the decimal parts as well as the whole parts of the numbers.

> You cannot redefine the way operators work with built-in data types. In other words, you cannot modify the way the plus sign works with integers. You can only specify the way the plus sign works with your own data types. You also cannot change operator precedence. If you overload the multiplication operator, *, to work on your own `class` data, the overloaded * has the same precedence as the regular multiplication operator.

In effect, the plus sign (and all the other operators) are already overloaded. That is, there actually is a plus routine that handles integers and a plus routine that handles floating-points. Of course, the same holds true in C as well. However, unlike C, you can take advantage of this knowledge in C++ by writing *more* addition operations. If C++ "sees" one of its built-in data types on both sides of the plus sign, it executes its built-in routine. If C++ "sees" one of *your* data types on either side of the plus sign, it looks to see whether you wrote an overloaded operator function that tells it what to do. If C++ finds an overloaded operator function, it executes it. Otherwise, it issues an error telling you that it does not know how to sum that type of data.

Many operators are already overloaded.

> Overloading is how C++ knows when to perform a bitwise shift with >> and when to perform input extraction: it uses the context of the >> operator. If the `cin` object is on the left, C++ knows that the >> means to extract from the standard input device instead of performing a bitwise shift of two integers.

An operator overloaded function looks just like any other C++ function, with one exception: the name of the function must be `operator`, followed by the operator you want to overload. In other words, here are the four function names you use to overload +, -, *, and /:

- `operator+()`
- `operator-()`

- `operator*()`

- `operator/()`

Going back to the employee salary example, suppose that you had the following C++ `class` definition:

```
class Employee{
   char name[30];
   int empnum;
   float salary;
public:
   Employee(char [], int, float);  // Constructor
   ~Employee();  // Destructor
   double operator+(Employee & e);  // Overloaded +
};
```

The function named `operator+()` is overloading the plus sign. Don't let the syntax fool you into thinking that the `operator+()` function is difficult to understand; it is not. It is just like any other function, except that it has a funny name, `operator+()`. The function returns a `double` argument and requires an `Employee` object argument.

As you might know from C, the plus sign is called a *binary* operator because it takes two arguments, one on each side of the plus sign. Because the `operator+()` function takes only one argument, can you see how the function works with a second argument (the argument on the other side of the plus sign)? Because `operator+()` is a member function, the first argument is already secretly passed to the function using the `*this` pointer.

Here is the implementation of the `operator+()` function as it would later appear:

```
double Employee::operator+(Employee & e)
{
   double sum;  // Defines a temporary place
   sum = salary + e.salary;
   return sum;  // Returns the sum
}
```

The function returns a double floating-point value taken from the two `class` salaries used in the function. The `*this` pointer tells C++ which `salary` member to work on, and the passed argument `e` (actually the second of the two arguments to the plus sign after `*this`) lets C++ find the `e.salary` member. By using a reference symbol, `&`, you pass the second plus sign argument by reference, overriding the default passing by value, so a copy does not get made of the argument, and the overloaded operator function is made more efficient. C++ programmers almost universally use references in their overloaded operator functions.

To further illustrate the function and its arguments, here is what C++ actually "sees" when it compiles the function:

```
double Employee::operator+(*this, Employee & e)
{
    double sum;   // Defines a temporary place
    sum = this->salary + e.salary;
    return sum;   // Returns the sum
}
```

Here is *one* way to call the overloaded plus sign function when you want to add two employee salaries together:

```
total_sal = personnel[0].operator+(personnel[1]);  // Finds total
```

In other words, take the first person's salary and add the second person's salary to it.

There is not much that is interesting about the syntax of calling operator+() this way. As a matter of fact, it is downright difficult, and you will be lucky to understand it without analyzing it for a few minutes (and you should do that, even though a better way will be explained soon). Obviously, the C way of calling a function to add these two values would not only be easier to understand, but it probably would be less error-prone. However, C++ does not stop here.

As described earlier, when the C++ compiler sees a plus sign, it looks at the data types on either side of the plus sign. If it recognizes the types as any of the built-in types, it performs the expected addition. If, however, C++ sees a user-defined data type (a class or a struct) on either side of the plus sign, *it first looks for a matching operator+() function.* If C++ finds an operator+() function, it executes it. If C++ does not find an operator+() function, it issues an error that basically says "I do not know how to add a data type like this one."

Given this automatic search for an operator+() function, you do not have to spell out the function call, like this:

```
total_sal = personnel[0].operator+(personnel[1]);  // Finds total
```

Rather, you only have to do this:

```
total_sal = personnel[0] + personnel[1];  // Finds total
```

The operator+() function kicks into effect when C++ sees an Employee object on each side of the plus sign. C++ now works on your own data types naturally. You do not have to remember fancy function names when you want to perform a simple operation with one of your data types; you only need to write an overloaded operator function that describes what the operator means to that data type. In the earlier example, the member array name and the member integer empnum are not affected or used by the operator+() function because the operator+() function does not use them. You can code an addition operation to work with whatever data members make the most sense.

All overloaded operators must take a class as an argument so that C++ can distinguish the overloaded operator from the operator's built-in purpose.

As another example, the following program tracks a class with five values. These might be five coordinates in a vector used for advanced calculus. Notice that the program contains a constructor that initializes the lists. main() declares and defines three lists: L1 has each element equal to 10, L2 has each element equal to 50, and L3 is equal to all zeroes. Three operations, +, -, and *, are overloaded to work on the lists. The class must contain overloaded operator functions, but look at how simply main() manipulates the class values. The C++ language is literally extended so that its operators work on abstract data types.

You might wonder why the List class is made up of five scalar variables and not an integer array. Overloading arrays requires that you overload the subscript operator, [], as shown later in this chapter.

LIST1.CPP. Manipulates a List class.

```cpp
// Filename: LIST1.CPP
// Manipulates a List class.
#include <iostream.h>

class List {
    int a,c,b,d,e;  // List values
public:
    List(int num);  // Constructor
    void printit(void);  // Prints the List
    List operator+(List & L);   // Overloads plus
    List operator-(List & L);   // Overloads minus
    List operator*(List & L);   // Overloads multiplication
};

List::List(int num)  // Constructor
{
    a=b=c=d=e=num;  // Initializes each List element
}

void List::printit(void)
```

```
{
   cout << "The result: ";
   cout << a << ", " << b << ", " << c << ", ";
   cout << d << ", " << e << "\n\n";
}

// Here are the implementation functions
// for the overloaded operators
List List::operator+(List & arg)
{
   List temp(0);  // Creates a temporary array to hold added values
   temp.a = arg.a + a;  // Adds each value together
   temp.b = arg.b + b;
   temp.c = arg.c + c;
   temp.d = arg.d + d;
   temp.e = arg.e + e;
   return temp;
}

List List::operator-(List & arg)
{
   List temp(0);  // Creates a temporary array to hold added values
   temp.a = arg.a - a;  // Subtracts the values
   temp.b = arg.b - b;
   temp.c = arg.c - c;
   temp.d = arg.d - d;
   temp.e = arg.e - e;
   return temp;
}

List List::operator*(List & arg)
{
   List temp(0);  // Creates a temporary array to hold added values
   temp.a = arg.a * a;  // Multiplies the values
   temp.b = arg.b * b;
   temp.c = arg.c * c;
   temp.d = arg.d * d;
   temp.e = arg.e * e;
   return temp;
}

///////////// Class ends here /////////////

void main()
{
   List L1(10), L2(50), L3(0);  // Defines and initializes three Lists
```

continues

195

LIST1.CPP. continued

```
// Uses the overloaded math operators
L3 = L1 + L2;  // Adds the two Lists and stores result in third
L3.printit();  // Prints the resulting List

L3 = L2 - L1;  // Subtracts the two Lists and stores result in third
L3.printit();  // Prints the resulting List

L3 = L1 * L2;  // Multiplies the two Lists and stores result in third
L3.printit();  // Prints the resulting List
};
```

Here is the output:

```
The result: 60, 60, 60, 60, 60
The result: -40, -40, -40, -40, -40
The result: 500, 500, 500, 500, 500
```

Should printit() be a member function of the List class? The function works closely with the List class and needs to access the List class members. Therefore, you might think that making printit() a member function makes a lot of sense. However, there is a way that you can make main() even clearer. Instead of calling a function to print the values, you can overload the << output operator so that it "knows how" to work directly with the List class, as described in the next section.

Overloading I/O

As mentioned earlier, the << operator is already overloaded. << is both a bitwise left-shift operator and, in C++, an output operator when cout appears on its left side. If you were to compile a C++ program that attempted to output with <<, and you failed to include iostream.h, you would receive an error similar to the following:

```
Undefined symbol 'cout'
```

The error occurs because iostream.h overloads << and describes the cout object. cout is an object of an output stream class named ostream. iostream.h includes definitions that overload the >> operator for input as well. In other words, iostream.h includes overloaded operator functions that look like this:

```
ostream & operator<<(ostream & c, int n);
```

along with several other overloadings that accept floating-points, characters, and all the

other built-in and user-defined data types. Unlike the overloaded operator functions you've seen so far, this one takes two arguments, an output stream and an integer. Because the operator<<() function is not a member of the ostream class, but is a friend of the class, it requires the two arguments because the *this pointer is not known as it would be if this were a member function of the ostream class. You will read about similar function constructs later in the section entitled "Overloading as friends." For now, do not be too concerned about the exact syntax of this function.

Notice that the overloaded << function returns a reference to the output stream ostream. Even though the concept of ostream is new to you, there is nothing difficult about it. Consider the following statement:

```
cout << 15 << 25;   // Outputs two integers to the output device
```

C++ knows to use the overloaded << output operator instead of the bitwise left-shift, because it sees the cout output object instead of an integer variable on the left side of <<. C++ sends 15 to the output cout object. Because the << overloaded function returns an output stream object, the 25 is then sent to *that* returned cout object. In other words, because the overloaded << operator returns a reference to a cout object, you can "stack" the commands. Figure 12.1 shows the progression of the operator's output.

```
cout << 15 << 25;
    \     /
   cout << 25;
      \   /
       cout
```

Figure 12.1. The overloaded << operator must return an output object so that you can stack several output values together on one line.

If operator<<() did not return a reference to the output stream object, you would be forced to separate the output command into two commands, like this:

```
cout << 15;
cout << 25;
```

Putting the output operator on hold for a moment, look back at the class List program shown in the preceding section. Try to determine whether this would be allowed in the main() program:

```
L3 = L1 + L2 + L2 + L1;   // Adds lots of Lists together
```

There is no problem with adding four List objects together like this because the operator+() function returns a List object. The function does not return a reference to the List object, but it returns a copy of it (returns it "by value"). You cannot return a reference to a variable that is going out of scope because the reference to an out-of-scope variable would be meaningless.

197

As you are beginning to see, the cryptic look of overloaded operator functions is not that difficult to decipher. You probably are beginning to understand how to overload the output operator to work with your own data types. Here is the List program with an overloaded output operator:

LIST2.CPP. Manipulates a List class.

```cpp
// Filename: LIST2.CPP
// Manipulates a List class.
#include <iostream.h>

class List {
   int a,c,b,d,e;  // List values
public:
   List(int num);  // Constructor
   List operator+(List & L);  // Overloads plus
   List operator-(List & L);  // Overloads minus
   List operator*(List & L);  // Overloads multiplication
   friend ostream & operator<< (ostream & out, List & L);
};

List::List(int num)  // Constructor
{
   a=b=c=d=e=num;  // Initializes each List element
}

// Here are the implementation functions
// for the overloaded operators
ostream & operator<< (ostream & out, List & L)
{
   out << "The result: ";
   out << L.a << ", " << L.b << ", " << L.c << ", ";
   out << L.d << ", " << L.e << "\n\n";
   return out;
}

List List::operator+(List & arg)
{
   List temp(0);  // Creates a temporary array to hold added values
   temp.a = arg.a + a;  // Adds each value together
   temp.b = arg.b + b;
   temp.c = arg.c + c;
   temp.d = arg.d + d;
   temp.e = arg.e + e;
   return temp;
}
```

198

```
List List::operator-(List & arg)
{
   List temp(0);   // Creates a temporary array to hold added values
   temp.a = arg.a - a;   // Subtracts the values
   temp.b = arg.b - b;
   temp.c = arg.c - c;
   temp.d = arg.d - d;
   temp.e = arg.e - e;
   return temp;
}

List List::operator*(List & arg)
{
   List temp(0);   // Creates a temporary array to hold added values
   temp.a = arg.a * a;   // Multiplies the values
   temp.b = arg.b * b;
   temp.c = arg.c * c;
   temp.d = arg.d * d;
   temp.e = arg.e * e;
   return temp;
}

///////////// Class ends here /////////////

void main()
{
   List L1(10), L2(50), L3(0);   // Defines and initializes three Lists

   // Use the overloaded math operators
   L3 = L1 + L2;   // Adds the two Lists and stores result in third
   cout << L3;     // Prints the resulting List

   L3 = L2 - L1;   // Subtracts the two Lists and stores result in third
   cout << L3;     // Prints the resulting List

   L3 = L1 * L2;   // Multiplies the two Lists and stores result in third
   cout << L3;     // Prints the resulting List
};
```

This program produces the same output as the preceding one. This version of the program is no shorter than the last one; the output function was simply turned into an overloaded << operator function. Brevity is not the reason for the change; main() became as stream-lined as it could. You now can work with your own data types as if they were built-in. You can concentrate more fully on your application and worry less about the details of the data and functions.

Overloading operators makes the class perform the detailed chores.

As you might imagine, you can define the output operator to display your own data types in any manner you would like. Your overloaded operator function becomes the code that C++ executes when it sees one of your objects on the right side of <<. If your class had many data members, your overloaded output operator function might be extremely long, but again, in keeping with the spirit of C++, the class is doing all the work, leaving the regular program very clean and free of petty details.

The output operator appears to know how to work with your own data types, and in reality, it really does because your overloaded operator<<() function describes what to do. As in the preceding program, most overloaded operator functions are friends of the class (although this is not always a strict requirement). If operator<<() were not a friend, it could not access the private data members unless it were a member function. The section entitled "Overloading as friends" addresses more detailed uses of friend functions for operator overloading.

You can overload the input operator as well. Consider the following Date class:

```
class Date {
    int day;
    int month;
    int year;
    friend istream & operator>> (istream & in, Date & d);
};
```

Notice that the overloaded input operator uses the input stream class named istream (defined in iostream.h along with ostream). One implementation of the operator>>() function might be this:

```
istream & operator>> (istream & in, Date & d)
{
    cout << endl;
    cout << "What is the month number (i.e., 7)? ";
    in >> d.month;  // Gets the month from the input device
    cout << "What is the day number (i.e., 28)? ";
    in >> d.day;  // Gets the day from the input device
    cout << "What is the year (i.e., 1993)? ";
    in >> d.year;  // Gets the year from the input device
    return in;  // Allows for stacking of the >> operator
};
```

All your regular program has to do to get a date from the user is to execute this statement:

```
cin >> today;
```

200

The user input session would begin, looking something like this:

```
What is the month number (i.e., 7)? 11
What is the day number (i.e., 28)? 9
What is the year (i.e., 1993)? 1993
```

As with the output operator, the input operator function can be as complex as you want it to be. Because that complexity is hidden inside the overloaded >>, the main program remains free of the clutter and function calls that other languages must contain for such specialized I/O. When you overload the >> input operator, do not pass the second argument as a const because >> will be changing it. Here is another example of an overloaded >> input operator function:

```
// Notice that second argument does not have 'const'
istream & operator>> (istream & in, Person & p)
{
    cout << "What is the Employee's name? ";
    in >> p.name;
    cout << "What is " << p.name << "'s age? ";
    in >> p.age;
    cout << "What is " << p.name << "'s salary? ";
    in >> p.salary;
    return in;
}
```

Overloading as *friends*

You saw the I/O operators overloaded as friend functions in the preceding section. Many operator overloading functions are friend functions because they need access to the private internal data of the class on which they work.

As a general rule, if an overloaded operator changes one of its operands, it should be a member function. For example, if you overload +=, -=, *=, /=, %=, ++, and - -, the overloaded operator functions should be members because they change one of the operands. If the overloaded operator does not change one of its operands, it should be a friend function. Here is the List class program with all of its overloaded operator functions declared as friend functions. Notice another improvement in the class: The parameters are passed with the const keyword to further protect their values because the overloaded operators in this program are not meant to change any of the arguments.

LIST3.CPP. Manipulates a List class with friends.

```cpp
// Filename: LIST3.CPP
// Manipulates a List class with friends.
#include <iostream.h>

class List {
   int a,c,b,d,e;   // List values
public:
   List(const int num);   // Constructor
   // Overloads some operators next
   friend List operator+(List & L1, const List & L2);
   friend List operator-(List & L1, const List & L2);
   friend List operator*(List & L1, const List & L3);
   friend ostream & operator<< (ostream & out, const List & l);
};

List::List(const int num)   // Constructor
{
   a=b=c=d=e=num;   // Initializes each List element
}

// Here are the implementation functions
// for the overloaded operators
ostream & operator<< (ostream & out, const List & L)
{
   out << "The result: ";
   out << L.a << ", " << L.b << ", " << L.c << ", ";
   out << L.d << ", " << L.e << "\n\n";
   return out;
}

List operator+(List & arg, const List & L)
{
   List temp(0);   // Creates a temporary array to hold added values
   temp.a = arg.a + L.a;   // Adds each value together
   temp.b = arg.b + L.b;
   temp.c = arg.c + L.c;
   temp.d = arg.d + L.d;
   temp.e = arg.e + L.e;
   return temp;
}

List operator-(List & arg, const List & L)
{
   List temp(0);   // Creates a temporary array to hold added values
   temp.a = L.a - arg.a;   // Subtracts the values
   temp.b = L.b - arg.b;
```

```
      temp.c = L.c - arg.c;
      temp.d = L.d - arg.d;
      temp.e = L.e - arg.e;
      return temp;
}

List operator*(List & arg, const List & L)
{
      List temp(0);  // Creates a temporary array to hold added values
      temp.a = arg.a * L.a;  // Multiplies the values
      temp.b = arg.b * L.b;
      temp.c = arg.c * L.c;
      temp.d = arg.d * L.d;
      temp.e = arg.e * L.e;
      return temp;
}

//////////////// Class ends here ////////////////

void main()
{
      List L1(10), L2(50), L3(0);  // Defines and initializes three Lists

      // Uses the overloaded math operators
      L3 = L1 + L2;  // Adds the two Lists and stores result in third
      cout << L3;     // Prints the resulting List

      L3 = L2 - L1;  // Subtracts the two Lists and stores result in third
      cout << L3;     // Prints the resulting List

      L3 = L1 * L2;  // Multiplies the two Lists and stores result in third
      cout << L3;     // Prints the resulting List
};
```

Because the operator overloading functions are now `friend` functions, they have no automatic access to `*this`, so both operands (the items on either side of the operator) must be passed to each of the functions. When they were member functions, only one operand had to be passed, because `*this` was passed by the compiler and `*this` represented the left side of the operator. In other words, because they are friends, the functions have no automatic access to `*this`, so the functions require two arguments in their parameter lists.

> The only operators you cannot make `friends` of a class are `*` (the dereference operator), `()`, `->`, `[]`, and `=`. These operators inherently define `lvalues` (values that might occur on the left side of an assignment operation, for example) and they inherently change the class for which they are defined. Therefore, keep these overloaded operator functions members of their class.

Sometimes, you must use a `friend` overloaded operator.

One situation *requires* you to use a `friend` overloaded operator function. As you know now, C++ uses the data type of the operand to determine whether to use a built-in operator or one of your overloaded operators. Suppose that you wanted the `List` class to be able to add a constant integer value to a `List` object such as this:

```
L3 = L1 + 25;  // Adds 25 to each of the List elements
```

You can use an overloaded operator member function for this if you want to. The `*this` pointer would point to the `List` object, and the function's argument would be the integer value that you added to each of the `List` members. The problem creeps in when you want to do this:

```
L3 = 25 + L1;  // Adds 25 to each of the List elements
```

C++ sees the integer 25 on the left side of the plus sign and attempts to perform a regular addition. The addition fails when the operator attempts to work with the `L1` `List` object. The built-in addition sign does not know how to handle the addition of a `List` object. Therefore, you must overload the `List` `operator+()` function so that it receives either a `List` class object on both sides, a `List` class object on the left side and an integer on the right, or an integer on the left side and a `List` class object on the right. Here is a `List` class header that handles the three addition possibilities:

```
class List {
   int a,c,b,d,e;  // List values
public:
   List(const int num);  // Constructor
   // Overloads some operators next
   friend List operator+(List & L1, List & arg2);  // L3=L1+L2;
   friend List operator+(List & L1, const int i);  // L3=L1+25;
   friend List operator+(const int i, List & L1);  // L3=25+L1;
   friend List operator-(List & L1, const List & L2);
   friend List operator*(List & L1, const List & L3);
   friend ostream & operator<< (ostream & out, const List & l);
};
```

The hidden *this pointer gets in the way if you declare the operator+(const int i, List &L1) function as a member and not as a friend. Remembering that all member functions receive the hidden *this pointer as their first argument means that the only way C++ calls a member overloaded operator function is when a class object appears on the left side of the operator.

this gets in the way of some overloaded operator member functions.

Overloading Typecasts

The List class program you've seen so far includes an overloaded typecast operator. You might not see it right away. The program can typecast an integer to a List object. Here is an example:

```
cout << List(9);
```

The program converts the 9 to a List object. What really happens is that all five members—a, b, c, d, and e—are assigned the value of 9. The constructor function does the conversion. Notice that the constructor takes an integer argument and converts it to a List. You could write several other constructor functions that would convert floats, chars, or any other data type to the List.

But what if you wanted to convert a List to an int? Of course, because the List is made up of five values, converting it to an int might not make sense, but you might have abstract data types that you want to convert to one of the built-in types, so you need to know how to do it. For this example, assume that to convert a List object to an int, the first data member, a, is the value sent to the integer. In other words, if the members a through e contained the values 10 through 14, the class would return a 10 when you typecast it to an integer. Here is a function that overloads the int typecast for the List class:

```
List::operator int()
{
    return a;
};
```

Your typecast conversion functions can be much longer than this, and you can overload any of the typecast data types in this manner. No return type is needed because C++ always assumes that you are returning the proper data type (and it is your responsibility to return the correct type) when you overload a typecast operator. Be sure to put a space between the operator and the data type keyword. Unlike the other operators, typecast names begin with characters. The following is not allowed:

```
List::operatorint()  // INVALID
```

205

> **TIP**
>
> You can typecast a List to an int either by calling the typecast with the C/C++ calling convention:
>
> ```
> num = (int)L3;  // Converts the L3 object to an integer
> ```
>
> or with the new C++ calling convention (described in Chapter 2, "C++ Data and Program Basics"):
>
> ```
> num = int(L3);  // Converts the L3 object to an integer
> ```

Overloading ++ and -- Operators

Beginning in the AT&T 2.1 C++ specification, you can overload the prefix and postfix ++ and -- operators. (Before 2.1, C++ did not distinguish between overloaded prefix and postfix operators.)

Suppose that you wanted to overload the List class object so that it would work with the prefix increment (++) and decrement (--) operators. In other words, if you write this in the main program:

```
++L1;  // Adds one to each of L1's five values
--L2;  // Subtracts one from each of L2's five values
```

all five values of L1—a, b, c, d, and e—will increment by one, and the five values of L2 will decrement by one. The following overloaded operator functions perform these two operations. Because they change member data, they are best left as member functions of the List class:

```
List & List::operator++()
{
    ++a; ++b; ++c; ++d; ++e;
}

List & List::operator--()
{
    --a; --b; --c; --d; --e;
}
```

Because these are the implementations of member functions, no parameters have to be passed because the hidden *this pointer ensures that the correct five values increment and decrement.

You can overload the other unary operators, + and -, just as easily. You only have to return the properly converted data member.

If you want to overload postfix increments and decrements, C++ requires a special notation to distinguish the postfix functions from the prefix ones you just saw. C++ (starting with AT&T version 2.1) looks for an int argument in the increment or decrement overloaded operator. If C++ sees one, it performs that operation when you postfix increment or decrement, and it performs the prefix increment and decrement otherwise. An example here is worth a thousand words of description.

When you request a prefix increment like this:

```
++L1;   // Adds one to each of L1's five values
```

C++ looks for an overloaded postfix operator function without an integer argument like the ones you saw earlier in this section. However, when you request a postfix increment operator like this:

```
L1++;   // Postfixes the increment
```

C++ looks for an overloaded postfix function like this one:

```
List & List::operator++(int)   // Designates postfix
{
   a++; b++; c++; d++; e++;
}
```

The int argument is called a *dummy argument.* That is, C++ does not really expect or want an integer argument. If you were to pass it one, C++ would ignore it. The int simply tells C++ to call that overloaded function if a postfix increment operation (or decrement, as the case may be) is called for, and to call the other overloaded increment or decrement (prefix) function otherwise.

In summary, if you overload both the postfix and the prefix increment operators, you code the following statement:

```
L3 = ++L1 * L2++;   // Contains both prefix and postfix
```

C++ executes the operator++() function to increment L1 and will execute the operator++(int) function when it is time to increment L2. The actual code inside these two functions is not as critical as when they are called. Both functions add one to the List class's five values, but operator++(int) does so only after the rest of the expression, including the assignment to L3, finishes.

Overloading Subscripts

Because the List program uses five values for each object, and because this program calls these objects List class objects, the class is perfectly suited for an array of five values. If you replace the a, b, c, d, e, and f members with a five-element array, you have the following class header (leaving out many of the overloaded operator functions shown throughout this chapter):

```
class List {
   int L[5];
public:
   List();  // Constructor
};
```

The individual data members are now part of an integer array. Nevertheless, the List objects are *not* integer arrays. If you declare a List object as follows:

```
List L1;
```

you should not access one of L1's elements like this:

```
num = L1[2];  // INVALID
```

The individual array elements of L1 are private, so you could not access them in the main program. Not only that, but L1 *is not an array!* L1 is an object. If you want the primary program to access individual elements from the array inside L1, you have to write a function to overload the subscript ([]) operator.

Here is code to overload [] for the List object:

```
int & operator[](const int sub)
{
   if ((sub < 0) ¦¦ (sub > 4))
     { cerr << "Invalid subscript.  " << sub;
       cerr << " is not within the range of 0 to 4.\n";
       exit(1);  // Aborts the program
     }
   return ( L[sub] );
}
```

Because the return value is a reference, the subscript operator works as an lvalue and as an access value to the List class. Both of the following work on the List object:

```
num = L1[2];   // Assigns the third L1 element to num
L2[2] = num;   // Assigns num to the third L1 element
```

Overloading Comparisons

At this point, overloading relational and logical operators is very easy. Here is an example of applying the relational != operator to the List class. You can overload the other relational and logical operators similarly.

```
friend List operator!= (const List &L1, const List &L2)
{
   for (int ctr = 0; ctr < 5; ctr++)
      { if (L1[ctr] != L2[ctr])
            { return 0; }  // An element was found to be unequal
      }
   return 1;  // Every element was equal to each other
}
```

Overloading = and Using the Copy Constructor

One final overloaded operator, the assignment operator, =, deserves special attention. As you can see from the title of this section, this discussion also describes a special type of constructor called the *copy constructor*. The copy constructor defines and initializes a new object *from an existing object*. A brief review of constructors is in order before an example is presented. Although this section more appropriately falls within Chapter 10, "Constructor and Destructor Functions," at that time you were not prepared to read about the copy constructor because you had yet to see friend functions or overloaded operators.

C++ is one of those subjects that is difficult to learn sequentially. It is like the "cart before the horse" syndrome in that you should learn about copy constructors when you learn about the regular constructors, but you do not understand enough at that point to fully grasp copy constructors. Many C++ texts include the copy constructor in their original constructor sections, but you might better appreciate the need for the copy constructor at this point in this book.

There are three places where you need constructors:

1. When you want to define a new object, as in:

   ```
   List L1;  // Constructs a new object
   ```

   C++ constructs a new L1 object, initializing it only if a default constructor assigns L1 values.

2. When you want to define a new object and initialize it with values:

   ```
   List L1(10);  // Constructs and initializes a new object
   ```

   You saw examples of both #1 and #2 in Chapter 10, "Constructor and Destructor Functions."

3. When you want to define a new object *and initialize it from another object,* like this:

   ```
   List L1(10);  // Constructs and initializes a new object
   List L2 = L1;  // Constructs L2 based on v1's contents
   ```

The different constructor variant appears in the second line of #3. It may at first appear that C++ makes an exact duplicate of the L1 object and places that duplicate into the newly reserved memory for L2. Basically, that *is* what happens, but that is not always what you want C++ to do.

Unless you specify a copy constructor, C++ calls an internal member function that reserves the object's storage and then performs a memberwise copy of the objects. The same thing happens if you do not overload the =, but use an assignment between objects. This is called the *default copy constructor.* The default copy constructor is C++'s way of copying every member of one object to another.

> There are three places where C++ calls the copy constructor, and all three places cause problems unless you want a memberwise copy. C++ calls the default memberwise copy constructor if you do not supply a better one when:
>
> 1. You define and initialize one object with another (as done in #3, discussed earlier).
>
> 2. You pass an object by value to a function (whereby a copy is made).
>
> 3. You return an object by value from a function.

Whenever a class contains a pointer to heap memory, you do not want a memberwise copy constructor called. For one thing, you do not want the newly-defined object to hold the same pointer value as the object from which it is initialized. If you perform a destructor function call on one of the objects, the other then points to deallocated heap memory, causing all sorts of problems.

Memberwise copying causes pointers to be copied, but not the data they point to.

Copy constructors are simple, and you can overcome many bugs and potential bugs if you get used to supplying them. Although copy constructors are especially important when your object contains a pointer, many C++ programmers write a default constructor for all their objects to eliminate problems down the road.

The assignment operator, =, performs the same memberwise copy and has the same problem with pointers that the copy constructors do. Whenever you assign one object to another, C++ uses the copy constructor to perform the assignment unless you override the constructor. The List class does not require a copy constructor or an overloaded assignment operator, because a memberwise copy is fine for it. When the previous programs in this chapter assigned values to L3, as in:

```
L3 = L1 + L2;  // Adds the two Lists and stores result in third
```

the operator+() function created an object that contained the sum of L1 and L2, then the default copy constructor copied that object, member by member, into the memory reserved for L3.

To see the copy constructor and overloaded assignment operator in action, consider this version of a String class program. Because C++ does not have a built-in string data type (neither does C, as you know), many C++ programmers create a string class to simulate a string data type. Because the string memory is reserved from the heap, it is vital that a copy constructor and an assignment constructor be supplied.

STRING.CPP. A simple string class program.

```
// Filename: STRING.CPP
// A simple string class program
#include <iostream.h>
#include <string.h>

class String {
   char *st;  // Pointer to heap memory where string data is stored
public:
   String();                 // Default constructor
   String(const char *);     // Initializes constructor
   String(const String & s); // Copy constructor
   ~String();                // Destructor
```

continues

211

STRING.CPP. continued

```cpp
    String & operator=(const String & s);   // Assignment operator
    friend ostream & operator<< (ostream & out, const String & s);
};

String::String()
{
    st = 0;   // Ensures empty string
}

String::String(const char * s)
{
    st = new char[strlen(s) + 1];   // Reserves enough heap for string copy
    strcpy(st, s);
}

String::String(const String & s)   // Copy constructor
{
    int newlen = strlen(s.st) + 1;   // Gets length of string to copy
    st = new char[newlen];
    strcpy(st, s.st);   // Keeps the pointers only from being copied
}

String& String::operator=(const String& s)   // Assignment operator
{
    if (this==&s)
      {return *this;}
    delete [] st;   // Deallocates the old string
    st = new char[strlen(s.st)+1];   // Makes room for the new one
    strcpy(st, s.st);
    return *this;   // Makes sure that you allow stacked assignments
}   // Without this, C++ would copy the pointer, but not the data

String::~String()
{
    delete [] st;   // Frees the string's space
}

ostream & operator<< (ostream & out, const String & s)
{
    out << s.st << endl;
    return out;
}

void main()
{
    String s1;   // Default constructor. This string will be empty
    cout << s1;   // Prints nothing
```

```
String s2("This is the Second string.");  // Initializes constructor
cout << s2;  // Prints contents of the string

String s3=s2;  // Uses copy constructor
cout << s3;

String s4;
s4 = "This is a 4th string.";  // No way in C!
cout << s4;
}
```

With the overloaded assignment function, you can see that you can directly assign a string constant list, This is a 4th string, to a String object. There is no need for strcpy() in main(). Here is the program's output:

```
This is the Second string.
This is the Second string.
This is a 4th string.
```

The assignment operator should *always* destruct (in this case, *deallocate* because the string was allocated to begin with) the value being assigned to. The operator=() function in the preceding program performs a delete of the assignment's target string before it constructs (allocates) and assigns the source string. As a rule of thumb, write your assignment operators as if they were a combination destructor/copy constructor call. By destructing the target string, you clean up its memory.

Destructing the target string first is good, but it poses yet another problem that you should deal with when writing the assignment operator. Before doing anything else, test to see whether the assignment target is already equal to the source being assigned. If they are, return and don't perform the assignment. You might have this situation in main():

```
s1 = s1;
```

If you destructed the target string, you also would destruct the source string on the right! Although such an assignment is a waste of time, the code using the class might actually have such a statement. If it does, instead of returning with nothing changed, you will really cause problems if you destroy before checking to see whether they are already equal.

There is another drawback to not having an assignment operator declared, other than confusing C++ when you assign values directly to an object. Suppose that you did this:

```
String s1("C++ is more fun");
String s2("than a barrel of monkeys.");
```

So far, the initialization constructor creates two strings on the heap, as shown in Figure 12.2.

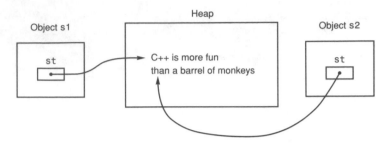

Figure 12.2. Each object contains a `String` *pointer that points to data in the heap.*

Consider what could happen if you attempted to do the following *without* the overloaded assignment operator:

```
s2 = s1;  // Whoops, lost some memory
```

C++ would perform an exact duplication of s1 to s2, resulting in the situation you see in Figure 12.3.

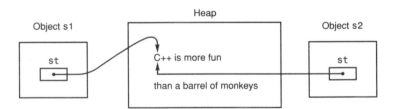

Figure 12.3. Without the assignment operator function, C++ copies the pointers but does not deallocate the extra heap data.

The memory originally pointed to by s2 is lost and will remain allocated, but you can never use it or deallocate it. The second problem is that if *either* of these two objects goes out of scope, the destructor deallocates the heap memory, leaving the other object pointing to deallocated memory.

Copy Constructors vs. Overloaded = Summary

A copy constructor is called by the compiler whenever it needs to create a copy of an object from another object. C++ calls either your copy constructor if you have defined one or the built-in memberwise copy constructor if you have not defined a copy constructor.

C++ calls the copy constructor *only* when it creates a new object from an existing one. You might at first think that the following statement calls an overloaded assignment operator function:

```
Ball basket = foot;  // Creates a basket object from
                     // the foot object
```

but because `basket` needs to be created, C++ calls the copy constructor. Nevertheless, if both `foot` and `basket` already exist, the following statement calls the overloaded assignment operator function (assuming that you've supplied one):

```
basket = foot;  // Copies the basket object to the foot
                // object
```

Final Design Note

Despite the interesting effects you have learned in this chapter, do not overload every single operator for every single class in your programs. It is possible that someday you might need an operator for a class that you did not predict when you wrote the first version of the program. If you find that you need additional operators as time goes by, write their overloaded code *then*. That is one of the primary advantages of C++: You can extend the language without affecting the rest of the program.

Also, whatever operators you do overload, try to leave the overloaded operators similar to their original built-in meanings, or make sure that the overloaded operators behave in a way that makes sense. You could overload the subtraction operator so that it multiplies and then takes the square root of a `class` object, but the results would be unclear, tricky, and downright bad coding.

Summary

The syntax for the various overloaded operators, although easy to understand when you take it apart, is difficult to grasp at first. Do not worry too much about understanding and memorizing the syntax needed to overload every operator. Concentrate instead on understanding the higher-level need for operator overloading. By overloading operators, you are teaching C++ how to operate on your own data types. As soon as you teach C++ how to act with your own data types, you can move on to the more important job of tackling

215

your application and let C++ worry about the petty details of inputting, outputting, and operating on your data.

Most beginning C++ programmers rightfully copy existing code, especially operator overloading functions, modifying the parts that need changing to work with their `class` objects. This chapter gives you the ammunition to overload your C++ program operators. As soon as you do, your main program can start working for you instead of adding to your programming frustrations.

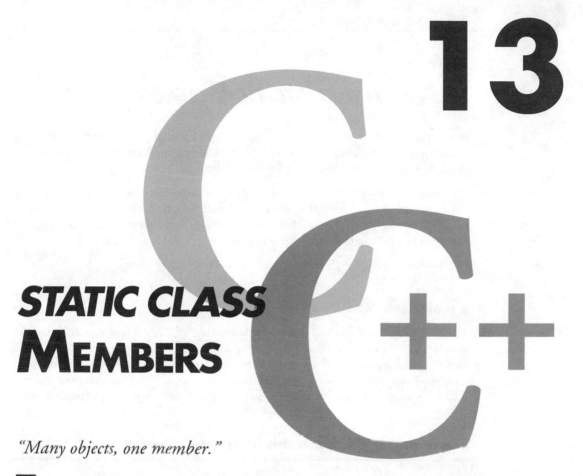

STATIC CLASS MEMBERS

"Many objects, one member."

The static keyword means something special when you use it with classes. Before reading about its usage in C++, think for a moment about the word itself; *static* usually means stable, as opposed to unstable, changing, and dynamic. static members have a special stability in C++ in that, unlike other types of members, static members exist outside of their class objects. This chapter attempts to show you how to use static members and static functions.

In this chapter, you will learn:

- How the static keyword differs in C++ and C
- How to declare static members
- How to declare static functions
- When to use static members and when to stay away from them
- How to declare static objects

Reviewing *static* Basics

Before you delve into static members and functions, a brief review is in order. In C++, static has three different uses. Two of those uses—static local variables and static global variables and functions—overlap the C language's static usage.

static variables are the opposite of auto variables.

In both C and C++, the opposite of a static variable is an auto variable, meaning *automatic*. All local variables are automatic by default; you do not have to specify the auto keyword. In other words, both of the following variable declarations are equivalent as long as they define the variables locally (inside a block):

```
int locval = 0;   // A local automatic variable
```

and

```
auto int locval = 0;   // A local automatic variable
```

All automatic variables disappear when they go out of scope. (This should be review, because it holds true in both C and C++.) For example, the following program does not use the local variable properly. The program attempts to use a local variable to keep track of the number of times main() calls count(), but the counter variable, ct, keeps going out of scope (disappearing) when count() finishes, so ct resets to 1 each time main() calls count().

STATIC1.CPP. Demonstrates improper use of auto variables.

```cpp
// Filename: STATIC1.CPP
// Demonstrates improper use of auto variables.
#include <iostream.h>
void count(void);

void main()
{
   cout << "At the top of main():\n\n";

   // Calls a function five times
   count();
   count();
   count();
   count();
   count();

   cout << "\nmain() just finished\n";
}

void count(void)
```

```
{
   // The following variable, ct, is automatic and local

   int ct=1;   // C++ assigns 1 EVERY TIME function executes

   cout << "count() called " << ct << " time(s) so far\n";
   ct++;
}
```

Here is the program's output:

```
At the top of main():
count() called 1 time(s) so far
count() called 1 time(s) so far
count() called 1 time(s) so far
count() called 1 time(s) so far
count() called 1 time(s) so far
main() just finished
```

Obviously, the local variable ct should *not* be an automatic variable because it keeps going away (going out of scope) when its block ends (the closing brace at the end of count()). main() calls count() five times, but the output does not keep track of those five times. count() resets ct to 1 each time main() calls count().

A static variable is one that does not lose its value when it goes out of scope. The following program is exactly like the preceding one, except that the local ct variable inside count() is static, not auto.

STATIC2.CPP. Demonstrates `static` **variables.**

```
// Filename: STATIC2.CPP
// Demonstrates static variables.
#include <iostream.h>
void count(void);

void main()
{
   cout << "At the top of main():\n\n";

   // Calls a function five times
   count();
   count();
   count();
   count();
   count();
```

continues

219

STATIC2.CPP. continued

```
   cout << "\nmain() just finished\n";
}

void count(void)
{
   static int ct=1;   // C++ assigns 1 only the FIRST time
   cout << "count() called " << ct << " time(s) so far\n";
   ct++;
}
```

Here is the program's output:

```
At the top of main():
count() called 1 time(s) so far
count() called 2 time(s) so far
count() called 3 time(s) so far
count() called 4 time(s) so far
count() called 5 time(s) so far
main() just finished
```

All global variables work like static variables, but they do not need the static keyword. For example, in the following program, g1 is a global variable that is a static variable. Its definition's location (between functions) makes it static.

STATIC3.CPP. Global variables retain their static duration.

```
// Filename: STATIC3.CPP
// Global variables retain their static duration.
#include <iostream.h>
void count(void);
main()
{
   cout << "At the top of main():\n\n";

   // Calls a function five times
   count();
   count();
   count();
   count();
   count();

   cout << "\nmain() just finished\n";
```

```
}

int ct=1;   // Global so that it retains its value past this point

void count(void)
{
   cout << "count() called " << ct << " time(s) so far\n";
   ct++;
}
```

Even though all global variables have static duration, putting the static keyword in front of global variables changes their duration slightly. If your program is a stand-alone program, without any other program that will be linked to it, the following global variable definitions do exactly the same thing:

static global variables and functions induce file scope.

```
float gl_pay = 12.50;   // static Global variable
```

and

```
static float gl_pay = 12.50;   // static Global variable
```

The subtle difference between these two definitions occurs only when several program files are linked together. Global variables with the explicit static keyword are static and global *only to the source file in which they are defined.* Global variables without the static keyword are static and global across more than one source file. The following statement in another program file:

```
extern float gl;   // Global variable is defined in another file
```

allows its source code to access another program's global variable called gl as long as the original program's gl does not have the static keyword before it.

The same file scope limitation applies to functions you designate as static. The following function cannot be referenced by another program linked to this one because of the static keyword:

```
static float doub(float x)   // Can be called only
{                            // from this program
   return (2*x);
}
```

Without the static keyword, however, the function is accessible from any program linked to that one, as long as the linked program contains the following external reference to the function:

```
extern float doub(float x);   // Function exists in another file
```

221

static class Member Data

In addition to the static possibilities discussed in the previous section, C++ introduces a new static feature. Members of a class—either data members or member functions—can be static, and when they are, they take on new meaning.

To declare a class data member static, simply precede the member name with static. The following class declaration contains a static data member called total.

```
class People {
   char name[30];
   int age;
public:
   static int total;  // Static across all objects
   People();
   ~People();
   Getit();
};
```

static data members exist only once.

total exists *only once in the program no matter how many* People *objects you define.* For example, suppose that you were to define three People class objects with this statement:

```
People emp1, emp2, emp3;  // Defines three People objects
```

222

Two of the data members, name and age, exist for all three objects. The data member total exists only once. Figure 13.1 shows how the objects use the same total but different names and ages.

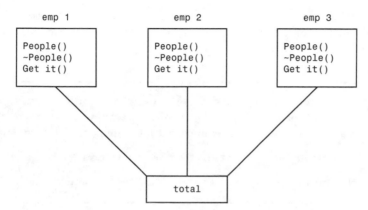

Figure 13.1. Each object, except for the static member named total, has a copy of the data. Each object shares the same total.

The action of static remains unaffected whether you declare the static member in the private or the public section of the class. If total were moved to the private section in the People class, Figure 13.1 would remain the same. The access specifier specifies only how visible the static member is to the rest of the program.

static data members are perfect for tracking statistics about objects and keeping track of counts and totals of the objects constructed. As each object gets constructed, your constructor could increment a static counter in the class, and as objects go out of scope, your destructor could decrement the static counter. Because only one occurrence of the static counter exists, no matter how many objects exist, the counter's integrity is unaffected by objects going in and out of scope.

Because static data members really do not reside with the individual objects, you must explicitly define the static member if you want it to be a value other than zero. In other words, C++ initializes total in the People class to zero if you do nothing. To initialize a

static member, precede the member name with the `class` name, followed by the scope resolution operator, `::`. This statement initializes the `People` class `total` data member to 1:

```
int People::total = 1;  // Initializes the static member
```

You could initialize `total` either before `main()`, inside `main()`, or between or inside any other function in the program.

> Even though C++ automatically initializes `static` data members to 0, you make your intentions clearer if you always explicitly initialize the `static` data members, even when you want them to be zero. For example, the following statement is unneeded:
>
> ```
> int People::total = 0;  // Initializes the static member
> ```
>
> but using it shows that you intended to zero out the `total` static data member.

Here is a complete program that uses a `static` data member. The program enables the user to enter three employees, then prints the employees to the screen. The program is simplistic, but it illustrates the use of a `static` data member. In this and other such programs, the `static` member acts almost like a global variable in that there is one copy of the variable that the object's member functions can access. Pay special attention to the way that the `static` variable is accessed. Because no single `Person` object is associated with the `static` variable `count`, the program accesses the `count` variable by preceding it with the `class` name instead of with an object name as would be done with regular, non-static members. The constructor's sole job is to increment the `static` variable `count`, and the destructor's job is to decrement `count`.

COUNTEMP.CPP. Uses a static variable to track the number of employee objects.

```
// Filename: COUNTEMP.CPP
// Uses a static variable to
// track the number of employee objects.
#include <iostream.h>
#include <iomanip.h>

class Person {
   char * name;  // Constructor allocates the name for each object
   int age;
   float salary;
```

```
public:
   static int count;  // Only one of these will exist
   Person();  // Constructor
   ~Person();  // Destructor
   friend istream & operator>> (istream & in, Person & p);
   friend ostream & operator<< (ostream & out, const Person & p);
};

// Member and friend functions follow
// The next two are small enough to have
// been inline with the preceding class
inline Person::Person()  // Constructor adds 1 to the static count
{
   name = new char[30];
   Person::count++;  // Must access count using the class name
}

inline Person::~Person()  // Destructor subtracts 1 from the static count
{
   delete [] name;
   Person::count—;  // Must access count using the class name
}

ostream & operator<< (ostream & out, const Person & p)
{
   out << setprecision(2);  // Two decimal places
   out << "Name:\t" << p.name << "\nAge:\t";
   out << p.age << "\nSalary:\t$" << p.salary << "\n" << endl;
   return out;
}

istream & operator>> (istream & in, Person & p)
{
   cout << "\nThis will be employee #" << Person::count << endl;
   cout << "What is the Employee's name? ";
   in >> p.name;
   cout << "What is " << p.name << "'s age? ";
   in >> p.age;
   cout << "What is " << p.name << "'s salary? ";
   in >> p.salary;
   return in;
}

int Person::count = 0;  // Initializes the static variable

void main()
{
```

continues

COUNTEMP.CPP. continued

```
    Person *emp1 = new Person;  // Bumps up employee count
    cin >> *emp1;  //Gets next employee's information
    Person *emp2 = new Person;
    cin >> *emp2;

    Person *emp3 = new Person;
    cin >> *emp3;

    cout << "\n";

    cout << *emp1;
    cout << *emp2;
    cout << *emp3;

    delete emp1;
    delete emp2;
    delete emp3;
}
```

main() could access count as well by referring to it using any of the three employee objects (such as emp1.count) or by using the scope resolution operator (as in Person::count). Here is the program's output. The static variable count keeps track of the employees as the user enters the data.

```
This will be employee #1
What is the Employee's name? Webster
What is Webster's age? 26
What is Webster's salary? 121.23

This will be employee #2
What is the Employee's name? Smith
What is Smith's age? 43
What is Smith's salary? 385.65

This will be employee #3
What is the Employee's name? Johnson
What is Johnson's age? 33
What is Johnson's salary? 254.78

Name:   Webster
Age:    26
Salary: $121.23

Name:   Smith
Age:    43
Salary: $385.65
```

```
Name:    Johnson
Age:     33
Salary: $254.78
```

Use *static* to Count Several Objects

You can use a static member to keep track of several different kinds of objects within the same class. For example, you might write a program to keep track of a coin collection. The Coin class might contain five static member counter variables, one for each Coin denomination (penny_ct, nickle_ct, dime_ct, quarter_ct, and half_dollar_ct).

In the Coin constructor, the argument you send it (for example, 1, 5, 10, 25, or 50) would indicate which kind of Coin you were constructing. In the primary program, for instance, if you wanted to construct a new nickle object, you might call this constructor:

```
Coin collection[next] = coin(5);  // Constructs a nickle
```

The Coin constructor function could contain a switch to check the argument and update the correct static counter. For example, this could be the first part of the Coin constructor:

```
Coin::Coin(int denom) {  // Constructor
   switch (denom) {
      case 1  : penny_ct++;       t_coins++; break;
      case 5  : nickle_ct++;      t_coins++; break;
      case 10 : dime_ct++;        t_coins++; break;
      case 25 : quarter_ct++;     t_coins++; break;
      case 50 : half_dollar_ct++; t_coins++; break;
      default: bad_denom_err();  break;
   }
   // Rest of constructor, if any, follows
```

(An enumerated set of constants, or a set of const ints, would better represent the denominations and make the code more readable, but too long, for this example.) The correct static member counter increments every time a coin of that denomination is constructed. Also, a total coin counter, t_coins, increments as well. At any time during the program's execution, you would have a running count of each denomination and of the total number of coins in the system.

static Member Functions

Member functions can be static as well. Unlike regular static functions that have file scope (as discussed in the first section of this chapter), static member functions have *external linkage*—that is, they can be called from across programs linked together. static member functions are not attached to any specific object. In other words, you do not have to refer to a specific object to execute static member functions.

For example, you have to call a regular member function with an object like this:

```
emp1.triple();  // Passes a triple message to the emp1 object
```

To call a static member function, you can use the class name and the scope resolution operator, like this:

```
Person::triple();  // Calls the static triple function
```

You can still call static functions using an object, but the code is not quite as clear because the static function has no attachment to that object. static member functions do *not* have a *this pointer, and you must pass the static function a pointer to an object if you want the static function to work with that object.

> Use static member functions to manipulate static data members. If you need to initialize or manipulate static data members when you have yet to create an object (called *object instantiation*), you can do so because you can execute static member functions using the class name. C++ programmers also use static member functions to manipulate global variables in their programs, although most programmers generally stay away from global variables because a global's scope is too broad for safety.

Here is a simple program that uses two static functions to work with a global variable, glob, and a static variable, st.

STATIC4.CPP. Uses static member functions to manipulate a global variable and a static data member.

```
// Filename: STATIC4.CPP
// Uses static member functions to manipulate a global variable and
// a static data member, even though no objects are defined at all.
```

```
#include <iostream.h>
int glob = 234;  // Global variable

class Statshow {
    int num;  // Never used
    char ch;  // Never used
public:
    static int st;  // Static data member
    static void sum_glob();
    static void sum_stat();
};

void Statshow::sum_glob()
{
    glob -= 34;  // Subtracts from global variable
}

void Statshow::sum_stat()
{
    st *= 3;  // Multiplies the static data member
}

int Statshow::st = 3;  // Must initialize static members

void main()
{
    cout << "At the top of main():\n" << "glob is " << glob << endl;
    cout << "st is " << Statshow::st << endl;

    Statshow::sum_glob();  // Static function that changes global
    cout << "\nAfter the change, glob is " << glob << endl;

    Statshow::sum_stat();  // Static function that changes static member
    cout << "After the change, st is " << Statshow::st << endl;
}
```

Here is the program's output:

```
At the top of main():
glob is 234
st is 3

After the change, glob is 200
After the change, st is 9
```

static Objects

Although static class objects rarely are used, you can declare them. As with any variable, a class variable is static if:

1. You define it globally (outside of any function).

2. You define it with the static keyword.

C++ calls a global static *object's constructor before* main() *even begins.*

If you define a global class variable, C++ calls the object's constructor *before* main() executes. To understand this, look at the following program. main() does *absolutely nothing*, and yet several messages print when the static global variables are created.

STATIC5.CPP. Program with static global objects.

```
// Filename: STATIC5.CPP
// Program with static global objects
#include <stdio.h>

class Stobj {
     int i;
 public:
    Stobj();  // Constructor
    ~Stobj();  // Destructor
};

Stobj::Stobj()
{
   printf("\nConstructor being called.\n");
   printf("What do you want i to be? ");
   scanf(" %d", &i);
};

Stobj::~Stobj()
{
   printf("\ni was %d before it gets destroyed.\n", i);
   i=0;
   printf("Destructor just called.\n");
}

Stobj o1;        // Declares two static objects. o1 has external
static Stobj o2;  // linkage and o2 has internal linkage (can be used
                  // only in this program, not declared as extern in
                  // another) because of the static keyword
```

230

```
void main()  // Nothing here!
{}
```

> The static object's constructor and destructor functions contain the C-style printf() and scanf() I/O functions. Although cout and cin are superior to the I/O functions, do not use cout and cin inside static constructors and destructors. Because cout and cin are objects, and so are the static objects you are constructing, the compiler might not have constructed cout and cin before it constructs your static objects (the order of these objects is not defined in C++). Although cout and cin often work in static constructors and destructors, they do not always. Sometimes C++ issues an error saying that you are attempting to use cout and cin objects before they are defined and constructed.

The program's output appears next. A lot goes on, considering that main() is empty!

```
Constructor being called.
What do you want i to be? 3

Constructor being called.
What do you want i to be? 5

i was 5 before it gets destroyed.
Destructor just called.

i was 3 before it gets destroyed.
Destructor just called.
```

Although watching constructors being called when there is no main() is interesting, you should limit your use of global variables because they do not offer the protection and safety of local variables, and even less so than class variables. A local static object is just like any other local object, except that it retains its value when it goes out of scope.

Summary

This chapter reviewed the basics of the static keyword. For many local and global variables, static means the same thing in C++ that it does in C. The difference appears when you use static inside a class.

A static class member exists only once for a class, no matter how many class objects you define. static variables are sometimes called *class variables* because they belong to the class and not to a specific object. C++ treats a static data member almost like a global variable because there is only one occurrence of the static data member. In other words, the objects of the class share the static value. static values let objects "talk" to one another and also keep statistics about the class (such as the number of objects constructed at anyone time if the constructor increments the static variable's count).

A static function works only with static class data and other static class member functions. You do not have to define a class object to access and change a static member; static functions can access static members any time you need access to the static members.

This wraps up another C++ milestone. You are now on your way to mastering OOP with C++. (You probably don't even blink now when you hear the words *OOP, member functions,* and *constructor!*) The next chapter begins one of the last large topics of the book. You are ready to learn about the ins and outs of *inheritance.* One object can inherit characteristics and behaviors of other objects. Before this book gets ahead of itself, take a break so that you can face inheritance with a fresh thinking cap.

Part IV

C++

INHERITANCE AND VIRTUAL FUNCTIONS

14

THE NEED FOR INHERITANCE

"Achieve success the good old-fashioned way: inherit it."

Inheritance dominates all walks of life. People, animals, and plants all inherit from the gene patterns of their ancestors. Genetic inheritance is the single most important determinant in life's final product. The more scientists discover about the genetic makeup of people, the more keys they find that unlock solutions to disease and physical limitations. Inheritance makes the creation of life much simpler. Instead of life's being formed from scratch, the inheritance patterns supply the puzzle pieces that only have to be put together, not created anew.

Despite all that is known about the benefits of inheritance, the history of computer programming seems slow to catch up. For years, programmers wrote programs from scratch, "reinventing the wheel" all along the way. Throughout the '70s and '80s, programmers realized that something had to be done to break the bottleneck of programming jobs that flooded the industry. Today, that bottleneck still exists, but for the first time, a real solution is available. C++ enables you to inherit objects from other objects, making the concepts of extensibility, maintainability, and reusability real for the first time in programming history.

With a build-up like that, you've just got to read further. In this chapter, you will learn:

- The background of class inheritance

- The difference between a base and a derived class

- How to inherit from existing classes

- How to use the access specifiers `private`, `public`, and `protected` when inheriting classes

- How to call inherited member functions

Inheriting to Simplify

Inheriting makes your programming much easier because you have to write less code. The more you inherit from existing programs, the less you need to do to get the current problem solved. In C, you simulate inheriting when you create libraries of functions. You can piece together functions you wrote for other programs and bring copies of them into your new programs.

Using existing code just doesn't always work.

Today's programmers know that using an existing piece of code usually is easier than writing it from scratch, yet using existing code is sometimes just as difficult as writing it again. For one thing, existing code rarely works *exactly* like the code you need, so you must modify it to make it work the way you want it to. Because of poor documentation and an on-again, off-again adherence to structured programming techniques, existing code is not always easy to modify. Sometimes more subtle bugs creep into existing code that you attempt to make work than would appear if you were to design and write the code from scratch. Even the simple act of block-copying the lines of code from one program to another can be tricky. You can miss lines, copy too many lines, or copy lines to the wrong place.

If all this sounds like overkill, it really is not. If existing code libraries were truly reusable, you would immediately see a gain in programming productivity. What programmers need is a real, lifelike inheritance language: existing, debugged, working programs from which you can inherit pieces that suit your needs. As with real-life inheritance, you might want to improve on the inherited code by adding key features and getting rid of unneeded ones (the bad genes). At the very least, you might want to inherit code so that fewer bugs creep into the code and you are up and running with a working application faster.

With inheritance, you can write complex applications quickly. C++ does the major work for you. You do not have to worry about copying lines of code or rewriting it so that it suits

your exact needs. With C++ inheritance, you only need to specify the new features of (or the ones you want removed from) the inherited code.

Derivation Fundamentals

Before diving into C++ inheritance specifics, you should take some time to familiarize yourself with basic inheritance concepts. C++ utilizes a hierarchical inheritance system. That is, you inherit one class from another, creating new classes from existing ones.

> You can inherit only classes, not regular functions and variables, in C++. This poses no limitation, for as you have seen, classes hold the real power in OOP C++ programs.

The inherited classes are called *derived* classes or, sometimes, *child* classes. In theory, the chain of derived classes starts with one original class. The primary class that begins the inheritance is called the *base* class or the *parent* class. For example, Figure 14.1 shows classes represented as boxes, with the class names in each box. Box A represents the base class, and boxes B, C, D, and E represent derived classes.

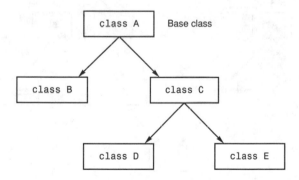

Figure 14.1. The relationships between the base class and its derived classes.

Although one can take semantics too far, class C is really a base class from which classes D and E are derived. To class D, class C is a base class, although to the overall inherited "family tree," class A is the primary base class.

237

The layered, hierarchical idea of OOP inheritance should be familiar to you. You probably notice how similar derived classes look to subdirectory structures in MS-DOS and UNIX. The root directory acts like a base class, and all subdirectories, the derived directories, extend down from the root to form other directory relationships.

Figure 14.1 shows *single inheritance*—that is, every derived class is inherited from a single class. In single inheritance, every class has one and only one parent class. Each parent class, however, can have many child classes.

C++ supports the use of *multiple inheritance* as well. If a child class has more than one parent class, the child class is being inherited through multiple inheritance. Figure 14.2 shows two occurrences of multiple inheritance (class AB and class B23). You might need multiple inheritance when a class needs to inherit behaviors and properties from more than one class. Although the idea is simple and seemingly useful, you rarely need multiple inheritance. If you find yourself wanting to use multiple inheritance, immediately suspect a problem with your class design. Almost every useful inheritance of classes can be done with single inheritance. Some programs might have several base classes with many derived classes from each of them, but they do not constitute multiple inheritance because each of the derived classes has at most one parent class.

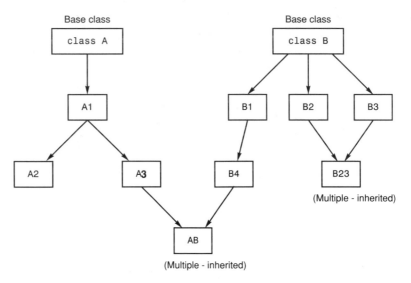

Figure 14.2. Multiple inheritance with derived classes having one or more parent classes. The two base classes in this figure are A and B.

The C++ Difference

There is much debate over multiple inheritance in the C++ world. Some programmers believe that only single inheritance should be allowed. At first, this seems limiting, but one of the original OOP languages, SmallTalk, allows only single inheritance, and SmallTalk programmers do not seem to miss multiple inheritance. In SmallTalk, a pure inheritance language, you must inherit every object from a single, generic, high-level base object. (C++ is sometimes called a *hybrid OOP language* because it does not always act like a pure OOP language. C++ allows multiple inheritance, and you can create a base class from scratch without using a single built-in generic class first.)

If only single inheritance were allowed, *every* class would have to derive from one base class. This is a lot like a hard disk. The disk has one root directory, and every other directory, no matter how complicated or eclectic the other subdirectories are, extends from the root.

It looks as though the proposed ANSI C++ committee is going to let multiple inheritance stay in the language. The biggest drawback to retaining multiple inheritance is the tendency to use it when you do not have to. As you will see a little later, multiple inheritance introduces all sorts of ambiguities and bugs into your code, so beware when thinking about using it.

Most C++ programmers will use multiple inheritance because the iostream.h header file includes the I/O class that is itself composed of multiple inheritance. The I/O class (discussed in detail in Chapter 18, "Advanced C++ Input/Output") is tested, debugged, and fully safe to use. When you write your own programs, however, attempt to find the most generic base class possible and try to inherit everything from that base class.

Why Do You Need Inheritance?

This book takes the philosophy that you should understand the need for a concept before you learn the concept's description and terminology. You saw the importance of data hiding before learning about `private` access and encapsulation. You saw how to send several different objects the same message before you heard the word *polymorphism*. (Actually, you saw only the surface of polymorphism; you will see polymorphism in much more depth after learning some inheritance fundamentals.)

All this aside, the preceding section explained many concepts and new terms before showing you much need for those terms. In this chapter's defense, most programmers are already familiar with some form of the inherited parent-child relationship. As mentioned earlier, directory structures use parent-child inheritance, as do many linked list behaviors such as binary trees, database files, and combined spreadsheet file systems. You also are familiar with the need to classify things into a tree structure in real life. Species of animals derive from other species, and you can classify nonliving, real-life objects in a derived hierarchy as well.

Most knowledge you gain is built on current knowledge.

It is the grouping of inherited objects that lets people learn a lot about new things. When you learn chemistry (if you ever have the desire), your chemistry professors will use your existing knowledge of algebraic math to describe chemical formulas. When you learned algebraic math, your math professors used concepts in earlier math courses to teach algebra. When you first learned about math, your schoolteachers used apples and oranges to teach you about addition and subtraction.

In other words, people learn best when they relate what they already know to the new subject. Instead of learning every new subject from scratch, people compare and contrast with something else. They learn how the new subject relates to what they already know. This book is a self-proving example of this concept. This book, especially the earlier chapters, bases every new C++ topic on something you already know and are comfortable with in C. Figure 14.3 shows how C++ relates to other programming languages. Each language is based on (inherited from) another language, and all go back to the original base language—the 1s and 0s of machine language.

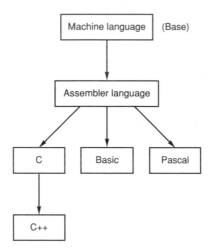

Figure 14.3. The inheritance model explains how C++ fits into the overall programming picture.

Therefore, when code inheritance is a built-in language feature, you can start with a basic class and create new classes from that base. As your programs become more complex, your reuse of code becomes greater, and the complexity does not get in the way of the programming problem as easily as it would without inheritance.

Inheritance Specifics

When one class inherits from another, the derived class inherits all public data and functions from the base class. Therefore, you have to specify only the additional data and functions to the derived class. To get started, here is a class header that keeps track of a person's name and address:

```
class NameAdr  {
public:
    char name[30];
    char addr[30];
    char city[10];
    char st[2];
    char zip[5];
    NameAdr get_info();  // Prompts for name and address info
    void print();  // Prints the name and address info
    NameAdr();  // Constructor
    ~NameAdr();  // Destructor
};
```

A little study of this class reveals a difference from the rest of the classes in this book. All members, both data and functions, are public. You know by now that many class members are better left private to achieve the data hiding encapsulation advantages of C++. The access specifiers, private and public, have more implications when you use them with inheritance. Making all members of NameAdr public for now helps streamline the introductory section of inheritance you see here.

Suppose that a hospital's data processing department were writing a C++ information system to track all the hospital's people. A hospital might want to track several types of people. For example, the hospital would want to track patients, employees, and suppliers. Not much is special about the NameAdr class just shown. As a matter of fact, it is so generic that the hospital will need much more information for any person it tracks.

One of the benefits of the NameAdr class is its plain-vanilla body. Because every patient, employee, and supplier will name a name, address, city, state, and zip code, the class is useful, but it must go further. Because all three types of people's classes might use this class,

including its `get_info()` and `print()` functions, the `NameAdr` class is a good base class candidate.

> When you want to update a program, inherit the class code you want to update. You then add all the new code in one place (the derived class code), where is it easier to debug and maintain.

The patient class needs much more than the `NameAdr` class, such as a diagnosis code, a balance owed, a home phone number, a primary doctor code, and a birthdate (data members). Also, you would need to send the patient a bill (member function). In reality there would be much more, but to keep things reasonable, this example stays with these new patient data members. Therefore, you might want a derived `Patient` class that inherits the `NameAdr` class and adds the additional data. Here is such a `Patient` class:

```
class Patient : NameAdr  {
   char diag_code[2];  // Diagnosis code
   double balance;  // Balance owed
   char phone[10];
   char dr_code[2];  // Doctor code
   char bdate[6];  // Birthdate
public:
   void send_bill();  // Send bill function
};
```

Some important considerations are in order before you get too comfortable with this class. The derived class has some potential problems that should be fixed, but don't sweat the details yet. Rather, concentrate on the inheritance concepts.

Separate the derived class from the base class with a colon, :.

When you inherit a derived class from a base class, you have to insert only a colon (:) and the base `class` name before the derived class's opening brace. The first line of the `Patient` class means "Define a new class named `Patient` and inherit the `NameAdr` class as a basis for the `Patient` class." Every member (because of the `public` access specifier in the base class `NameAdr`) is inherited into the derived class, as shown in Figure 14.4.

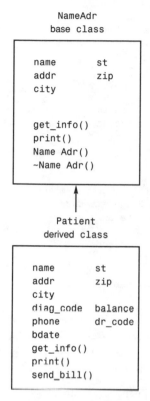

Figure 14.4. The derived class NameAdr *receives all public members of the base class* Patient.

Constructors and destructors are never inherited. You must write new constructors and destructors for each derived class that requires them. Chapter 15, "Inheritance Issues," explains how to construct and destruct with inheritance.

Because the base class rarely has all public members, you have to learn how to inherit classes with private members as well. The problem is that C++ simply does not let you do this! Here are the two classes again. This time, many of the base class's members are private:

```
class NameAdr  {
   char name[30];  // None of these private
   char addr[30];  // members will ever be
   char city[10];  // inherited!
   char st[2];
   char zip[5];
public:
   NameAdr get_info();  // Prompts for name and address info
   void print();  // Prints the name and address info
   NameAdr();  // Constructor
   ~NameAdr();  // Destructor
};

class Patient : NameAdr  {  // Derived class
   char diag_code[2];  // Diagnosis code
   double balance;  // Balance owed
   char phone[10];
   char dr_code[2];  // Doctor code
   char bdate[6];  // Birthdate
public:
   void send_bill();  // Send bill function
};
```

The following private members of NameAdr are *not* inherited in Patient: name, addr, city, st, and zip. You do not want these to be accessible to the rest of the program, but only to member functions that deserve access. However, if you cannot inherit these private members, what good is inheritance?

The base class protected specifier makes private members available to the derived class.

The answer would be "not much," except that C++ offers a third access specifier called *protected* that fixes the problem nicely. Here is the same class header with the protected specifier in place of the default private specifier in the base class:

```
class NameAdr  {
protected:
   char name[30];  // All of these members
   char addr[30];  // are now inherited
   char city[10];
   char st[2];
   char zip[5];
public:
   NameAdr get_info();  // Prompts for name and address info
   void print();  // Prints the name and address info
   NameAdr();  // Constructor
   ~NameAdr();  // Destructor
};

class Patient : NameAdr  {  // Derived class
   char diag_code[2];  // Diagnosis code
```

```
   double balance;   // Balance owed
   char phone[10];
   char dr_code[2];  // Doctor code
   char bdate[6];    // Birthdate
public:
   void send_bill();  // Send bill function
};
```

To summarize, `private` members can be used only by their class's own member functions. `public` members can be used by the entire program, as well as by any inherited classes. `protected` members are available to their class's own members and to derived classes, but not to the rest of the program.

> If possible, try to inherit only the `public` base class members if your application allows. This keeps `private` members `private`, allowing access to them only through `public` member functions, even to derived classes.

One final observation is in order: All `class` objects have a base class representation, but not all classes have to represent objects. A base class is not always used to define objects; some base classes exist only to provide a common class from which you inherit other, more specific classes.

Receiving Inherited Members

One last piece of the `private-public-protected` puzzle must be put into place before every *base* is covered (pun intended). The preceding section explained the syntax needed to inherit one class from another and also showed how to direct access specifiers so that the base `class` members can be available or not available to their derived classes.

The final part of your simple inheritance instruction is how inherited members appear *in the derived class.* In other words, although you now understand how the three access specifiers work in the base class, you do not yet know the answers to the following questions:

1. Are base `public` class members inherited as `public`, `private`, or `protected` in the derived class?

2. Are base `protected` class members inherited as `public`, `protected`, or `private` in the derived class?

3. Are base `private` `class` members inherited as `public`, `protected`, or `private` in the derived class?

In other words, you need to know how inherited members end up in the derived class. Just because they were `public` in the base class does *not* mean that they will be `public` in the derived class. It depends on the *base* `class` *access.*

Base `class`
access determines
how the derived
class receives
inherited
members.

The base `class` access is either `private`, `protected`, or `public`. If you do not specify a base `class` access, C++ assumes that you want `private` inheritance. This usually is *not* what you want, but C++ plays it safe. Put the base `class` access specifier after the colon, `:`, and before the derived `class` name when you inherit a class. As an example, the following `class` definition inherits from a base class called `NameAdr`, using `public` base `class` access:

```
class Patient : public NameAdr  { // Public base class
```

The `public` keyword is different from the `private`, `protected`, and `public` keywords in the `NameAdr` base class, although it is related in how it works.

The following `class` definition inherits from the base class called `NameAdr`, using `protected` base `class` access:

```
class Patient : protected NameAdr  { // Protected base class
```

The following `class` definition inherits from the base class called `NameAdr`, using `private` base `class` access:

```
class Patient : private NameAdr  { // Private base class
```

and so does this because `private` is the default if you do not specify it:

```
class Patient : NameAdr  { // Private base class
```

Therefore, the complete `class` header shown in the preceding section was inherited using a `private` base `class` access because no base `class` access was specified.

The base `class` access works in the following ways:

1. If the base `class` access is `private`, *all* the base class's members (both data and functions) will be `private` in the derived class, no matter what they were in the base class.

2. If the base `class` access is `protected`, the base class's `private` members (both data and functions) remain `private` in the derived class, the base class's pro- tected members remain `protected` (inheritable, but still hidden from the rest of the program), and the `public` members change to `protected` members when they are brought into the derived class. The base `class` members stay whatever they are in the base class (which implies that another class might derive the

members differently). The base `class` access specifies only how inherited members are treated in the derived class.

3. If the base `class` access is `public`, the base class's `private` members (both data and functions) remain `private`, the base class's `protected` members remain `protected` (inheritable, but still hidden from the rest of the program), and the `public` members remain `public` members when they are brought into the derived class. The base `class` members stay whatever they are to the base class. The base `class` access specifies only how inherited members are treated in the derived class.

> Remember as you read about inheritance that *base* `class` *access* refers to the `public`, `protected`, or `private` access specifier used in the derived class's first line. The base `class` access only dictates how the derived class receives the base `class` members. The base `class` access is different from (but related to) the access specifiers listed with the members inside the base class itself.

Despite C++'s default `private` base `class` access, you will almost always want to override `private` with `public`. A derived class is not very usable if all its members are `private`, as would be the case if you did not specify the `public` base `class` access. A `protected` base `class` access is more lenient than `private`, but again, when you inherit, you almost always need `public` base `class` access for functionality.

Summarizing the Possibilities

Things might seem a little fuzzy to you at this point. There are a total of nine combinations of `private`, `protected`, and `public` access specifiers and base class specifiers. The members of the base class can be any of the three access specifiers, and at the same time, derived classes can indicate any of the three base `class` access specifiers. In other words, the derived classes determine how they interpret the base class, but the base class has final control over who inherits its members.

If you are reading this chapter, but not trying examples on your own, you might be tempted to skim through these combinations and get to them when you need them. Try not to do that. Before moving on to the next few chapters, you must understand the ins and outs of the three access specifiers, both in the base class and in the derived class's base access specifiers. You do not have to memorize every combination, but you should be able to follow the combinations when you need to. To help put all this together, examples of every possible access combination are included in the program segments that follow. They clearly show you how inherited classes access members from their parent classes.

In these sample `class` headers, the base class `NameAdr` has three different types of members—`public`, `protected`, and `private`. The derived class's first line determines how the derivation will treat the three types of base `class` members.

```
class NameAdr  {
private:  // private keyword unneeded here
   char name[30];
   char addr[30];
   char city[10];
   char st[2];
   char zip[5];
protected:
   NameAdr get_info();  // Prompts for name and address info
public:
   void print();  // Prints the name and address info
   NameAdr();  // Constructor
   ~NameAdr();  // Destructor
};

class Patient : private NameAdr  {  // Derived class as private
   char diag_code[2];  // Diagnosis code
   double balance;  // Balance owed
   char phone[10];
   char dr_code[2];  // Doctor code
   char bdate[6];  // Birthdate
public:
   void send_bill();  // Send bill function
};
```

The `Patient` class inherits all of `NameAdr`'s members, but those members are all `private` to `Patient`. Therefore, if another class inherits from `Patient`, the members that `Patient` got from `NameAdr` will be `private`. Of course, some other class can inherit from `NameAdr` and get different results if it uses a different base `class` access, such as `protected` or `public`. Figure 14.5 shows the resulting `Patient` class as soon as it privately inherits `NameAdr`.

The `private` keyword could be left off the class `Patient`'s first line and the results would remain the same because `private` is the default base `class` access.

The following `class` header defines `Patient` as inheriting from `NameAdr` with the `protected` base `class` access:

```
class NameAdr  {
private:  // private keyword unneeded here
```

```
   char name[30];
   char addr[30];
   char city[10];
   char st[2];
   char zip[5];
protected:
   NameAdr get_info();  // Prompts for name and address info
public:
   void print();  // Prints the name and address info
   NameAdr();  // Constructor
   ~NameAdr();  // Destructor
};

class Patient : protected NameAdr  {  // Derived class as protected
   char diag_code[2];  // Diagnosis code
   double balance;  // Balance owed
   char phone[10];
   char dr_code[2];  // Doctor code
   char bdate[6];  // Birthdate
public:
   void send_bill();  // Send bill function
};
```

Patient inherits all of NameAdr here also. The private members of NameAdr remain private when they get to Patient. The protected members of NameAdr remain protected. The public members of NameAdr change to protected when they get to Patient. If another class inherited from Patient, it would think that Patient had 13 members (count them, but remember that the constructor and destructor will never be derived to Patient), of which 10 would be private, 2 would be protected, and 1 would be public. Figure 14.6 shows the resulting Patient class and its members' access specifiers.

```
                          Patient class

┌─────────────────────────────────────────────────────┐
│                                                       │
│  private members: name        st                      │
│                   addr        zip                      │
│                   city        print()                  │
│                   get_info()  balance                  │
│                   diag_code() dr_code                  │
│                   phone                                │
│                   bdate                                │
│                                                       │
│                                                       │
│  public members: send_bill()                          │
│                                                       │
└─────────────────────────────────────────────────────┘
```

Figure 14.5. The resulting Patient *class after inheriting from* NameAdr *with a private base class access.*

```
                        Patient class

    ┌─────────────────────────────────────────────────────┐
    │  private members:      name         st              │
    │                        addr         zip             │
    │                        city         diag_code       │
    │                        balance      phone           │
    │                        dr_code      bdate           │
    │                                                      │
    │  protected members:    get_info()                   │
    │                        print()                      │
    │                                                      │
    │  public members:       send_bill()                  │
    └─────────────────────────────────────────────────────┘
```

Figure 14.6. The resulting `Patient` *class after inheriting from* `NameAdr` *with a* `protected` *base* class *access.*

The following `class` header defines `Patient` as inheriting from `NameAdr` with the `public` base class access:

```
class NameAdr  {
private:  // private keyword unneeded here
   char name[30];
   char addr[30];
   char city[10];
   char st[2];
   char zip[5];
protected:
   NameAdr get_info();  // Prompts for name and address info
public:
   void print();  // Prints the name and address info
   NameAdr();  // Constructor
   ~NameAdr();  // Destructor
};

class Patient : public NameAdr  {  // Derived class as public
   char diag_code[2];  // Diagnosis code
   double balance;  // Balance owed
   char phone[10];
   char dr_code[2];  // Doctor code
   char bdate[6];  // Birthdate
public:
   void send_bill();  // Send bill function
};
```

`Patient` inherits all of `NameAdr` here also. The `private` members of `NameAdr` remain `private` when they get to `Patient`. The `protected` members of `NameAdr` remain `protected`.

The public members of NameAdr remain public when they get to Patient. If another class inherited from Patient, it would think that Patient had 13 members, of which 10 would be private, 1 would be protected, and 2 would be public. Figure 14.7 shows the resulting Patient class and its members' access specifiers. The public base class access is the most commonly used in C++ programming.

```
              Patient class

┌─────────────────────────────────────────────────┐
│                                                   │
│  private members:     name        st             │
│                       addr        zip            │
│                       city        diag_code      │
│                       balance     phone          │
│                       dr_code     bdate          │
│                                                   │
│  protected members:   get_info()                 │
│                                                   │
│                                                   │
│  public members:      print()                    │
│                       send_bill()                │
│                                                   │
└─────────────────────────────────────────────────┘
```

Figure 14.7. The resulting Patient *class after inheriting from* NameAdr *with a* public *base class access.*

Here is a more complete class header that the hospital might use. It uses the NameAdr as a base class for three other classes: Patient, Employee, and Supplier. Because there are two types of employees, hourly and salaried, the Employee class is a parent class to two more classes, Hourly and Salaried.

When a class inherits from another derived class, the newly derived class cannot have more freedom to the original base class than its parent. In other words, because Employee inherits NameAdr as protected, Hourly cannot have public access to addr because addr is a private member in Employee.

INHER1.CPP. Uses NameAdr as a base class for three other classes.

```
// Filename: INHER1.CPP
class NameAdr  {
private:  // private keyword unneeded here
   char name[30];
   char addr[30];
   char city[10];
   char st[2];
   char zip[5];
```

continues

INHER1.CPP. continued

```
protected:
   NameAdr get_info();  // Prompts for name and address info
public:
   void print();  // Prints the name and address info
   NameAdr();  // Constructor
   ~NameAdr();  // Destructor
};

class Patient : protected NameAdr {  // Derived class as protected
   char diag_code[2];  // Diagnosis code
   double balance;  // Balance owed
   char phone[10];
   char dr_code[2];  // Doctor code
   char bdate[6];  // Birthdate
public:
   void send_bill();  // Send bill function
};

class Supplier : protected NameAdr {  // Derived class as protected
   char vendorcode;
   double balance;
   char busphone[10];
   float discount;
public:
   void pay_bill();
};

class Employee : protected NameAdr {  // Derived class as protected
   char dept_code;
   int withholding;
   char ins_plan;  // Insurance plan
public:
   void send_paycheck();
};

class Hourly : public Employee {  // Derived class from another one
   float rate;
public:
   double comp_pay();  // Computes pay function
};

class Salaried : public Employee {  // Derived class from another one
   float annual;
   int yrs_vested;  // Years employee has been vested in insurance
public:
   double comp_pay();  // Computes pay function
};
```

Figure 14.8 shows how this `class` header inheritance structure looks. Many more inherited classes could be added, but for now, concentrate on the inheritance syntax and the workings of the access specifiers.

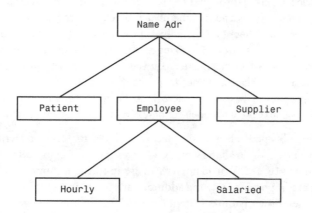

Figure 14.8. A more complete `class` *header that depends on three layers of inheritance.*

You can see how easy it is to extend a class. One of the smallest-looking classes in the `NameAdr` header file is actually the largest class. The class `Salaried` has a total of 10 members. To C++, it looks like this:

```
class Salaried {  // After inheritance, Salaried looks like this
    char name[30];
    char addr[30];
    char city[10];
    char st[2];
    char zip[5];
    char dept_code;
    int withholding;
    char ins_plan;  // Insurance plan
    float annual;
    int yrs_vested;  // Years employee has been vested in insurance
protected:
    NameAdr get_info();  // Prompts for name and address info
    void print();  // Prints the name and address info
public:
    void send_paycheck();
    double comp_pay();  // Computes pay function
};
```

If the base class changes, all inherited classes will include those changes.

Of course, this expanded `Salaried` class never appears in the program as you see it here, but this is how C++ views the class as soon as inheritance takes place. Take a moment to follow this expanded view of `Salaried`. Follow its inheritance along the way from the original `NameAdr` base class, through the `Employee` class, and finally into `Salaried`. Do you see why `send_paycheck()` is a `public` member and not a `protected` or a `private` member of `Salaried`? `send_paycheck()` originally appears as a `public` member in `Employee`. Because `Salaried` inherits from `Employee` with `public` base class access, all `public` members of `Employee` will be `public` in `Salaried`. Do you see why `print()` is `protected`? In the original class it appears in, `NameAdr`, `print()` is `public`. When `Employee` inherits, it inherits with `protected` base class access, so `print()` becomes `protected`. Because `Salaried` inherits `Employee` with a `public` base class access, `print()` remains `protected`.

The epitome of C++ power begins to surface here. The actual code you write for `Salaried` is very small; you let C++ do all the work. C++ takes care of bringing all the inherited class information into `Salaried`. You do not have to use an editor to copy the code (introducing errors), but more important, only the additions are stored in `Salaried`. Therefore, if the base class changes, or if any of the parent classes along the way changes, C++ makes sure that all derived classes then include those changes automatically. All your new code is in one place, but so is the old code, the base class, as well. If you were still copying functions from libraries, and the function code changed, *you would have to change the copied code everywhere in the program that you copied it.* Even more frustrating, if you copied that code to other source files, you would have to load each of those files, make the changes or copy the modified code back into the files, recompile them, and then hope that the changes you made would not affect something else in the programs.

Another powerful advantage that inheritance gives you is the ability to reuse and add to functionality in the derived classes without having the source code to the base class. You can purchase precompiled class libraries and inherit from those libraries, adding your own members and reusing ones from the compiled code. Many C++ programmers program Windows applications, using one of the many Windows class libraries available from Borland and other vendors. When you need a special window class, you only have to inherit one of the generic window classes that come with the library, tailoring it to suit your specific needs.

With C++ and its inheritance of classes, programming groups can begin to be productive and move from a maintenance mode into a productivity mode. When a system changes, instead of looking for ramifications in every source file that might use those changes, you only have to change the base class; C++ takes care of the rest of the code that uses that base class.

You will see in the next chapter how to remove functionality from parent classes, taking away data and functions that the derived class does not need while maintaining other members it does need. Derived classes cannot always use every member of their parent classes. Also, a derived class can modify the behavior of a parent class member so that a member function or a data member is different in the derived class.

Introduction to Using Inheritance

As soon as you set up your class inheritance, you can call member functions using the inherited `class` objects (more accurately in C++ terminology, you can send an inherited object a message). For example, to declare a `Salaried` object, you would define one, like this:

```
Salaried Jones;  // Creates a Salaried object
```

As soon as you initialize the data members of `Jones`, you could compute the pay for `Jones` like this:

```
Jones.comp_pay();  // Computes the pay for Jones
```

Given the `class` structure shown earlier, the primary program cannot send the `print()` message to `Jones` like this:

```
Jones.print();  // INVALID; print() is protected
```

Because `print()` is protected for `Salaried` objects, `print()` can be inherited and used only by derived objects and `NameAdr` objects (where `print()` is public). As you can see, objects can receive messages within their `class` scope. Inheritance is a structured way of setting up your classes in an ordered, uncluttered manner, making your program maintenance much less troublesome by keeping all changes in one place. As soon as the inheritance takes place, the derived objects follow the scope, `public` rules, and `private` rules with which you are familiar.

If a base class has the same function as a derived class (and in the examples you have seen so far, they all do), the derived class has priority (called the *dominance rule*). For example, consider the following `class` definitions:

The derived class dominates.

```
class Base {  // Base class
   int i;
public:
   void print() { cout << i; }
};

class Derived1 : public Base {  // First derivation
   int j;
public:
   void print() { cout << i << "\n" << j << "\n"; }
};

class Derived2 : public Derived1 {  // Second derivation
   int k;
public:
   void print() { cout << i << "\n" << j << "\n" << j << "\n";
};
```

If the program creates three objects—a Base, a Derived1, and a Derived2 object—like this:

```
Base    A;  // Defines a Base object named A
Derived1 B;  // Defines a Derived1 object named B
Derived2 C;  // Defines a Derived2 object named C
```

the following statement executes the print() member function of Derived2:

```
C.print();  // Assumes that the program initialized members of C
```

The following statement executes the print() member function of Derived1:

```
B.print();  // Assumes that the program initialized members of B
```

Finally, the following statement executes the print() member function of Base:

```
A.print();  // Assumes that the program initialized member in A
```

None of the versions represents overloaded functions. They do not match the pattern of overloaded functions because their signatures (their parameter lists) all match. Each class has its own version of print(); that is, each succeeding derived class overrides the preceding class's (the parent class's) print().

The preceding example is straightforward and offers no surprises. Changing the class a little creates some differences, but C++ still works as you might expect, as the following example shows:

```
class Base {  // Base class
   int i;
public:
   void print() { cout << i; }
```

```
};

class Derived1 : public Base {  // First derivation
   int j;
};

class Derived2 : public Derived1 {  // Second derivation
   int k;
};
```

This class example shows much less code in the derived classes. Both of the derived classes, Derived1 and Derived2, inherit the print() function. If you send the print() message to a Derived1 or a Derived2 object, however, only i prints because neither Derived1 nor Derived2 overrode the print() function.

Summary

You are on your way to tackling inheritance. As you design and write C++ programs, you will create many classes. When you find yourself designing two classes that have similar features, consider their commonalties and turn their common members into a base class from which you can inherit the others. Not only will you finish the program faster, but you will have fewer bugs and you will control future maintenance.

The next couple of chapters show you more uses for inheritance and also show you how to extend the functionality of derived classes and modify the behavior of inherited class data. There is much yet for you to learn about inheritance before you will see its true power. Chapter 15, "Inheritance Issues," discusses how constructors and destructors work with inherited objects and how you can override some of the default inheritance features to make them work for you.

INHERITANCE ISSUES

"A child class must take care of its parent."

There is much more for you to learn about inheritance before you will fully grasp the power behind OOP, but you are well on your way. Because constructors play an important role in inheritance, you must understand their ordering and execution in the hierarchy of inheritance. Not everything in C++ can be inherited, so you also must learn the limitations of inheritance.

This chapter takes you another step closer to mastering inheritance. After this chapter, you will be prepared for one of the most important concepts (and the least understood, it seems) of C++ and OOP. Chapter 17, "Virtual Functions," discusses virtual functions, the apex of OOP and polymorphism. Virtual functions also are one of the last new features of C++, so as soon as you tackle them, you are on your way to being a master C++ programmer.

In this chapter, you will learn about:

- Constructor initialization lists
- The role inheritance plays with constructor functions

- How to override a base class's `private`, `protected`, or `public` access

- Inheritance limitations

- The hows and caveats of multiple inheritance

Constructor Initialization Lists

C++ offers an alternative syntax for constructor functions that you should begin getting used to. Many constructor functions do not include any assignment statements, yet the constructor initializes member data. To show you the alternative syntax, here is a simple constructor function like many you have seen so far in this book:

```
class Store {
   int num;
   double sales;
public:
   Store(int n, double s) { num=n; sales=s; };
   ~Store();  // Implemented elsewhere
   print();  // Implemented elsewhere
};
```

By this time, you know that the constructor could have been implemented later in the code and only prototyped inside the class, like this:

```
class Store {
   int num;
   double sales;
public:
   Store(int n, double s) ;
   ~Store();  // Implemented elsewhere
   print();  // Implemented elsewhere
};

inline Store::Store(int n, double s)  {
   num = n;
   sales = s;
};
// Rest of code follows
```

There really is no difference between these two implementations of the constructor function, and you should now be comfortable with both. Just as you are comfortable with both, however, C++ changes things. There is yet another way to construct objects: by initializing their members. Most C++ programmers prefer this newer method. You can construct an object using a *constructor initialization list*.

The constructor initialization list replaces the constructor's assignment statements. You must precede a constructor initialization list with a colon, :, inserting the list between the constructor argument list and the constructor's opening brace. The preceding Store class looks like this if you replace the body of the constructor function with an initialization list:

A constructor initialization list replaces multiple constructor assignment statements.

```
class Store {
   int num;
   double sales;
public:
   Store(int n, double s) : num(n), sales(s) {};
   ~Store();  // Implemented elsewhere
   print();   // Implemented elsewhere
};
```

Notice that there is no need for a constructor body because the initialization list takes care of the initialization of the members. C++ programmers prefer to initialize data members with an initialization list for three reasons:

1. A constructor should not *assign;* it should *initialize.* Although the difference might be only in semantics in many cases, the spirit of the constructor is better achieved with an initialization list. The body of the constructor might still contain additional code, but it needs no direct assignment of data members.

2. When you implement inheritance, the initialization list offers a more streamlined transition toward understanding base class construction. (The next section explains what is meant by *base class construction.*)

3. const and reference members cannot be assigned values, so you *must* initialize them.

Inheritance with Constructors

When you work with a derived class, you must remember that the class is not just a stand-alone class, but that it is a conglomerate of a parent class. If a base class constructor requires an argument—that is, if it requires more than a default constructor—the derived class must supply the argument by calling the base class constructor. A derived class has to worry about only its immediate base class (its parent class). If there is a chain of derived classes, each one takes care of its immediate parent class so that the constructors will "trickle up" properly.

A derived class must construct its base class.

To construct a parent class, add an argument list to the derived class constructor function. C++ will use that extra argument list to initialize the base class constructor. If your derived class function header were to look like this by itself:

```
Derived::Derived(int i, float x)   // Partial constructor
```

then you must tack the base class constructor call, using an initialization list, onto the end with a separating colon, like this:

```
Derived::Derived(int i, float x) : Base(char * c, int j);
```

The extra syntax at first seems like just another responsibility for you to worry about. It is, but for a good reason. You must make sure that the base class is properly constructed, for if it is not, your derived class can never be fully constructed. The argument list in the base class constructor list *must be in the same order as the inherited base class constructor arguments.* In the full constructor just shown, you can tell by looking at the base class constructor argument list that two data members, a character pointer and an integer, were inherited from the base class.

C++ requires the order of the base class constructor argument list to be the same as the exact order of data members you inherit for good reason. If you change the order—for instance, if the char * and int were swapped in the preceding constructor—the base class data members would get incorrect types, and bad data would result.

To give you a better idea of how a base class construction works and why you need to bother with it, here is a program that uses a base and a derived class to initialize and print some inventory items. No base class (Inventory) objects are defined, only derived class objects (the Auto and Machine class objects). Even though the program uses no base class objects, the two derived classes still must initialize their base class data items, or the inheritance will not be complete.

This is a long program, but most of it consists of straightforward class descriptions and functions. (Notice that the base class contains an initialization list for your review.) As with most C++ programs, the main() implementation code is very short. The rest of this section that follows the program listing describes some of the program's features.

INHCONST.CPP. Inventory program that derives two classes from a base class that needs to be constructed.

```
// Filename: INHCONST.CPP
// Inventory program that derives two classes from a
// base class that needs to be constructed
#include <iostream.h>
#include <iomanip.h>
#include <string.h>
////////// Base class follows //////////
class Inventory {  // Base class
    int quant, reorder;  // Number on hand and reorder quantity
    double price;  // Price of item
```

```
   char * descrip;   // Description
public:
   Inventory(int q, int r, double p, char *);   // Constructor
   ~Inventory();   // Destructor
   void print();
   int get_quant()    { return quant; }
   int get_reorder() { return reorder; }
   double get_price() { return price; }
};

Inventory::Inventory(int q, int r, double p, char * d) :
   quant(q), reorder(r), price(p)  // Initialization list
{
   descrip = new char[strlen(d)+1];   // Leaves room for terminator
   strcpy(descrip, d);
}

Inventory::~Inventory()
{
   delete descrip;   // Returns string space to the free store
}

inline void Inventory::print()
{
   cout << "Description: " << descrip << endl;
}

////////// First derived class follows //////////
class Auto : public Inventory {
   char * dealer;
public:
   Auto(int, int, double, char *, char *);   // Constructor
   ~Auto();
   void print();
   char * get_dealer() { return dealer; }
};

Auto::Auto(int q, int r, double p, char * d, char * dea) :
          Inventory(q, r, p, d)   // ** Calls base constructor!
{
   dealer = new char[strlen(dea)+1];   // Room for terminator
   strcpy(dealer, dea);
}

Auto::~Auto() {
   delete dealer;
}
```

continues

INHCONST.CPP. continued

```cpp
void Auto::print()  // Redefines base class's print()
{
   cout << setiosflags(ios::fixed);
   cout << "Dealer: " << dealer << endl;
}

////////// Second derived class follows //////////
class Machine : public Inventory {
   char * vendor;
public:
   Machine(int, int, double, char *, char *);   // Constructor
   ~Machine();
   void print();
   char * get_vendor() { return vendor; }
};

Machine::Machine(int q, int r, double p, char * d, char * ven) :
          Inventory(q, r, p, d)  // ** Calls base constructor!
{
   vendor = new char[strlen(ven)+1];  // Room for terminator
   strcpy(vendor, ven);
}

Machine::~Machine()  {
   delete vendor;
}

void Machine::print()  // Redefines base class's print()
{
   cout << setiosflags(ios::fixed);
   cout << "Vendor: " << vendor << endl;
}

////////// Implementation follows //////////
void main()
{
   // Constructs two different types of inventory items
   // As each is constructed, the base Inventory constructor
   // is also called by the derived class constructor functions

   Auto    car(3, 1, 8745.99, "4-door", "GM");
   Machine rotor(11, 5, 54.67, "High voltage", "Aztec");

   // Now, calls some of the base class functions to show you that
   // each inherited class also inherited the base class objects
   cout << setprecision(2);  // Two decimal points
```

```
    cout << "The car's data: \n";
    car.print();  // Derived print function overrides base class's

    // The following are inherited function calls
    cout << "Quantity: " << car.get_quant() << "\n";
    cout << "Reorder: " << car.get_reorder() << "\n";
    cout << "Price: $" << car.get_price() << "\n";

    // Uses the base class's print() function now
    // Because it is the same name as the derived class's, you
    // must qualify it with the scope resolution operator
    car.Inventory::print();
    cout << "\n\n";

    cout << "The machine's data: \n";
    rotor.print();  // Derived print function overrides base class's

    // The following are inherited function calls
    cout << "Quantity: " << rotor.get_quant() << "\n";
    cout << "Reorder: " << rotor.get_reorder() << "\n";
    cout << "Price: $" << rotor.get_price() << "\n";

    // Uses the base class's print() function now
    // Because it is the same name as the derived class's, you
    // must qualify it with the scope resolution operator
    rotor.Inventory::print();
    cout << "\n\n";
}
```

The program's output appears as follows. Study the main() function to see how the output is generated.

```
The car's data:
Dealer: GM
Quantity: 3
Reorder: 1
Price: $8745.99
Description: 4-door

The machine's data:
Vendor: Aztec
Quantity: 11
Reorder: 5
Price: $54.67
Description: High voltage
```

The first two lines in `main()` construct derived `class` objects. They are repeated here to help this discussion:

```
Auto    car(3, 1, 8745.99, "4-door", "GM");
Machine rotor(11, 5, 54.67, "High voltage", "Aztec");
```

The `Inventory` base class for each object also is being constructed, because the `Auto` and the `Machine` constructor functions send the appropriate values to the `Inventory` constructor function. For example, the `Auto` constructor function header shown here:

```
Auto::Auto(int q, int r, double p, char * d, char * dea) :
        Inventory(q, r, p, d)  // ** Calls base constructor!
```

constructs an `Auto` object, but it calls the `Inventory` constructor (the code following the colon), passing the `Inventory` constructor the values q, r, p, and d. The order of the arguments is critical. Because the `Inventory` constructor expects the arguments in that order, the `Auto` constructor must pass the `Inventory` constructor those arguments in that order.

Pre-AT&T 2.1 C++ compilers did not require the base `class` name before the base `class` argument list. With those older C++ compilers, you did not need to specify `Inventory` in front of the argument list for the base class. Modern C++ compilers require the base `class` name.

If you wanted to create an `Inventory` object, you could easily do so with the following definition:

```
Inventory item(12, 6, 12.59, "Widget");  // Constructs Inventory object
```

If you passed the `print()` message to the `item` object, like this:

```
item.print();  // Prints the item's data members
```

as opposed to the derived `Auto` members printing with this:

```
car.print();  // Prints the car's data members
```

the hidden `*this` pointer ensures that C++ sends the proper message to the proper object.

> If a derived class is derived from a base class that is itself derived from a base class, C++ traces back up through the inheritance tree, constructing the first base class, then each succeeding derived class, until all the objects are created. Therefore, if class A is the base class for B, and class B is the base class for C, when you create a C object, C++ first creates an A object, then a B object, then a C object. After all, a child cannot exist if its parent never existed. Figure 15.1 shows this relationship. If you create a C object, you can be assured that C++ first creates an A and a B object (as long as you supply the appropriate base `class` constructor code).

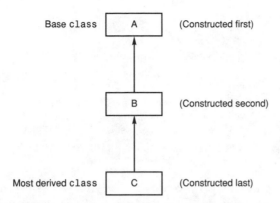

Figure 15.1. The "most base" base class constructs first, then all the others through the inheritance tree until the "most derived" class is constructed.

These two lines in main():

```
car.Inventory::print();
```

and

```
rotor.Inventory::print();
```

show that nothing is for certain. Just because your derived classes override the base class's print() member function, that does not remove the base class member function from your usable domain of available functions. C++ sends the base class's print() message to the object when you resolve the base class scope with ::, as was done with these two statements. As you can see, you can call a base class function using a base class object, even if that function is overriden in a derived class.

Derived functions are not the only items in C++ that you can override. You also can change individual members' public, private, and protected access when you inherit as described in the next section.

Base *class* Constructor Considerations

The base class may or may not need a specific constructor called from a derived class. Here are the possibilities:

If a base class constructor requires arguments, the derived class must call the base class constructor, specifying those arguments as you just saw. If the derived class

continues

267

continued

does not "take care of its parent," C++ issues an error because it does not have enough information to construct the base `class` object.

If a base class does not need a constructor, or requires only a default constructor, C++ calls the constructor when you define the derived `class` object. Therefore, you do not need to do anything special with the base `class` constructor. Derived classes need to worry about specifying a base `class` constructor only when the default base constructor will not suffice.

If the derived class does not have a constructor, an error will result if the base class requires a constructor. If the base class needs only a default constructor, however, C++ calls it when it defines the derived `class` object.

There might be times when your derived class does not need a constructor for itself, but you must supply one simply to call a base `class` constructor with arguments.

C++ requires no action on your part to call base class destructors.

Although you must call a base `class` constructor if there is no default constructor, you do not have to worry about the base `class` destructor. C++ calls the base class destructor automatically (or uses a default destructor if you do not supply your own) when a derived object goes out of scope. First, C++ calls the base `class` destructor, then the derived `class` destructor (the opposite order of constructor calls).

Overriding Individual Members' Inherited Access

Now that you understand how each of the `public-protected-private` access combinations works, you should know that you can override any of them for specific members if you prefer. For example, suppose that you inherit a class using the base class `protected` access. That means that every `private` member in the inherited class remains `private`, the `protected` member in the inherited class remains `protected`, and the `public` member in the inherited class converts to `protected` as well. Here is an example of such an inheritance:

```
class Abc {
   int i;
protected:
   char * name;
public:
```

268

```
    float stuff;
    void print();
    Abc get_vals();
    Abc();
    ~Abc();
};

class Xyz : protected Abc {  // Inherits public as protected
    float additional;
public:
    Xyz();
    ~Xyz();
};
```

If you wanted print() to remain public in Xyz, but still keep get_vals() protected, you could do so. Instead of inheriting all of class Xyz as protected, you could override the print()'s access like this:

```
class Abc {
    int i;
protected:
    char * name;
public:
    float stuff;
    void print();
    Abc get_vals();
    Abc();
    ~Abc();
};

class Xyz : protected Abc {  // Inherits public as protected
    float additional;
public:
    Abc::print;  // This is now public, not protected
    Xyz();
    ~Xyz();
};
```

Any of the rest of the program can send the print() message to any Xyz or Abc object. Inside the class Xyz, print() is overriden to be public instead of the protected access it would otherwise have. If print() were to remain protected, only members of Xyz could use print(), not the rest of the program.

For safety, you can go the other direction as well. A base class might have public members that you want to be private in the inherited class. In this next version of the class example, stuff would have been inherited as protected, but the Xyz class changes its inherited access to private:

```
class Abc {
   int i;
protected:
   char * name;
public:
   float stuff;
   void print();
   Abc get_vals();
   Abc();
   ~Abc();
};

class Xyz : protected Abc {  // Inherits public as protected
   float additional;
   Abc::stuff;  // This is now private, not protected
public:
   Abc::print;  // This is now public, not protected
   Xyz();
   ~Xyz();
};
```

A derived class can call the original base class function (instead of having to repeat all the code from the base class function) by prefixing the base class before the function name. For example, the following Der class function calls the base class function:

```
class Der : protected BaseDer  {
   fun() { BaseDer::fun();  // Calls the base class
                            // version
   // Rest of derived function version follows
```

Inheritance Limitations

As mentioned in the preceding section, derived classes never inherit base class constructor functions. There is good reason for this limitation. Constructors execute when their objects go into scope. Because the inherited objects are different from their base objects (with more or fewer data members and member functions), you need specific constructors and destructors for each kind of object.

Actually, none of the following C++ operations is inheritable:

- Constructor functions, including copy constructors

- Destructor functions

- `friend` functions

- Overloaded `new` operators

- Overloaded assignment (=) operators

- `static` data members and member functions

Multiple Inheritance

All the inheritance examples you have seen so far have been examples of single inheritance. That is, each derived class had one and only one parent class. Of course, a base class can have several derived classes, as shown in Figure 15.2. However, each derived class has only one parent class.

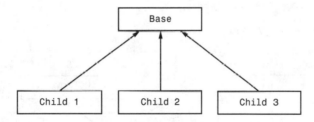

Figure 15.2. A base class might have several child classes.

Multiple inheritance enables you to inherit properties and behaviors from more than one class. That is, a class can have more than one parent class. Figure 15.3 shows what such a class structure looks like. In the figure, a class `Date` and a class `Time` are used as base classes for a `DateTime` class that works with both sets of members.

Here is the code to implement the multiple inheritance of the `DateTime` class:

```
#include <iostream.h>

class Date {
    int day;
```

271

```
    int month;
    int year;
public:
    Date();
    ~Date();
    void display();   // Displays the date
    Date get();
    void set();
};

class Time {
    int hour;
    int minute;
    int second;
public:
    Time();
    ~Time();
    void display();   // Displays the time
    Time get();   // Returns the time
    void set();   // Sets the time
};


class DateTime : public Date, public Time {
    int digital;
public:
    void display();   // Prints date and time
};
```

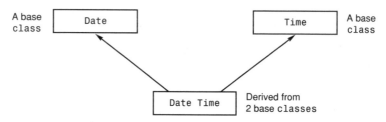

Figure 15.3. Multiple inheritance in action. The derived `DateTime` *class has two parent classes (two base classes).*

The `DateTime` class includes every member of both the `Date` and the `Time` classes. Suppose that you were to create a `DateTime` object, like this:

```
DateTime watch;   // Defines an object
```

Assuming that you wrote the implementation code for display(), you could display the watch object with the following statement:

```
watch.display();   // Passes display message to watch object
```

Everything is fine at this point. Nevertheless, *many* problems can creep into code when you use multiple inheritance. For example, suppose that DateTime did not redefine the other two classes' display() functions. C++ would find this an ambiguous statement:

```
watch.display();   // Ambiguous
```

Because DateTime inherited two versions of display(), C++ has no idea which version of display() to call. display() is an ambiguous function call.

It might seem as if C++ should not allow these two functions to be inherited into a single class, but it does because you can resolve the ambiguity. If you wanted to call either the Date display() function or the Time display() function using the watch object, you could, using the scope resolution operator as both the following statements do:

```
watch.Date::display();   // Displays the date members
```

or

```
watch.Time::display();   // Displays the time members
```

The ambiguity of multiple inheritance seems as though it would be easy to overcome, and in most instances it is. Nevertheless, your programming workload is expanded greatly when you use multiple inheritance. As an example, remember that earlier you learned to construct a base class object, using an initialization list, before constructing the derived object. What if an object has *two* base classes? What if it has *four?* The syntax and bookkeeping required on your part, and, more importantly, the maintenance problems you would incur, just do not seem to justify any advantages multiple inheritance might have.

Virtual Base Classes

Someday, try as you might, you might not be able to stay completely away from multiple inheritance—although the next section tries to talk you out of using it. Seriously, all sorts of strange inheritance patterns can creep into your code if you use multiple inheritance. This section explains how to work around one potential multiple inheritance problem that sometimes develops.

You might run into a situation where a base class becomes shared by two other classes. Sharing a base class does not necessarily cause a problem, because single inheritance is still

at work. For example, the following `class` definitions show two classes (similar to those seen earlier in this chapter) being inherited from a base class:

```
class Inventory {  // Base class
   // Base class code goes here
};

class Auto : public Inventory {  // Derived class
   // Derived Auto class code goes here
};

class Machine : public Inventory {  // Derived class
   // Derived Machine class code goes here
};
```

So far, this single inheritance offers nothing new. A problem can occur if you decide to inherit a new class from *both* `Auto` and `Machine`. For example, you might want to create a new class called `CustOrder` that consists of the two parent classes:

```
class CustOrder : public  Auto, public Machine {  // Multiple inheritance
   // Derived CustOrder class code goes here
};
```

Figure 15.4 shows the result of this inheritance. The `CustOrder` class includes two copies of the base class `Inventory`. You might run into conflicts with the two copies of the base class. You probably should share the base class instead of inheriting it multiple times.

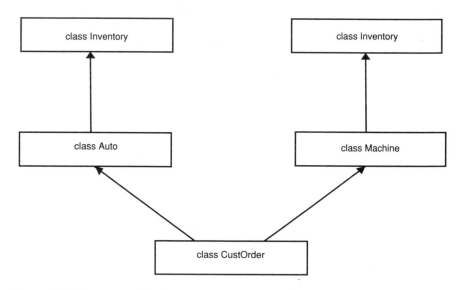

Figure 15.4. Two copies of the base class get into the resulting derived class.

If you want to share a base class, insert the `virtual` keyword in the base class access list of the derived classes. `virtual` ensures that a copy of the base class will not be used every time the base class is inherited. Here is the sample code with `virtual` added to the base class's derived classes:

Virtual base classes appear only once in the inheritance hierarchy.

```
class Inventory {  // Base class
   // Base class code goes here
};

class Auto : virtual public Inventory {  // Derives class virtually
   // Derived Auto class code goes here
};

class Machine : virtual public Inventory {  // Derives class virtually
   // Derived Machine class code goes here
};
```

Now when you inherit from both derived classes, you get only one copy of `Inventory`'s members. For example, when you define the `CustOrder` class like this:

```
class CustOrder : public  Auto, public Machine {  // Multiple inheritance
   // Derived CustOrder class code goes here
};
```

you get the improved situation shown in Figure 15.5.

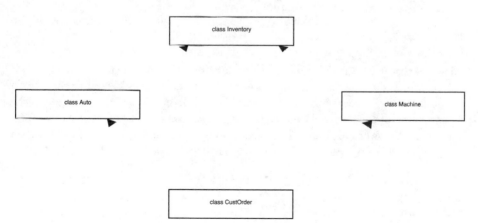

Figure 15.5. One copy of the base class ends up in the resulting derived class.

The only other consideration is your construction of the base class. Remember that you must construct the base class when you construct a derived class. In this example, the

derived classes are sharing one copy of the base class, so *the in-between base* class *constructors will not function when you define a* CustOrder *object.* Here is a skeleton of the implementation code for this CustOrder inheritance:

```
class Inventory {  // Base class
   int quant;
public:
   Inventory(int Q) {quant = Q; }
};

class Auto : virtual public Inventory {  // Derives class virtually
   char type;
public:
   Auto(char T, int Q) : Inventory(Q) {type = T; }
};

class Machine : virtual public Inventory {  // Derives class virtually
   float weight;
public:
   Machine(float W, int Q) : Inventory(Q) {weight = W; }
};

class CustOrder : public Auto, public Machine  {  // Multiple inheritance
   int ordnum;
public:
   CustOrder(int O, int Q, char C, float W)
                    : ordnum(O), Inventory(Q), Auto(C,Q), Machine(W,Q)
{};
};
```

The CustOrder constructor constructs not only itself (its only member ordnum), but it also constructs the base class and then its derived classes. This breaks the rule that if each child class takes care of its parent class, the trickle-up occurs automatically. The parent classes of CustOrder do not construct a base class object because they cannot. The virtual keyword tells Auto and Machine not to worry about their parent class when a CustOrder object is created, because CustOrder does all the work.

If you define an Auto or a Machine object like this:

```
Auto car('X', 7);
Machine widget(232.34, 6);
```

each object calls the base class constructor. The virtual keyword is meaningless to these objects (car and widget) because they inherit only one copy of Inventory anyway. If, however, you define a CustOrder object like this:

```
CustOrder johnson(12, 5, 'F', 2354.54);
```

johnson's constructor takes care of initializing its derived class and the base class.

Do You Need Multiple Inheritance?

An OOP language does not *require* multiple inheritance. Single inheritance is all you need. One of the original OOP languages, SmallTalk, offers only single inheritance, and SmallTalk programmers do not seem to miss multiple inheritance. As a matter of fact, SmallTalk programmers probably wonder why anyone would ever need multiple inheritance.

You do not need multiple inheritance.

If you find yourself wanting to inherit from two base classes, reconsider the inheritance. You might need to create a common parent class from those two individual classes, or you might be trying to derive a class that does too many unrelated tasks.

There is really only one useful place where a beginning C++ programmer (or even an advanced C++ programmer) would want to use multiple inheritance. Actually, you already have used multiple inheritance, but you just did not know it. The iostream.h header file contains multiple inheritance. Objects such as cin and cout are derived in iostream.h from two base classes named istream and ostream.

The iostream.h file is a tested and accurately implemented multiple inheritance class set. It is safe to use, and as a C++ programmer, you would be limiting yourself too much if you stayed away from it. Nevertheless, you should guard against implementing your own multiple inheritance classes until you are very comfortable with C++.

This author is so strongly against multiple inheritance that this book does not cover it in any more depth. If you have looked at other C++ books, you might be surprised at the lack of multiple inheritance coverage here. Please do not feel shortchanged. Multiple inheritance complicates your code in ways that are not needed. Although there might be cases where multiple inheritance is the only way to write a specific program, those cases are few and far between. Single inheritance is safer and easier to maintain.

Restricting Inheriting Functions

You have now seen inheritance in action. When you inherit a class, the derived class contains all the members of the inherited class as well as the members you specify explicitly. You can override the access rights of inherited members, as well as change the way an inherited member performs. As a review, here is a simple inheritance. Class B contains all the members of A, in addition to the ones defined for B:

```
class A {
   int i;
public:
   void print();
   get();
};

class B : public A {  // Inherits all of A's members
   int j;
public:
   display();
};
```

After the inheritance of A, B is expanded with additional members.

The following version of the A and B classes changes the way print() works, in effect redefining print() for the B class:

```
class A {
   int i;
public:
   void print();
   get();
};

class B : public A {  // Inherits all of A's members
   int j;
public:
   int print();  // Redefines print()
   display();
};
```

There might be times when you want to *restrict* inherited members. That is, you might want the inherited class to contain fewer members than its parent class, but still retain the functionality of the rest of the inherited class. There is no direct way of restricting inherited members in C++; you cannot actually decrease the number of inherited members, but you can change the way they work.

If the base class contains a data member that you do not want in the derived class, you can change the data to private (if it is not already) to limit its access from anywhere else in the program. However, that is about as far as you can go with data members. Some C++ programmers simply redefine inherited member functions they do not want so that the functions contain a null body (just braces with no code). Although these are artificial means of restricting member functionality, you have to work around it because C++ does not support member restriction explicitly.

Summary

This chapter explained several more advanced inheritance issues. The most critical issue is how derived classes must take care of their base classes—that is, how a derived class must call the base class's constructor. Because an inherited class often is dependent on its base's being constructed, you must ensure the proper construction yourself.

Multiple inheritance, although a powerful language element when used properly, is unnecessary for most C++ programs. Thankfully, single inheritance offers as much power as you probably will ever need. The advanced code needed for multiple inheritance makes it prone to bugs, and, at best, leads to maintenance headaches later.

There is much more to inheritance, and starting in Chapter 17, "Virtual Functions," you will learn the true meaning of *polymorphism*. You are truly an object-oriented programmer when you understand virtual functions. You might also be relieved to know that virtual functions are the last real C++ frontier. As soon as you learn about virtual functions, the rest of C++ is just a variation on what you already know.

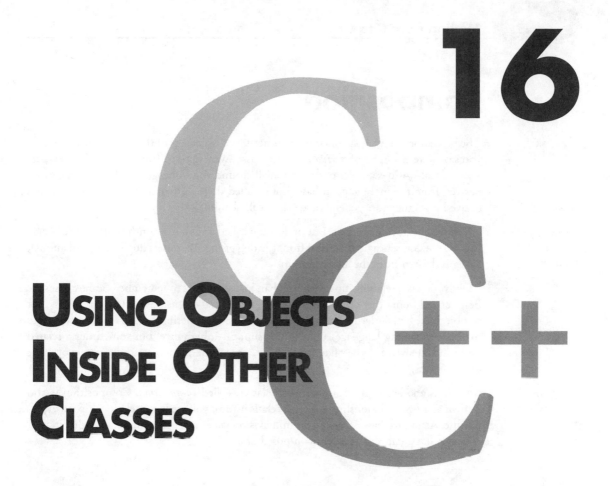

USING OBJECTS INSIDE OTHER CLASSES

16

"Compose a composition."

Inheritance does not always work, even when you want to create classes from other classes. Inheritance provides one type of class relationship, but there is another called *composition* that describes a different way to combine classes to create new ones. This chapter explains the ins and outs of putting class members inside objects.

In this chapter, you will learn about:

- The difference between inheritance and composition
- The *is-a* and *has-a* relationships
- How to make one object a member of another
- How to construct member objects

Composition

The preceding chapter explained many inheritance issues. All of the inheritance examples you saw were examples of *derivation:* new classes were derived from existing base classes. You see real-world examples of derivation all around you. A beagle is a dog, so beagles are derived from the more general base group called dogs. A dog is an animal, so dogs are derived from the more general base group called animals.

Derivation results in an is-a relationship.

It should be obvious why derivation is often called an *is-a* relationship. Because a beagle is-a type of dog, a beagle is derived from the dog group. Because a dog is-a type of animal, a dog is derived from the animal group.

Derivation is-a relationships are more than just semantics to remember. Some classes are best derived from other classes because they are natural extensions of their base class. Not all objects are best derived from other objects, however. Inheritance offers many advantages over programming languages that do not support inheritance, but sometimes a related object is not always a type of another object. Sometimes, an object *contains* one or more other objects.

Composition results in a has-a relationship.

There is another relationship between classes, called *composition*. Composition is also known as a *has-a* relationship. Like is-a relationships, you see has-a relationships in everyday life. An animal has-a heart, so an animal is *composed* of a heart (and many other items). A beagle has-a tail, so a beagle is composed of a tail.

Using Composition

C++ enables you to designate one class as a member of another, just as easily as you designate built-in data types inside classes. When you run into a class that is composed from another class, the has-a relationship applies, so you will want to compose one class from one or more other classes. For example, this Disk class contains only built-in data types:

```
class Disk  {
   int rpm;
   float price;
public:
   Disk(int R, int P) {R=rpm; P=price; }  // Constructor
};
```

The following PC class contains a member that is a class Disk data type:

```
class PC {
   long RAM;
   long ROM;
   char * cpu_type;
   float price;
   Disk storage;   // A member from another class
public:
   PC();   // Constructor
   ~PC();  // Destructor
};
```

Do not think that PC is derived from Disk. A PC is *not* a Disk, and a Disk is *not* a PC. The is-a relationship just does not apply in this example. There is no derivation relationship between Disk and PC, but there obviously is a relationship of some kind. You can compose a new class from as many classes as your application requires. The following PC class is composed of three other classes—Disk, Screen, and Keyboard—yet no derived inheritance exists or would even produce the same needed composition relationship.

```
class PC {
   long RAM;
   long ROM;
   char * cpu_type;
   float price;
   Disk storage;   // Three members that are other classes
   Keyboard kb;
   Screen   crt;
public:
   PC();   // Constructor
   ~PC();  // Destructor
};
```

So why is all this important? When you compose one class from one or more classes (that is, when one class has-a class as a member), you do not have to worry about derivation syntax, but you still need to construct that class member. The implementation code for PC must ensure that the constructor for Disk is called, or Disk cannot be a member of the PC class. An integer, long integer, or character needs no constructor because C++ already knows how to construct the built-in members. You must instruct C++ how to construct your class members, or C++ will be unable to construct the overall class (the *composed* class).

Constructing composed class members is easy, especially now that you have mastered the inheritance base constructor issues of Chapter 15, "Inheritance Issues." Actually, the syntax for constructing composed class members is even easier than constructing inherited base classes because you do not have to specify the inherited class in the derived class header.

283

The composed class's constructor must call the class member constructors.

To supply a constructor for a member class, put that member's constructor initialization list after the overall `class` constructor (the class that has the member). Although it is difficult to describe in words, the following code easily illustrates constructing a composed class. The code first defines the three component classes—`Disk`, `Keyboard`, and `Screen`. The `PC` class then is defined as being composed of the three individual classes. The constructor in `PC` might seem confusing at first, but the `PC` class is constructing all its own member objects in its constructor.

MEMCLAS1.CPP. Illustrates composition of classes within a class.

```
// Filename: MEMCLAS1.CPP
// Illustrates composition of classes within a class.
#include <iostream.h>
#include <iomanip.h>
#include <string.h>
enum scrntype {COLOR, MONO};

class Disk  {
   int rpm;
   float price;
public:
   Disk(int R, float P) : rpm(R), price(P) {}  // Constructor
   friend ostream & operator<< (ostream & out, const Disk & d);
};

ostream & operator<< (ostream & out, const Disk & d)
{
   out << setprecision(2);  // Two decimal places
   out << "\nDisk rpm: " << d.rpm << ", Disk price: $";
   out << d.price << endl;
   return out;
}

class Keyboard  {
   int numkeys;
   float price;
public:
   Keyboard(int N, float P) :
            numkeys(N), price(P) {};  // Constructor
   friend ostream & operator<< (ostream & out,
                                const Keyboard & kb);
};

ostream & operator<< (ostream & out, const Keyboard & kb)
{
```

```
      out << setprecision(2);  // Two decimal places
      out << "Keyboard keys: " << kb.numkeys;
      out << ", Keyboard price: $" << kb.price << endl;
      return out;
}

class Screen  {
   char colorflg;
   float price;
public:
   Screen(int C, float P) :
           colorflg(C), price(P) {};  // Constructor
   friend ostream & operator<< (ostream & out,
                                const Screen & crt);
};

ostream & operator<< (ostream & out, const Screen & crt)
{
   out << setprecision(2);  // Two decimal places
   out << "Screen type: ";
   out << ((crt.colorflg == COLOR) ? "Color" : "Monochrome");
   out << ", Screen price: $" << crt.price << endl;
   return out;
}

class PC {
   long RAM;
   long ROM;
   char * cpu_type;
   float price;
   Disk storage;  // Three members that are other classes
   Keyboard kb;
   Screen   crt;
public:
   PC(long, long, char *, float, int, float,
      int, float, int, float);
   ~PC() {delete cpu_type;}  // Destructor
   friend ostream & operator<< (ostream & out, const PC & pc);
};

PC::PC(long RA, long RO, char * C, float P, int DR, float DP,
       int KN, float KP, int SC, float SP)
       : storage(DR, DP), kb(KN, KP), crt(SC, SP)  {
   RAM = RA; ROM = RO;
   cpu_type = new char [strlen(C)+1];
   strcpy(cpu_type, C);
   price = P;
}
```

continues

MEMCLAS1.CPP. continued

```
ostream & operator<< (ostream & out, const PC & pc)
{
    cout << setiosflags(ios::fixed);
    out << setprecision(2);  // Two decimal places
    out << "\nThe computer information:\n";
    out << "RAM: " << pc.RAM << "K, ROM: " << pc.ROM << "K\n";
    out << "CPU: " << pc.cpu_type << ", System price: $";
    out << pc.price << pc.storage << pc.kb << pc.crt;
    return out;
};

void main()
{
    PC computer(640, 45, "Zytel", 999.93, 200, 136.54, 120,
                47.45, COLOR, 19.85);
    cout <<  computer;
}
```

Here is the program's output:

```
The computer information:
RAM: 640K, ROM: 45K
CPU: Zytel, System price: $999.93
Disk rpm: 200, Disk price: $136.54
Keyboard keys: 120, Keyboard price: $47.45
Screen type: Color, Screen price: $19.85
```

As with derivation, you do not need to worry about calling destructors for composed members. C++ calls the proper destructors when the composed classes go out of scope. C++ first calls the destructor for the composed object, then calls the destructor for any remaining member objects. The order of destructor calls is the opposite of the order of constructor calls. C++ first constructs a `Disk`, `Keyboard`, and `Screen` before it constructs the `computer` object. In the preceding program, when the compiler sees this:

```
PC computer(640, 45, "Zytel", 999.93, 200, 136.54, 120,
            47.45, TRUE, 19.85);
```

C++ searches for the computer constructor and finds this constructor definition:

```
PC::PC(long RA, long RO, char * C, float P, int DR, float DP,
       int KN, float KP, int SC, float SP)
       : storage(DR, DP), kb(KN, KP), crt(SC, SP)  {
```

The compiler initializes the three member objects—storage, kb, and crt—with the values you supplied in the computer object's definition. The rest of the PC constructor body initializes the regular PC members.

> The overloaded << operator function in the PC class indicates why C++ must construct member objects before it constructs the composed object. For PC's operator<< function to output the individual object members, those members' operator<< had to be defined first.

The ordering of the construction is a direct result of your supplying an initialization list in the PC constructor function. If you do not supply initialization lists, C++ tries to construct the member objects, using default constructors if possible.

When the computer object goes out of scope (the end of main() in this example), C++ calls the destructor function for computer, then calls a destructor for the remaining three member objects. You do not have to do anything special to dictate the destructor order. If you do not supply destructor functions for the composed object, or for any of the member objects, C++ uses a default destructor.

Here is the order of constructors when the computer object is defined:

storage, kb, crt, and computer

Here is the order of destructors when the computer object goes out of scope:

computer, crt, kb, and storage

You can define individual objects for the Screen, Keyboard, or Disk classes if you want to. Just because they are composed into PC does not take away their individuality as classes. This main() function defines four objects: an individual Screen object, an individual Keyboard object, an individual Disk object, and a composed PC object.

MEMCLAS2.CPP. Defines four objects.

```
// Filename: MEMCLAS2.CPP
void main()
{
   Disk floppy(88, 45.75);  // Creates a Disk object
   cout << floppy;
   Keyboard keys(120, 12.33);  // Creates a Keyboard object
```

continues

MEMCLAS2.CPP. continued

```
    cout << keys;
    Screen monitor(MONO, 130.92);   // Creates a Screen object
    cout << monitor;
    PC computer(640, 45, "Zytel", 999.93, 200, 136.54, 120,
                47.45, COLOR, 19.85);
    cout <<  computer;
}
```

Here is the output of this code (assuming that its class header and implementation code are identical to that in MEMCLAS1.CPP):

```
Disk rpm: 88, Disk price: $45.75
Keyboard keys: 120, Keyboard price: $12.33
Screen type: Monochrome, Screen price: $130.92

The computer information:
RAM: 640K, ROM: 45K
CPU: Zytel, System price: $999.93
Disk rpm: 200, Disk price: $136.54
Keyboard keys: 120, Keyboard price: $47.45
Screen type: Color, Screen price: $19.85
```

You also can construct additional PC constructors that take objects as arguments. Suppose that you needed to compose individual Disk, Keyboard, and Screen objects and then compose a Computer object from those three objects. You could do so with the following constructor:

```
PC::PC(long RA, long RO, char * C, float P,
       Disk & d, Keyboard & k, Screen & s)
       : storage(d), kb(k), crt(s)  {
   RAM = RA; ROM = RO;
   cpu_type = new char [strlen(C)+1];
   strcpy(cpu_type, C);
   price = P;
}
```

This method keeps the constructor list from having so many individual arguments that make up every member of every object in the composition. Using this PC constructor, you could construct the three component objects, then the composed object, using this main() code section:

MEMCLAS3.CPP. Constructs the three component objects, then the composed object.

```
// Filename: MEMCLAS3.CPP
void main()
{
   Disk floppy(88, 45.75);  // Creates a Disk object
   cout << floppy;
   Keyboard keys(120, 12.33);  // Creates a Keyboard object
   cout << keys;
   Screen monitor(MONO, 130.92);  // Creates a Screen object
   cout << monitor;
   PC computer(640, 45, "Zytel", 999.93, floppy, keys, monitor);
   cout <<  computer;
}
```

Here is the program's output:

```
Disk rpm: 88, Disk price: $45.75
Keyboard keys: 120, Keyboard price: $12.33
Screen type: Monochrome, Screen price: $130.92

The computer information:
RAM: 640K, ROM: 45K
CPU: Zytel, System price: $999.93
Disk rpm: 88, Disk price: $45.75
Keyboard keys: 120, Keyboard price: $12.33
Screen type: Monochrome, Screen price: $130.92
```

Efficiency and the Need for Initialization

Although the previous member object initialization constructors are a little tricky to learn at first, they are very efficient. The last constructor shown in the preceding section includes two parts: an initialization list section and an assignment section. Figure 16.1 labels the parts of the constructor so that you can understand which section is which.

You write less efficient code if you move the initialization list section for the member objects down into the assignment section like this:

```
PC::PC(long RA, long RO, char * C, float P,
      Disk & d, Keyboard & k, Screen & s)
{
   Disk storage(d);   // These three lines
   Keyboard kb(k);    // used to be in the
   Screen crt(s);     // initialization list
```

289

```
     RAM = RA; ROM = RO;  // The rest of the assignments
     cpu_type = new char [strlen(C)+1];
     strcpy(cpu_type, C);
     price = P;
}
```

Constructor name   Argument list

```
     PC::PC(long RA, long RO, char * C, float P,
            Disk & d, Keyboard & k, Screen & s)
Initialization ──────►  : storage(d), kb(k), crt(s)  {
section        RAM = RA; ROM = RO;
                 cpu type = new char [strlen(C)+1];    Assignment
                 strcpy(cpu type, C);                  section
                 price = P;
             }
```

Figure 16.1. The parts of a constructor with an initialization list.

C++ has to construct the member objects before it constructs the PC object. Because no initialization list is used, the compiler uses default constructors for the three objects. When the body of the PC constructor begins (the assignment section), C++ must initialize the Disk, Keyboard, and Screen objects all over again (it first initialized them with the default constructors).

Another reason for learning how to declare initialization lists goes beyond efficiency. If any class member is a const or a reference, you *must* use an initialization list. Neither constants nor references can be assigned the initial values inside the assignment section. As soon as the objects are constructed using the default constructor just mentioned, you cannot then assign values to constants and references.

Assignment Considerations

Consider the following code in place of main() in MEMCLAS1.CPP:

```
main()
   Disk floppy(88, 45.75);   // Creates a Disk object
   cout << floppy;
   Keyboard keys(120, 12.33);   // Creates a Keyboard object
   cout << keys;
   Screen monitor(MONO, 130.92);   // Creates a Screen object
   cout << monitor;

   // New lines follow
   PC computer1(640, 45, "Zytel", 999.93, floppy, keys, monitor);
   PC computer2(256, 64, "APC", 697.84, floppy, keys, monitor);
   cout <<  computer1;
   cout <<  computer2;
   computer2 = computer1;  // Assignment here
   cout <<  computer2;
}
```

After creating two PC objects and printing them, the program assigns one PC object to the other using assignment.

When you assign one composed object to another, you should understand exactly how C++ makes the assignment. If you supply no operator=() function, C++ uses a default memberwise assignment. This is nothing new. C++ always uses a default memberwise assignment when you do not supply an overloaded assignment operator, whether an object contains another object or not.

With composition, however, there is another layer of assignments. The assignment rules are easy:

1. If a class object member has an operator=() function defined in its own class listing, C++ uses that function to assign the member object when it copies that member.

2. If a class object member has no operator=() function defined in its own class listing, C++ uses a memberwise copy when it copies that member.

These two rules are the same rules C++ uses for the overall composed class.

Figure 16.2 shows an X object being assigned to an A object. X is composed of two other objects, Y and Z. Assuming that Y has an overloaded operator=() function, that function is used for that member's assignment, and the default memberwise assignment is used for the rest of the X object.

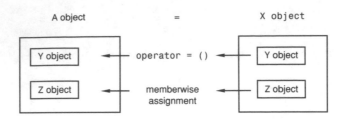

Figure 16.2. C++ assigns object members without an operator=() *function using memberwise copy.*

To show assignment in action, the following program is a rewritten version of the previous ones in this chapter. The constructors for the objects now have default values so that they can be used as default constructors. main() first creates a system1 object using the default constructors (because no arguments are passed to system1's constructor). main() then creates system2, which has specific values specified. When main() assigns system2 to system1, it uses two overloaded operator=()s, one for PC and one for Disk. C++ uses default assignment for the other member objects.

MEMCLAS4.CPP. Illustrates composition of classes within a class.

```cpp
// Filename: MEMCLAS4.CPP
// Illustrates composition of classes within a class.
#include <iostream.h>
#include <iomanip.h>
#include <string.h>
enum scrntype {COLOR, MONO};

class Disk   {
   int rpm;
   float price;
public:
   Disk(int R=0, float P=0.0) :
        rpm(R), price(P) {}   // Constructor
   Disk & operator=(const Disk & d);   // Assignment operator
   friend ostream & operator<< (ostream & out,
                                const Disk & d);
};

Disk & Disk::operator=(const Disk & d)   // Assignment operator
{
   rpm = d.rpm;
```

```
      price = d.price;
      return *this;
}

ostream & operator<< (ostream & out, const Disk & d)
{
      out << setprecision(2);  // Two decimal places
      out << "\nDisk rpm: " << d.rpm << ", Disk price: $";
      out << d.price << endl;
      return out;
}

class Keyboard  {
      int numkeys;
      float price;
public:
      Keyboard(int N=0, float P=0.0) :
               numkeys(N), price(P) {};  // Constructor
      friend ostream & operator<< (ostream & out,
                                    const Keyboard & kb);
};

ostream & operator<< (ostream & out, const Keyboard & kb)
{
      out << setprecision(2);  // Two decimal places
      out << "Keyboard keys: " << kb.numkeys;
      out << ", Keyboard price: $" << kb.price << endl;
      return out;
}

class Screen  {
      char colorflg;
      float price;
public:
      Screen(int C=0, float P=0.0) :
            colorflg(C), price(P) {};  // Constructor
      friend ostream & operator<< (ostream & out,
                                    const Screen & crt);
};

ostream & operator<< (ostream & out, const Screen & crt)
{
      out << setprecision(2);  // Two decimal places
      out << "Screen type: ";
      out << ((crt.colorflg == COLOR) ? "Color" : "Monochrome");
      out << ", Screen price: $" << crt.price << endl;
      return out;
```

continues

MEMCLAS4.CPP. continued

```cpp
class PC {
   long RAM;
   long ROM;
   char * cpu_type;
   float price;
   Disk storage;   // Three members that are other classes
   Keyboard kb;
   Screen   crt;
public:
   PC() {RAM=0; ROM=0; cpu_type=0; price=0.0;}
   PC(long RA, long RO, char * C, float P, int DR, float DP,
       int KN, float KP, int SC, float SP);
   ~PC() {delete cpu_type;}   // Destructor
   PC & operator=(const PC & p);   // Overload the assignment
   friend ostream & operator<< (ostream & out, const PC & pc);
};

PC::PC(long RA, long RO, char * C, float P, int DR, float DP,
       int KN, float KP, int SC, float SP)
      : storage(DR, DP), kb(KN, KP), crt(SC, SP)  {
   RAM = RA; ROM = RO;
   cpu_type = new char [strlen(C)+1];
   strcpy(cpu_type, C);
   price = P;
}

PC & PC::operator=(const PC & p)  // Overloads the assignment
{
   if (this == &p) return *this;  // Triggers if same ob=ob;
   delete cpu_type;
   cpu_type = new char [strlen(p.cpu_type)+1];
   strcpy(cpu_type, p.cpu_type);  // Handles the string
   // Assigns the regular members
   RAM = p.RAM;
   ROM = p.ROM;
   price = p.price;
   storage = p.storage;  // The overloaded = used here only
   kb = p.kb;  // Default = used here
   crt = p.crt;  // Default = used here
   return *this;
}

ostream & operator<< (ostream & out, const PC & pc)
{
   cout << setiosflags(ios::fixed);
   out << setprecision(2);   // Two decimal places
```

```
    out << "RAM: " << pc.RAM << "K, ROM: " << pc.ROM << "K\n";
    out << "CPU: " << pc.cpu_type << ", System price: $";
    cout << pc.price << pc.storage << pc.kb << pc.crt;
    return out;
};

void main()
{
    PC system1;   // Default constructors just to define an object
    PC system2(640, 45, "Zytel", 999.93, 200, 136.54, 120,
               47.45, COLOR, 19.85);

    // At this point, there are two objects. The system1 object
    // has default values (all 0s) and system2 has true values.
    cout << "\nBefore the assignment:\nFirst system:\n";
    cout << system1;   // Shows that the first object has no data
    cout << "\nSecond system:\n";
    cout << system2;   // Shows that the second object has data

    system1 = system2;
    cout << "\nAfter the assignment, the first system is now:\n";
    cout << system1;
}
```

Here is the program's output:

```
Before the assignment:
First system:
RAM: 0K, ROM: 0K
CPU: , System price: $0
Disk rpm: 0, Disk price: $0
Keyboard keys: 0, Keyboard price: $0
Screen type: Color, Screen price: $0

Second system:
RAM: 640K, ROM: 45K
CPU: Zytel, System price: $999.93
Disk rpm: 200, Disk price: $136.54
Keyboard keys: 120, Keyboard price: $47.45
Screen type: Color, Screen price: $19.85

After the assignment, the first system is now:
RAM: 640K, ROM: 45K
CPU: Zytel, System price: $999.93
Disk rpm: 200, Disk price: $136.54
Keyboard keys: 120, Keyboard price: $47.45
Screen type: Color, Screen price: $19.85
```

295

In this program, the default assignments would suffice in the Disk object, as they do in the other two member objects. Disk contains only scalar (non-array) data. However, a default assignment would not work with the PC class because the character pointer, not the actual cpu_type data, would be copied.

Summary

Many composition and inheritance needs will arise as you program in C++. The primary difficulty of derivation and inheritance is constructing the base classes, but initialization lists provide the means for the construction. There is very little difference in the syntax between derivation and composition constructors.

Now you know the fundamentals of inheritance and composition. You should understand the importance of constructing the base classes, whether you derive or compose new classes from existing classes. It is now time to tackle the true frontier of inheritance. Many people feel that you are not a true C++ programmer until you understand virtual functions. Luckily, virtual functions sound more difficult than they are, as you will see in the next chapter.

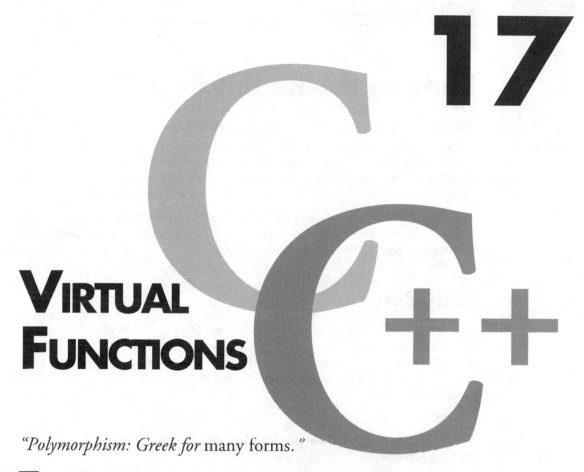

VIRTUAL FUNCTIONS

"Polymorphism: Greek for many forms."

This chapter ties inheritance and polymorphism together into a nice package that produces code that models the real world. With virtual functions, your C++ programs behave just as their real-world counterparts behave. The closer your code gets to modeling the real world, the faster you will finish your programming jobs and the quicker you can move programs into productive use.

In this chapter, you will learn:

- The difference between early and late binding
- How to use virtual functions
- How the internal vtable works
- About abstract base classes
- About pure virtual functions

Early and Late Binding

C compiles using early binding.

This chapter teaches you a little about both C and C++ that you might not know. The concepts of *early binding* and *late binding* do not typically arise during discussions of procedural non-OOP programming languages. Most programming languages produce compiled code with early binding, sometimes called *static binding*, and because there is no binding other than early binding in those languages, there is no need to delve into it.

C++ produces compiled code using the two binding methods (both early binding and late binding, sometimes called *dynamic binding*). As a C++ programmer, you must understand the difference between the two binding methods.

Early Binding

Early binding refers to C's requirement that all direct function calls be known at compile time. This means that a C compiler looks through the program, hunting for function calls so that it can resolve those function calls during the compilation. C includes the called function addresses in the resulting object file. Look at the following program to see early binding in action.

EARBIND.C. C and C++ perform early binding on this program.

```
/* Filename: EARBIND.C
   C and C++ perform early binding on this program. */
#include <stdio.h>
void print_age(int age);
int get_age(int age);

void main()
{
   int age=0;

   age = get_age(age);  /* Gets the user's age */
   print_age(age);  /* Prints a message based */
}                    /* on the user's age */

int get_age(int age)
{
   printf("How old are you? ");
   scanf(" %d", &age);
```

```
   return age;
}

void print_age(int age)
{
   if (age < 18)
      { printf("Register to vote when you are old enough!\n"); }
   else
      { printf("I hope you vote every four years!\n"); }
}
```

This program contains three functions—main(), get_age(), and print_age(). You can easily trace through the program's execution. You know, beyond a shadow of a doubt, the order of the function calls. So does the C compiler. The functions executed in this program are the following:

```
main()
get_age()
print_age()
```

As soon as the C compiler locates all three functions, it can complete its task. The compiler binds the function calls directly into its object code. Again, because the concept of early binding is so obvious to you, you might be tempted to make it more difficult than it is. If this were a C++ program, the C++ compiler would also use early binding. Nothing about this program requires late binding, the opposite of early binding.

Late Binding

Early binding makes some programs impossible to write, specifically some OOP programs. The programs you have seen so far in this book do not require late binding, but the programs in this chapter do. Therefore, you must understand the concept of late binding before proceeding to virtual functions.

If you have done much C programming, you might be thinking about another way to call functions. Instead of calling each function by name, you know that you can create a pointer to functions. Instead of calling the function directly, you can dereference the function pointer to execute the function. When you do this, the C compiler does not really know what functions will be called when it compiles the program. The compiler knows only that when the program is run, the function pointers will specify the proper functions to execute.

It is possible to achieve some late binding in C.

299

The following C program displays a menu and then waits for the user to type a selection. When the user selects an option, that option's matching function executes. You will not find a switch or if statement in the entire program, yet the program executes the proper function, based on the user's choice of four options.

POINTF.C. Demonstrates a menu without a switch or if statement.

```
/* Filename: POINTF.C
   Demonstrates a menu without a switch or if statement. */
#include <stdio.h>
#include <stdlib.h>
#include <conio.h>

void add_fun(void);  /* Function prototypes */
void change_fun(void);
void print_fun(void);
void quit_pgm(void);

void (*menu[])(void) = {add_fun, change_fun, print_fun,
                        quit_pgm};

main()
{
   int ans;
   clrscr();
   do
   {  printf("\n\n\nDo you want to:\n\n");
      printf("1. Add records\n");
      printf("2. Change records\n");
      printf("3. Print records\n");
      printf("4. Quit program\n");
      scanf("%d", &ans);

      menu[ans-1]();  /* Calls function without switch */
   } while (1);  /* Infinite loop */
}

void add_fun()
{
   /* Body of add function would go here */
}

void change_fun()
{
```

```
    /* Body of change function would go here */
}

void print_fun()
{
    /* Body of print function would go here */
}

void quit_pgm()
{
      exit(0);
}
```

In the program in the preceding section, EARBIND.C, you knew the order of function calls and so did the compiler. Of course, the data might determine the order of function calls in many programs, but whenever it is time for a function call, the compiler normally knows where that function is—but not in *this* program.

The line that defines the function pointer array:

```
void (*menu[])(void) = {add_fun, change_fun, print_fun, quit_pgm};
```

creates a table of addresses called menu. Figure 17.1 shows how the compiler treats this table.

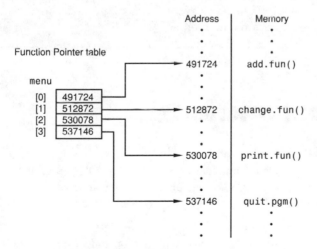

Figure 17.1. The menu function pointer table holds the function address that C uses to resolve function calls during program execution.

The following line calls one of the four functions, depending on the value of ans:

```
menu[ans-1]();   /* Calls appropriate function without switch */
```

Thanks to the table of function pointers, the compiler can put off the binding of the function call into the object code at this statement. The compiler simply inserts the menu table into the object code. At runtime (versus the compile time of early binding), the order of the functions is determined dynamically (hence the second name for late binding, dynamic binding).

When the compiled program gets to the function call statement, it uses ans to search the table of pointers, then finds the address of the function that it should actually call. Searching the function pointer table takes more time than directly calling the function by name. The trade-off of efficiency usually is minor when you use function pointers.

C++ also achieves late binding, but it uses a somewhat different approach. (You can use function pointers in C++ also, but you do not have to as often as in C.) C++ uses a table similar to the function pointer table shown in Figure 17.1 to perform its late binding. With late binding, C++ achieves true polymorphism. Before delving into that $50 word, read about virtual functions in the next section.

> It helps to understand that C and C++ achieve late binding by resolving function calls as late as possible (right before the functions execute). The function call code is hinted at but not defined until runtime.

Virtual Functions

Virtual functions offer additional advantages to your C++ programming. Some C++ programmers say that virtual functions produce the true OOP in C++. Late binding is inherent with virtual functions. Knowing this means that you already can guess that virtual functions offer some way for C++ to resolve function calls at runtime instead of at compile time.

Virtual functions add another layer of complexity for students moving from C to C++. Complexity is a relative term, however. Virtual functions are not difficult to understand, nor are they difficult to implement. You must learn some additional syntax and programming considerations that you do not have to cope with in C. Nevertheless, specifying and using virtual functions is one of the last primary C++ topics you must master.

> Do not confuse *virtual functions* with *virtual base classes* (discussed at the end of Chapter 15, "Inheritance Issues"). You use virtual base classes when you inherit a base class multiple times and want the base class shared between the inherited classes. Virtual functions are the mechanism that C++ uses to achieve late binding and true polymorphism.
>
> Although they are different concepts, the name *virtual* is similar for both virtual base classes and virtual functions. In both cases, *virtual* implies that a normal base class or function does not exist, but rather a placeholder exists that appears to look like a base class or a function.

You use virtual functions with inheritance. Inheritance sometimes puts requirements onto the compiler that you could not handle without virtual functions. To declare a virtual function, put the keyword `virtual` before the function name in the `class` header. The following base class declares two virtual functions and two nonvirtual functions:

The keyword `virtual` *labels a virtual function in a class.*

```
class Children  {
    int age;
    char * name;
public:
    int get_age();
    char * get_name();
    virtual void show();          // Two virtual function
    virtual int add(int, char *); // declarations
};
```

Using Virtual Functions

Virtual functions are best learned when you ease into them. The next program creates a good foundation from which you can learn the need for virtual functions. Nothing virtual exists in the first version. There is nothing in this program that you do not already know. It is simple, but take the time to study it. Then, as the succeeding sections add to it, you will understand the additions.

INHERNOV.CPP. Inheritance without virtual functions.

```
// Filename: INHERNOV.CPP
// Inheritance without virtual functions
```

continues

INHERNOV.CPP. continued

```cpp
#include <iostream.h>
#include <string.h>

class Person  {
   char * name;
   int age;
public:
   Person(char *, int);
   ~Person() { delete name; }  // Inline destructor code
   void display();  // Displays the complete Person
};

Person::Person(char * n, int a)  {  // Constructor
   name = new char [strlen(n)+1];
   strcpy(name, n);
   age = a;
}

void Person::display()  {
   cout << "\nName:\t" << name << endl;
   cout << "Age:\t" << age << endl;
}

///// First derived class /////
class Student : public Person  {
   char * id;  // Student ID
public:
   Student(char *, char *, int);
   ~Student() {delete id;}  // Inline destructor code
   void display();
};

Student::Student(char * i, char * n, int a) : Person(n, a) {
   id = new char [strlen(i)+1];
   strcpy(id, i);
}

void Student::display()  {  // Redefines the base display()
   Person::display();  // First, calls the base's version
   cout << "ID:\t" << id << endl;  // Adds to the output
}

///// Second derived class /////
class Teacher : public Person  {
   double salary;
public:
   Teacher(double s, char * n, int a) :
```

```
        salary(s), Person(n, a) {}
};

void main()
{
   Person  human("George Smith", 25);
   Student kid("8NB5", "Jane Marlin", 12);
   Teacher adult(32356.54, "Mr. Frazier", 35);

   // Now, displays each object
   human.display();
   kid.display();
   adult.display();
}
```

Here is the program's output:

```
Name:   George Smith
Age:    25

Name:   Jane Marlin
Age:    12
ID:     8NB5

Name:   Mr. Frazier
Age:    35
```

To help explain the program, Figure 17.2 describes the class hierarchy of INHERNOV.CPP.

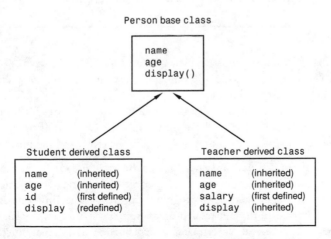

Figure 17.2. The classes Student *and* Teacher *are derived from* Person. *Notice that* Teacher *does not redefine* display(), *so it uses the base class's* display().

305

Non-students and non-teachers (the base class Person) have names and ages, and the base class display() function takes care of those two members. Because students also have a student ID, the Student display() function redefines the base class display() (in effect, not inheriting it, but inheriting only the base class data members). Because the program does not display teacher salaries, the Teacher class uses the inherited Person function, without redefining it.

You typically find virtual functions used with inheritance when derived classes inherit and redefine the base class functions. The INHERNOV.CPP program has both inheritance and base class function redefinition, so it is a possible candidate for a virtual function. If you made display() into a virtual function, the class header would look like this:

INHERV1.CPP. Inheritance with a virtual function.

```
// Filename: INHERV1.CPP
// Inheritance with a virtual function
#include <iostream.h>
#include <string.h>

class Person  {
   char * name;
   int age;
public:
   Person(char *, int);
   ~Person() { delete name; }  // Inline destructor code
   virtual void display();  // Virtualizes the function
}
```

The only change is the keyword virtual before the inherited display() function. virtual tells C++ to bind the display() function later, at runtime, not at compile time. As soon as you define a function as a virtual function, C++ creates a table in memory of future function addresses. The compiler directs all calls to the display() function to that table and not to a specific address. At runtime, the actual address of the function being called is resolved, the function's address is placed in the table, and the function executes.

After all this has been said, virtual does not help this program one bit! As a matter of fact, virtual slows down the program and generates larger compiled code (due to the indirect function call table). (Compile the two programs, putting virtual into one and leaving it out of the other. Notice the differences in program size.) From the output, you would never know that they were different. Nevertheless, as explained earlier, virtual functions are best learned gradually, and you are almost there. The next section describes a similar program that works *only* when you specify display() as virtual.

Requiring Virtual Functions

This section shows you two modified versions of the preceding program. Until now, the program created scalar objects of the Person, Student, and Teacher classes. As you know from your experience in C, you often need to work with pointers to objects instead of with scalar objects. In other words, you can work directly with an integer variable (a scalar object), but you often work with pointers to integers and other data types to improve your program's flexibility and allow advanced data structures such as linked lists. You might just as easily require pointers to class objects as well.

The difference between the following program and the Person base class program is in main(). (If you are typing these programs in as you read, do not include the virtual keyword this time around.) After the three different objects are created, an array of object pointers is created to hold each object. Each element of the object array points to a different type of object. The first element points to a Person object, the second element points to a Student object, and the third element points to a Teacher object.

> C++ enables you to create an array of pointers to different types of objects as long as those objects all belong to the same class inheritance hierarchy. You must use the base class when defining the array. Any derived class object can be pointed to by a base class pointer. (The reverse is not allowed, however. You cannot define a pointer using a derived class and then point to a base object with it.)

As soon as the program sets up an array of pointers to the three objects, a simple for loop displays all three objects. Study main() to see object pointers being used.

INHERV2.CPP. Inheritance with a virtual function.

```
// Filename: INHERV2.CPP
// Inheritance with a virtual function
#include <iostream.h>
#include <string.h>

class Person   {
   char * name;
   int age;
public:
   Person(char *, int);
   ~Person() { delete name; }   // Inline destructor code
```

continues

307

INHERV2.CPP. continued

```cpp
   void display();   // Displays the complete Person
};

Person::Person(char * n, int a)  {  // Constructor
   name = new char [strlen(n)+1];
   strcpy(name, n);
   age = a;
}

void Person::display()  {
   cout << "\nName:\t" << name << endl;
   cout << "Age:\t" << age << endl;
}

///// First derived class /////
class Student : public Person  {
   char * id;  // Student ID
public:
   Student(char *, char *, int);
   ~Student() {delete id;}  // Inline destructor code
   void display();
};

Student::Student(char * i, char * n, int a) : Person(n, a) {
   id = new char [strlen(i)+1];
   strcpy(id, i);
}

void Student::display()  {  // Redefines the base class display()
   Person::display();  // First, calls the base class's version
   cout << "ID:\t" << id << endl;   // Adds to the output
}
///// Second derived class /////
class Teacher : public Person  {
   double salary;
public:
   Teacher(double s, char * n, int a) : salary(s), Person(n, a) {}
};

void main()
{

   // Creates three objects
   Person  human("George Smith", 25);
   Student kid("8NB5", "Jane Marlin", 12);
   Teacher adult(32356.54, "Mr. Frazier", 35);
```

```
    Person * ptr[3];   // Defines three pointers to base objects
    ptr[0] = &human;   // Even though two of these assignments
    ptr[1] = &kid;     // are not being made to a Person base
    ptr[2] = &adult;   // object, C++ allows them

    // Displays each object. The pointers enable you
    // to display each object inside a for loop
    for (int ctr=0; ctr<3; ctr++)  {
       ptr[ctr]->display();  }
}
```

The for loop demonstrates that you can call the same member function using pointers of different types. In C++ terminology, you can pass three different types of objects the same message. All might seem fine, but the program has a problem. How does C++ know which object's display() to call? In other words, the compiler has to handle this statement somehow:

```
ptr[ctr]->display();
```

At compile time, the compiler has *no idea* exactly what to do here. The compiler does not know which object will be pointed to by ptr[ctr]. (In this simplistic program, you can glance up a few lines and tell, but what if these pointers were initialized based on user input? If the user wanted two Teacher objects, only one Student object, and no Person object, then the ptr[] array would contain a different assortment of data pointers than it does in this program.

Nevertheless, C++ must generate some code for the display() call. Because C++ has no idea exactly what type each ptr[] element will hold, C++ has no idea whether the program will have to use the base class display() or the redefined Student class display(). Because it has to make some assumption at compile time, C++ decides that it will use the base class display() for this statement, no matter what the ptr[] element contains at runtime. Early binding is taking place; the compiler must decide at compile time what code to generate for the statement.

Here is the output from the preceding program to show that C++ called the base class display() function, even though the middle object was a Student with its own display() function. If the Student display() function had executed, the student's ID would have printed. Because the base class display() function does not print the ID, and because the output does not contain the ID for the student (the second object), you can correctly conclude that C++ called the base display() each time.

```
Name:   George Smith
Age:    25
```

```
Name:    Jane Marlin
Age:     12          ── base display() incorrectly called

Name:    Mr. Frazier
Age:     35
```

The problem becomes even clearer when you consider what happens when you add the following three lines after the for loop in the preceding program:

```
human.display();
kid.display();   // NOT the same output as ptr[1]->display()!
adult.display();
```

Figure 17.3 shows the function call mechanism that C++ sets up for the pointers at compile time.

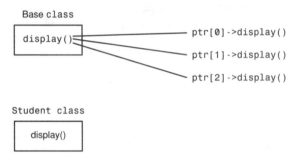

Figure 17.3. The base class display() *message should not have been used with the* ptr[1]
(Student) *object.*

Early Binding Again

The same early binding problem would result if you used references to invoke the object member functions. Suppose that you created a function that displayed whatever object was passed to it. The code might be:

```
void output(const Person & p)  {
   p.display();  // C++ has no idea which display() to
}                // call at compile time, so it uses the
                 // base display() unless you virtualize
                 // base
```

You need some way to tell the C++ compiler the following:

"I want you to use the `Student display()` function if the pointer contains a `Student` object, and I want you to use the base class `display()` function if the pointer contains either a `Person` or a `Teacher` object. You, C++, will know at runtime, not before, what objects are being pointed to by the pointer array."

The `virtual` keyword tells C++ exactly what objects are being pointed to. If you virtualize a base `class` function, C++ knows to perform late binding. C++ does *not* resolve the function call references at compile time. Using `virtual` tells C++ that you want to send the *same message* to *different* objects. Using `virtual` tells C++ to wait by not assuming that the base class will contain the function to call. Using `virtual` tells C++ that you want to perform polymorphism: You want to pass the same message to different objects to make your programming easier. You do not have to remember a different function name for every type of object to inherit from one common object. Instead, C++ sets up a table of pointers at compile time, using that table at runtime to resolve function call addresses, just as C and C++ both do when you call functions using function pointers.

virtual allows for polymorphism.

The only difference between the following program and the preceding one is the `virtual` keyword in the base class `display()` function. The output is now correct. Each object, at runtime, determines the function C++ calls to display.

INHERV3.CPP. Polymorphism.

```
// Filename: INHERV3.CPP
// Polymorphism
#include <iostream.h>
#include <string.h>

class Person  {
   char * name;
   int age;
public:
   Person(char *, int);
   ~Person() { delete name; }  // Inline destructor code
   virtual void display();  // ** Virtualized **
};

Person::Person(char * n, int a)  {  // Constructor
   name = new char [strlen(n)+1];
```

continues

311

INHERV3.CPP. continued

```
    strcpy(name, n);
    age = a;
}

void Person::display()  {
    cout << "\nName:\t" << name << endl;
    cout << "Age:\t" << age << endl;
}

///// First derived class /////
class Student : public Person  {
    char * id;  // Student ID
public:
    Student(char *, char *, int);
    ~Student() {delete id;}  // Inline destructor code
    void display();
};

Student::Student(char * i, char * n, int a) : Person(n, a) {
    id = new char [strlen(i)+1];
    strcpy(id, i);
}

void Student::display()  {  // Redefines the base class display()
    Person::display();  // First, calls the base class's version
    cout << "ID:\t" << id << endl;  // Adds to the output
}
///// Second derived class /////
class Teacher : public Person  {
    double salary;
public:
    Teacher(double s, char * n, int a) : salary(s), Person(n, a) {}
};

void main()
{

    // Creates three objects
    Person  human("George Smith", 25);
    Student kid("8NB5", "Jane Marlin", 12);
    Teacher adult(32356.54, "Mr. Frazier", 35);
```

```
Person * ptr[3];   // Defines three pointers to base objects
ptr[0] = &human;   // Even though two of these assignments
ptr[1] = &kid;     // are not being made to a Person base
ptr[2] = &adult;   // object, C++ allows them

    // Displays each object. The pointers enable you
    // to display each object inside a for loop
    for (int ctr=0; ctr<3; ctr++)  {
        ptr[ctr]->display();  }
}
```

Here is the output:

```
Name:   George Smith
Age:    25

Name:   Jane Marlin
Age:    12          — Student display() called here
ID:     8NB5

Name:   Mr. Frazier
Age:    35
```

Figure 17.4 shows the correct function call mechanism that C++ set up at runtime. The virtual keyword informed C++ that it was to look at the pointer's contents at runtime and make the function call based on the pointer's contents. Because the pointers are not initialized until runtime, C++ cannot determine which functions to call at compile time. In effect, the objects themselves decide which function actually executes.

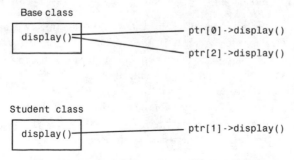

Figure 17.4. The base class display() *message was properly used with the* ptr[1] (Student) *object.*

Some C++ programmers prefer to put the `virtual` keyword in front of every derived function that comes from a virtual function in the base class. In other words, the preceding program could have `virtual` placed before `Student::display()`'s implementation code. No output changes occur when you place `virtual` in front of derived function names. You might want to put `virtual` in front of derived function names just to remind yourself that they derive from virtual functions.

Why Use Polymorphism?

The late binding of polymorphism is advantageous for C++ programmers. Late binding decreases your programming time. The preceding program is not stretching a point. Rather, it shows a powerful OOP mechanism that improves program coding.

In real life, people apply the same actions on different types of objects all the time. You might *play* the piano, *play* the trombone, *play* in the pool, and *play* football. All four activities are entirely different, but people use polymorphism to understand the four different meanings of *play*.

Wouldn't it be inefficient to create a new word for *play* for every different musical instrument? If you did, you might *play* the piano, *plung* the trombone, *plack* the clarinet, and *prog* the drums. Language would immediately become impractical to learn. It would take a lifetime to learn a different verb for every single activity, even though many of those activities are similar *in concept* but different in execution.

In the OOP programming world, when you write a program, creating families of objects through inheritance, you can use the same function name for similar activities on different types of objects. You do not need to have a different function name for every object. In the preceding program, `display()` suffices for every object derived from `Person`. You don't need a `displ_st()`, a `displ_te()`, and a `disp_pe()` function for the three kinds of objects in the inheritance. All those function names would only confuse you while you struggled to write the rest of the program, just as different verbs for the same actions would confuse people.

You might wonder why C++ does not default to virtual functions when you inherit from a base class. If it did, it would call only functions that matched the objects' types. One reason is that you might want C++ to use the base `class` function for all objects pointed to

by the object pointers. With `virtual`, you have the choice. Another (perhaps more important) reason that C++ gives you the option of specifying `virtual` is efficiency. Efficiency suffers slightly when you use virtual functions. The compiler must make extra decisions at runtime that early binding compiles do not require. The designers of C++ wanted to give you the option of deciding whether the efficiency trade-off is worth the advantage.

`friend` functions and regular program functions cannot be virtualized.

The Virtual Table

As a blossoming OOP programmer, you should begin to think about the internals that C++ must go through to accomplish polymorphism. C++ does not perform some kind of runtime compile, changing compiled code depending on the runtime contents of variables. Not only would that be inefficient, but it also would be virtually impossible (pun intended).

Recall how C resolves function pointers at runtime. It sets up an address table at compile time, but the compiler does not supply the addresses at that time. The function calls point to the function address table, not to actual functions as would be the case with early binding. At runtime, the proper addresses are loaded into the address table so that when a function call begins, C++ goes to that function's address table, dynamically, to get the proper address to call.

C++ performs polymorphism, resolving function addresses at runtime so that many objects can use the same function names, through the use of a table similar to the function pointer table. However, C++ goes a little further with its late binding table. The C++ late binding table is called a *virtual table*, also known as a *vtable*.

The virtual table (vtable) provides the means for polymorphism.

Each class containing virtual functions, as well as each derived class, has its own vtable. The preceding program, INHERV3.CPP, has a virtual function in the base class, with three classes altogether (`Person`, `Student`, and `Teacher`). Therefore, the compiler sets up three vtables, one for each class. The vtable contains addresses of each function in the base class. In this simple program, there is only one virtual function per class, so there is only one function address. If there were several virtual functions in each class, each vtable would contain several function addresses pointing to the functions.

Figure 17.5 shows the situation C++ first sets up when it compiles the program.

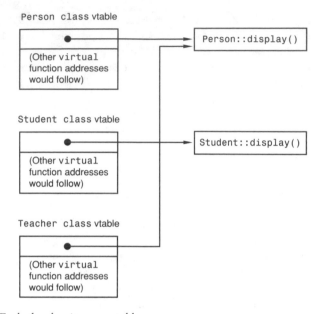

Figure 17.5. Each class has its own vtable.

Every object of a class contains a pointer, called the *vptr,* to the vtable. INHERV3.CPP contains three variables (three objects, or three instances of the class)—human, kid, and adult vtables. Each of those variables has the usual data members (human has name and age, kid also has id, and adult has salary). In addition to the data members, each of those class variables has an extra member, a vptr member. Each variable's vptr contains the address of (in effect points to) that variable's class vtable.

As Figure 17.6 shows, the variable's vptr points to the vtable, which in turn points to the virtual functions in the class. Note that if the Person class contained seven virtual functions, each of the vtables would contain seven function pointers.

> Different C++ compilers might implement virtual functions and the vtable differently. There is no requirement as to the vtable's internals. Nevertheless, the end result, polymorphism, is the important knowledge you need. If you had never seen the vtable's inner workings, you could still understand everything there is to understand about C++ and polymorphism.

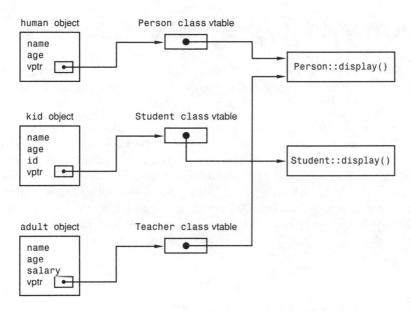

Figure 17.6. Each variable's vptr points to the class virtual function table.

Overriding the Virtualization

Just because a function is virtual, and just because that same function exists in a derived class, you are not limited to using the derived function. As with most aspects of C++, you can override the defaults of virtualization.

Whenever you want to call the base class function code instead of a derived class function, even when using the derived class object, preface the object with the base class scope resolution operator. In the preceding program, if you wanted to pass the base class display() message to the Student object, and the Student object were pointed to by ptr[1], you could do so with this:

```
ptr[1]->Person::display();  // Calls the base class display()
```

You might want to do this if you didn't want the student's ID printed. The ID would print if you let the virtual display() call remain as is.

317

Family of Type Patterns

Virtual functions provide a nice way of letting objects figure out what to do at runtime (polymorphism). Virtual functions make your life easier because you can use the same function name for similar activities, as described earlier.

Actually, virtual functions provide a more high-level advantage to C++ programming. The base class virtual functions explain what each derived object is capable of doing. Some derived objects might have additional functions, and some derived objects might redefine the base class functions, but each of the derived classes will have functions named the same as the base class's. In effect, you are saying, "All objects I derive will have these properties." In the preceding program, the base class explained, at a high level, that all objects in the program can be displayed (via a `display()` function). If there were a virtual `calculate()` function, all objects and derived objects could calculate. Each object might calculate in a different way, but they all could calculate.

Pure Virtual Functions and Abstract Base Classes

Abstract base classes provide the framework of their inherited classes.

Taking the concept of high-level base classes one step further, you might create a base class that contains virtual functions with *no code* in the functions. These virtual functions are called *pure virtual functions*. They have no code; they are purely virtual in that they do not define any code but act as a pattern for all derived classes.

Although you can specify a pure virtual function just by not putting code into the function's body, C++ provides another mechanism that ensures that the function is only inherited and never used. Instead of having a function body enclosed in braces (even empty braces), assign the function a 0, as done in the following statement:

```
virtual void display() = 0;  // Pure virtual function
```

The base class `display()` function is now defined as a pure virtual function. You cannot define any objects for a class that contains a pure virtual function. The class becomes an *abstract base class* because it defines the makeup of the family of classes, but it provides no code. Any class that contains one or more pure virtual functions is an abstract base class because you could never instantiate an object from that class (it is unfinished due to the `virtual` keyword).

Get in the habit of passing objects to describe virtual functions by reference or through a pointer. That way, if an object's member function is called, the function will use the virtual member functions.

Wrapping Up Virtual Functions

You might recall how inheritance affects constructor and destructor calls. When an inherited object goes out of scope, the compiler automatically calls the derived `class` destructor (supplying its own destructor if you do not), then calls the parent `class` destructor, trickling up through the inheritance hierarchy until the base `class` destructor performs its job.

For every base class from which you will derive other functions, make the base `class` destructor virtual. If you subsequently delete an object through its pointer (or a reference), C++ calls the object's own destructor. If the base `class` destructor were not virtual, C++ would try to use the base `class` destructor whenever you deleted the object with its pointer using `delete`.

To ensure that proper destructors are called, virtualize *any* destructor that resides in a class with virtual functions. If the program uses a pointer or a reference to the object, it will be properly destructed when you delete it.

You cannot call a constructor for an abstract base class. As you know from Chapter 15, "Inheritance Issues," you must construct a base `class` object, through an initialization list, before you can construct a derived object. Because the base class is virtual, and because you cannot create an abstract base `class` object, you never have to write a base `class` constructor (nor are you allowed to).

Some advanced applications have been documented that seemingly need to construct base `class` objects from an abstract base class. Although you cannot do this directly, there are ways to fool C++ into thinking that you constructed a base `class` object.

continues

> *continued*
>
> Sometimes, this can get as difficult as multiple inheritance. Therefore, this topic is beyond the scope of this book. You will stay busy enough with virtual functions to handle almost any programming situation you might encounter.

Summary

Now that you understand true polymorphism, you can take a deserved break. Just about any C++ article or book you read now will make sense to you. You have made it through the difficult sections, and as you found out, they were not that difficult.

While honing your C++ skills, keep reminding yourself that the designers of C++ did not design the language to be hard to use. They designed the language to be easier than traditional programming languages. Some of the concepts, such as virtual functions, are very new to you, but they exist to streamline your programming job. Being able to send generic messages to objects, and letting the objects figure out exactly what message to handle, takes much of the programming burden off you.

Part V

C C++

ADVANCED OBJECT-ORIENTED PROGRAMMING

ADVANCED C++ INPUT/OUTPUT

"Please file this for me."

Although this chapter is entitled "Advanced C++ Input/Output," you soon will learn that I/O in C++, even that considered "advanced," is not difficult at all. Now that you have worked your way through most of the C++/OOP topics, I/O will seem like an elementary change of pace. As a matter of fact, most of C++'s I/O, such as file I/O, is easier in C++ than in other languages, including C.

In this chapter, you will learn:

- About C's I/O stream class
- How to direct line I/O
- How to control sequential file I/O
- How to control random file I/O

The *iostream* Class Library

When you include iostream.h, you include an input/output stream class that almost every C++ program uses (as you have seen throughout this book). The base class is named `ios`. The derived classes extend from `ios` and the defined objects such as `cin` and `cout` that you are now very comfortable with. Figure 18.1 shows what the `ios` class hierarchy (without file I/O) looks like.

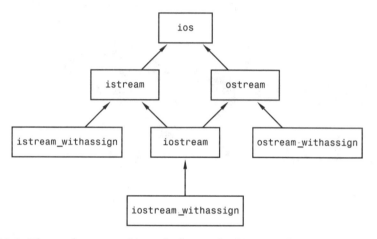

Figure 18.1. The `ios` *base* `class` *hierarchy for standard input and output in iostream.h.*

The `iostream`
properly
implements
multiple
inheritance.

Notice that the `iostream` class has two parent classes. The `ios` class includes multiple inheritance and is about as close to multiple inheritance as you should get for a while—maybe forever. As Chapter 15, "Inheritance Issues," points out, multiple inheritance is dangerously bug-prone, and you should not resort to using it except in very advanced situations where it might be worth the effort. Some programmers argue that no programming problem in the world requires multiple inheritance, and that you can accomplish the same advanced goals with single inheritance that you can with multiple inheritance.

The jury is still out. Multiple inheritance is a relatively new addition to C++. The AT&T specifications allowed only single inheritance until version 2.0. Nevertheless, the `ios` class is known to be about as bug-free as a class can get, and whether or not it should be rewritten using single inheritance is moot; the class works well now. Feel free to use it. More importantly, you *should* use it in place of the standard I/O functions you are used to in C. Not only is the `ios` class more efficient than `printf()` and the others, but it is easier to use as well.

Multiple inheritance streamlines input and output. As you might guess, the `istream` class handles input, and the `ostream` class handles output. The overloaded extraction operator, `>>`, is a member of `istream`, and the overloaded insertion operator, `<<`, is a member of `ostream`. The inherited `iostream` class supports both input and output, inheriting the properties of both its parents.

Some beginning C++ programmers confuse the two uses of `iostream`, but they are easy to remember. iostream.h is a file (you #include only files) that contains the `ios` class and its derivations. `iostream` happens to be the name of one of those derived classes.

The three derived classes `istream_withassign`, `ostream_withassign`, and `iostream_withassign` contain the same `class` definition as their parents, but they also define the assignment operator, `=`, so you can assign one stream to another. `cin` is an object instantiated from `istream_withassign`, and `cout`, `clog`, and `cerr` objects are instantiated from `ostream_withassign`.

A problem can arise in this section due to compiler differences. Different C++ compilers implement the `ios` class in different ways. Many (Borland's Turbo C++ compilers, for example) support the `ios` class described here.

There is more to the overall I/O `class` hierarchy than you see in Figure 18.1. The section entitled "File I/O" discusses file I/O.

Standard Input/Output

Throughout this book, you have seen many uses of the iostream.h file. `cin` is not a keyboard object. It is the standard input object, but most of the time `cin` is routed to the keyboard. The same holds true for `cout`, `cerr`, and `clog` directed to the screen; these are three output objects that are usually directed to the screen. Through the operating system, you can redirect `cin` and `cout`. (UNIX and mainframe programmers can redirect `cerr` and `log` as well.) Most C++ programmers let these objects represent the keyboard and the screen. If you want to perform I/O to the printer, a modem, or a disk file, you can use classes discussed throughout this chapter.

As mentioned earlier, different compilers implement I/O differently. The following sections discuss common I/O routines that are possible in C++. Consult your compiler manual for more specifics and other methods you can use.

The Input Member Functions

In C, you probably are familiar with the gets() function. gets() enables you to request an entire string from the input device. scanf() does not suffice because it stops receiving input at the first whitespace character. Here is a simple program that uses gets():

GETS.C. Gets a string from the keyboard into a character array.

```
/* Filename: GETS.C */
/* Gets a string from the keyboard into a character array. */
#include <stdio.h>
void main()
{
    char str[81];   /* Reserves space for 80 characters with null */

    printf("What is your full name? ");
    gets(str);

    printf("Thank you, %s, for answering me.", str);
}
```

Here is a sample output from the program:

```
What is your full name? Gennifer Roses
Thank you, Gennifer Roses, for answering me.
```

If the program requested the name using scanf(), then str would contain only the first name, Gennifer, because scanf() would stop getting input at the first space. Also, the program has no way to keep the user from entering strings longer than 80 characters. The designers of C offer another function named fgets() that enables you to specify the maximum length of string accepted from the user. The user still can enter a string longer than the length specified in fgets(), but C will ignore everything to the right of the maximum length specified.

If you used `fgets()` in the preceding program, the program would be a little more accurate because it would not allow an extra-long string to overwrite the `str` array. To use `fgets()`, you would replace `gets()` with `fgets()`, as seen in the following line:

```
fgets(str, 81);  /* Limits the characters read to 80 plus null */
```

The C++ `istream` class offers a very useful and flexible member function named `get()` that you can use for the input of strings. `get()` works like `fgets()` in that you specify the maximum number of characters in the input string. As with any member function, you execute `get()` by using it with an object—`cin.get()` is very easy indeed, as the following C++ program demonstrates.

GETS.CPP. Gets a string from the keyboard into a character array.

```cpp
// Filename: GETS.CPP
// Gets a string from the keyboard into a character array.
#include <iostream.h>
void main()
{
   char str[81];  // Reserves space for 80 characters with null

   cout << "What is your full name? ";
   cin.get(str, 80);

   cout << "Thank you, " << str << ", for answering me.";
}
```

There are many variations on `get()`, depending on your compiler. Most compilers overload `get()` so that it gets single characters as well as strings. Here are just a few prototypes for the overloaded `get()` functions that typically are available:

- `int get();`

  Returns the next character typed.

- `istream & get(char * str, int len, char='\n');`

  The function used in the preceding program. The `char=` specifies the character that you want to *end* the input with. For example, if you passed `'\t'` as the third argument, the input would stop when you pressed Tab, not when you pressed Enter. (Note that Enter would still have to end the input, but C++ would ignore

327

any characters after the Tab keypress.) Because '\n' is the default third argument, you do not have to specify it in most instances, such as in the preceding program, because Enter generally ends input.

- ```
  istream & get(char & c);
  ```

  Gets a character into the character variable c.

- ```
  istream & get(char & c, char='\n');
  ```

  Gets characters, sending them through the input stream, until the delimiter (the default is '\n') is input.

The get() function occasionally has a side effect. get() leaves the newline character on the input stream, letting it be the first character in the *next* get(). The newline means that you would have to perform an extra get() to grab that newline before you perform another get(). If you are inputting several values, you might be better off using a member function named getline() that is similar to C's fscanf(). getline() reads a line of text until it reaches a newline or until the length is reached. getline() discards the newline so that the next input is fresh. getline()'s prototype is

```
istream & getline(char *, int, char='\n');
```

If you want the end of input to be triggered by something other than a newline character, supply a third argument to override the default argument.

The Output Member Functions

Much of this chapter will be extremely easy for you. As you saw in the preceding section, performing character and string input is simple when you pass the get() message to cin. When you were reading the part of this book that first explains C++ I/O (Chapter 3, "Introduction to C++ Input and Output"), you would not have understood the usage of something such as cin.get() because you were unfamiliar with member functions. At that time, you thought that structs had only data members, as they do in C.

Even though you had not yet learned about member functions, you did learn in Chapter 3 how to perform some rather powerful output using the I/O manipulators. For example, if you wanted to print the mathematical value of pi to three decimal places, you could do something like this:

```
const int PI = 3.14159;
cout << setprecision(3) << PI;  // Outputs pi to two decimals
```

Chapter 3 also describes the base manipulators that enable you to print numbers in decimal, octal, or hexadecimal. You also learned about the setw() manipulator and several others that give you more control over cin and cout (Table 3.2 provides many of these).

Go back to Chapter 3 and find Table 3.3. You will now recognize something that you did not fully understand at the time. Table 3.3 describes the format flags available. Many of the format flags duplicate the I/O manipulators, but the format flags also offer conversions such as uppercase to lowercase. The part of the table you will now recognize is the scope resolution operators. For instance, to right-justify pi within a field of ten characters, you would pass the right-justify format flag to the setiosflags() manipulator like this:

```
cout << setw(10) << setiosflags(ios::right) << PI << '\n';
```

The ios:: should be obvious to you; right and the other iostream.h format flags are defined in the ios base class. It is the base class right that you are using and sending to setiosflags(). If you want to combine the format flags, you can do so by separating them with a bitwise OR operator, ¦. The following statement outputs a left-justified uppercase character:

```
cout << setiosflags(ios::uppercase ¦ ios::left) << c;
```

> Remember to include iomanip.h when you use the manipulators.

This chapter is not trying to rehash Chapter 3. However, a brief review was in order now that you understand classes and inheritance better.

There is a popular member function defined in ostream for use with the cout object—put(). put() outputs a single character. Here is an example that uses put():

put() works like C's putchar() function.

PUT.CPP. Demonstrates cout.put(), which outputs single characters.

```
// Filename: PUT.CPP
// Demonstrates cout.put(), which outputs single characters.
#include <iostream.h>
void main()
{
   char grade;
   int  score;
```

continues

329

PUT.CPP. continued

```
    cout << "What is your test score? ";
    cin >> score;

    if (score>=90)  {grade = 'A';} else
      if (score>=80)  {grade = 'B';} else
        if (score>=70)  {grade = 'C';} else
          if (score>=60)  {grade = 'D';} else
                {grade = 'F';};

    cout << "Your grade is ";
    cout.put(grade);  // Outputs the letter grade
}
```

Here is the program's output:

```
What is your test score? 78
Your grade is C
```

The put() member function might seem trivial at this point. If you study this grade program, you probably will wonder why put() was even used. After all, the second-to-last cout could have included the character variable, and one line would be saved. The advantage to using the ios library is that you can use the same I/O methods for files as well as for the standard input and output devices.

The C++ equivalents of fread() and fwrite() are read() and write().

fread() and fwrite() read and write complete streams of C data. You need to send only the starting address, an array length, and the size of each array element to write an entire floating-point array to a disk file.

C++ offers read() and write(), two functions borrowed from C and changed to work with objects. The prototypes of read() and write() are

```
istream & read(char *, int length);
```

and

```
ostream & write(char *, int length);
```

With read() and write(), you can write objects and arrays of objects to disk files. Suppose that you created an array of 100 People objects with the following statement:

```
People group[100];  // Defines an array of 100 People objects
```

After initializing the group array, you can write it to disk using the following statement:

```
diskfile.write((char *)group, sizeof(group));  // Writes
                                    // entire array of objects
```

330

Notice that to match the prototype (and in C++, matching the prototype is very critical) you must typecast the array of objects to be a character array. read() and write() both work with binary data only. Therefore, if you write data to a disk file, that data will be compressed into binary data that is not in ASCII format. Because of this, read() and write() are mirror images of each other. read() usually reads data written by another write().

File I/O

C++ file I/O is performed through the use of the fstream and related classes ifstream (for file input) and ofstream (for file output). fstream is also derived from ios, but multiple inheritance rears its ugly head again: iostream is *also* a parent class of fstream. Figure 18.2 tries to give you an idea of where ostream, ifstream, and fstream fit into things. The additional derived classes add complexity to the overall ios class, but luckily, you do not really need to understand the class inheritance hierarchy to use fstream effectively.

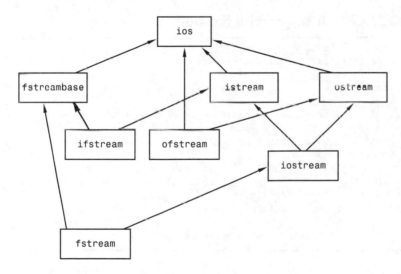

Figure 18.2. fstream, ifstream, *and* ofstream *are derived from* ios *as well as from other classes.*

The entire file stream class connection to the other ios class library resides in the header file named fstream.h. You must include fstream.h in any program that uses file I/O.

Because of the multiple inheritance, the I/O manipulators work with file I/O. Despite all this discussion about classes, file I/O in C++ is very similar to file I/O in C. There are several approaches to file I/O. Many of the more popular uses are explained in the following sections.

Simple File I/O

There are many ways to open a file using fstream and related classes. If you are performing straight sequential input or output, you can use ifstream and ofstream directly, saving an extra parameter over using the more general fstream.

The following program creates an output file and writes text to it. If the file exists, the file is overwritten with the new file. Overwriting existing files is a common feature of sequential output, and C does the same thing. To open and create an output file, you only have to create an output file object and pass that object a filename.

SEQOUT.CPP. A sequential file output program.

```
// Filename: SEQOUT.CPP
// A sequential file output program
#include <fstream.h>
void main()
{
   cout << "File creation program\n";  // Writes to the screen

   // Opens a file for output by calling the constructor for
   // an output file object
   ofstream outf("MYDATA.DAT");  // You could have used a
                                 // full pathname in the quotes
   outf << "Line 1 in the file.\n";
   outf << "Line 2 in the file.\n";

} // Output object goes out of scope here
```

The file object is named outf. One nice feature of object-oriented programming arises in this program: You do not have to close the output file object named outf. When outf goes out of scope, C++ calls the destructor for the output file, which closes the file. You could also output data to a disk file one character at a time if your data requires it. The following statement would output the character variable named c to the outf file object:

```
outf.put(c);  // Writes a character to the output file
```

> When you want to perform I/O with files and with the standard output devices (screen and keyboard), you do not have to include iostream.h because the fstream.h header file includes all the derived information found in iostream.h.

The following program turns things around by creating an input file object, named `inf`, and reads the strings from the data file created earlier.

SEQIN.CPP. A sequential file input program.

```
// Filename: SEQIN.CPP
// A sequential file input program
#include <fstream.h>
void main()
{
   char inbuf;  // Reserves a place to hold input

   cout << "File input program\n";  // Writes to the screen

   // Opens a file for input by calling the constructor for
   // an input file object
   ifstream inf("MYDATA.DAT");  // You could have used a
                                // full pathname in the quotes
   while (inf)  {
     inf.get(inbuf);  // Gets text a character at a time
     cout << inbuf;
   }
} // Output object goes out of scope here
```

Here is the program's output:

```
File input program
Line 1 in the file.
Line 2 in the file.
```

> The ifstream class returns a 0 (a null pointer) if the end of file condition is reached. Other error conditions are returned as well, so you should test the return value for your programs. The preceding program loops until it reaches a 0 value, which terminates the while loop. A later section describes file error checking.

The earlier section entitled "The Input Member Functions" describes the getline() member function. getline() is more appropriate if you are performing sequential I/O because the program reads one record at a time. When you use getline(), you must know the record terminating character (usually newline) or the record length if the file is fixed-length. For example, the following program reads the disk file one line at a time.

SEQBUF.CPP. A sequential file line input program.

```
// Filename: SEQBUF.CPP
// A sequential file line input program
#include <fstream.h>
void main()
{
   char inbuf[80];  // Reserves a place to hold input

   cout << "File input program\n";  // Writes to the screen

   // Opens a file for input by calling the constructor for
   // an input file object
   ifstream inf("MYDATA.DAT");  // You could have used a
                                // full pathname in the quotes
   while (inf)  {
     inf.getline(inbuf, 80);  // Gets text a line at a time
     cout << inbuf << "\n";  // Adds a newline
   }
} // Output object goes out of scope here
```

Because getline() stops at the newline character, you must add a newline to the end of the screen-printing cout, or the program will print the file contents without using newline.

Using read() and write(), you can read and write object variables to disk. The following program asks the user for three object values, writing each to the disk.

OBWRI.CPP. Writes three object variables to disk.

```
// Filename: OBWRI.CPP
// Writes three object variables to disk.
#include <fstream.h>
class Book  {  // Declares a book inventory class
   char title[20];
   char author[15];
   float price;
```

```
      int quantity;
public:
   void ask();   // Asks the user for the data
};   // Due to simplistic objects,
     // no constructors are needed
void Book::ask()  {
   cout << "\nWhat is the title? ";
   cin.getline(title, 19);
   cout << "Who is the author? ";
   cin.getline(author, 14);
   cout << "What is the price? ";
   cin >> price;
   cout << "How many are there? ";
   cin >> quantity;
   cin.get();  // Discards the newline at the end of quantity
}

void main()
{
   Book book1, book2, book3;   // Defines three books
   ofstream outf("BOOK.DAT");   // Creates an output file object

   cout << "* Book Inventory *\n";
   book1.ask();  // Gets data from user
   outf.write( (char *)&book1, sizeof(book1));   // Writes data

   book2.ask();
   outf.write( (char *)&book2, sizeof(book2));

   book3.ask();
   outf.write( (char *)&book3, sizeof(book3));
}
```

The only extra code in this program that you might not understand is the extra cin.get() at the end of the member function ask(). There are several ways to handle extra newlines that float through input streams, as you know from C. The cin >> quantity; statement puts your value into quantity, but when you press Enter to end the input, a newline is left on the input stream. When the program asks for the next book, that newline triggers an early termination of the title's getline. The extra input at the bottom of the class grabs the newline and does nothing with it, in effect discarding it.

The next program illustrates how you can use read() to read an entire array of objects from the disk. The three books entered in the preceding program are read and displayed in this program.

OBREAD.CPP. Reads three object variables to disk.

```cpp
// Filename: OBREAD.CPP
// Reads three object variables to disk.
#include <fstream.h>
#include <iomanip.h>

class Book  {  // Declares a book inventory class
   char title[20];
   char author[15];
   float price;
   int quantity;
public:
   void display();  // Displays the object's data
};

void Book::display()  {
   cout << setprecision(2);
   cout << "\nTitle:\t" << title;
   cout << "\nAuthor:\t" << author;
   cout << "\nPrice:\t" << price << "\tQuantity: " << quantity << endl;
}

void main()
{
   const int num = 3;
   Book books[num];  // Will hold all three objects in an array

   ifstream inf("BOOK.DAT");  // Creates an input file object

   inf.read((char *)&books, sizeof(books));

   for (int ctr=0; ctr<num; ctr++)  {
      books[ctr].display();  }
}
```

Notice how simple read() makes reading the entire array. In this example, only three books were read because the program that created the data file (OBWRI.CPP) wrote only three books. If there were 1,000 books in the data file, the only change you would have to make to the program would be the initialization of the num constant.

> You can append to an existing file, just as you can in C, but you must master the open() member function first. The next section describes open().

Random File I/O

Often, you need to read and write to the same open disk file. C++ offers object-oriented random file access modes, just as C does. The primary differences between the two access modes in C++ are that in random file access:

- You must use the fstream object, derived from iostream, so that you can perform input and output. The previous sequential program examples used istream for input and ostream for output.

- You have to specify an extra parameter on most fstream object member functions that indicates whether you are writing or reading.

- There is a seekg() function that corresponds to the fseek() function you use in C. With seekg(), you can move the file pointer to any location in the file that you want to read or write.

Your first responsibility when using random files (or, more specifically, the fstream class) is to create a file object. Then you must properly open that file. The previous programs did not require an open() because the class name determined the mode, input or output, in which you wanted C++ to open the file. The prototype of the open() member function follows:

```
void open(const char* filename, int mode);
```

The *filename* is the name of the file that you want to open, including a path if you wish. The *mode* is one of the several mode parameters shown in Table 18.1. There is a third argument whose value defaults to be openprot, but you do not need to worry about sending it a different value. openprot ensures that the file works in a read and write mode.

Table 18.1. The mode parameters for open().

Constant	Description
ios:in	Read mode
ios:out	Output mode
ios::app	Append mode
ios::ate	Seeks to the end of the file before reading or writing
ios::trunc	Erases the file if it exists (default for app)
ios::nocreate	Opens the file only if it exists
ios::noreplace	Opens the file only if it does not exist
ios::binary	Opens the file as a binary file (versus the default text mode)

You often use many of the values in Table 18.1 together by performing a bitwise OR on more than one of them in the open() function. The sample programs later in this chapter show some of the things that are possible with open().

You rarely have to close a file explicitly, unless you face either of the following situations:

1. You want to open the file in more than one different mode within the same program. For example, you might want to open a file for append, close it, and read the file from the beginning (although you can use seekg() to do the same thing without closing and reopening the file).

2. For safety, you want to close the file after the last statement in the program that uses it finishes. In case of a power failure or a data loss, the file will be better protected if it is closed.

You can close a file if you need to.

If you want to close the file, you only need to call the close() member function, such as inf.close().

The seekg() member function is familiar to you if you have used fseek() in C. seekg() moves the file pointer forward and backward in a file so that your next read or write will occur exactly at the point you want in the file. seekg() is overloaded, and it works two different ways depending on the arguments you pass it. The following statement shows one of the two seekg() methods.

```
datfile.seekg(278);  // Moves the file pointer to the 279th byte
```

When you specify only one long int argument, the argument specifies the exact byte position in the file that you want to move the file pointer to. You can call another version of seekg() like this:

```
datfile.seekg(53L, ios::cur);  // Moves pointer 53 more bytes
```

When you specify two arguments, the first long int argument is the *relative* position you want to move to in the file (the relative position can be negative). The second argument can be one of the values shown in Table 18.2. This second form of seekg() is much closer to that of C's fseek() function.

Table 18.2. The relative starting point for seekg().

Constant	Description
ios::beg	Beginning of the file
ios::cur	Current position in the file
ios::end	End of the file

The preceding seekg() moves the file pointer 53 bytes from the current position (from wherever it currently points). The next statement moves the file pointer 46 bytes from the end of the file:

```
datfile.seekg(-46L, ios::end);  // Moves pointer -46 from end
```

The next statement moves the file pointer to the beginning of the file, no matter where it was before the statement:

```
datfile.seekg(0L, ios::beg);  // Moves pointer to beginning
```

One last function often is helpful for reading and writing throughout a file. The tellg() member function returns information about a file. It is most often used to find the total number of records in a file. If an object is the same as a record, and it usually is if the file contains objects, you can determine the number of objects in a file with the next pair of statements:

```
myfile.seekg(0L, ios::end);  // Moves to end of file
num_objs = myfile.tellg() / sizeof(object);
```

Because tellg() returns the total number of bytes in the file, if you divide its return value by the record size, you will get the total number of records in the file.

Other Useful File Functions

You can erase a file with the remove() function prototyped in iostream.h. Suppose that you wanted to delete a file named XYZ.DAT on drive D: in a directory named MINE. You could do so with this statement:

```
remove("D:\MINE\XYZ.DAT");  // Erases a file
```

The filename could also be stored in a null-terminated character array.

You can print to a printer very easily using these I/O functions. All you need to do is specify a printer device in place of a filename when you open an output file. Common PC printer devices might be named PRN:, LPT:, LPT1:, LPT2, AUX:, COM1:, and COM2:. (The colons are optional.) UNIX and mainframe programmers must substitute their local printing devices. For example, the following short program opens the printer hooked to the PC's first parallel port and prints two lines to it.

PRINTIT.CPP. Prints a string to the printer.

```
// Filename: PRINTIT.CPP
// Prints a string to the printer.
```

continues

PRINTIT.CPP. continued

```
#include <fstream.h>

void main()
{
    ofstream prnt;  // Uses ofstream because printers are output only
    prnt.open("LPT1:");

    char *s = "This is going to the printer\n";
    prnt << s;
}
```

Of course, you need to be able to handle file I/O errors. Anytime you read or write, errors can occur. A floppy disk drive door might be left open, the printer might be out of paper, or you might try to read a file that does not exist.

An end-of-file condition is fairly easy to check for. One of the programs in this chapter, SEQIN.CPP, checks the file object itself. When you read from a file object, the file object contains a null pointer when you reach the end-of-file. You also can check a series of status bit member functions. Error checking is one of those topics that can be very compiler-specific, but most C++ compilers support the limited use of status bit functions.

The `ios` member functions you may use to check the status of the potential errors are shown in Table 18.3. Check for these problems after each read or write to a device other than the screen and keyboard.

Table 18.3. The status error member functions.

Function	Description
clear()	Clears the error status in case you want to retry the I/O
eof()	Returns true if end-of-file is reached
fail()	Returns true if an error occurred
good()	Returns true if the last I/O operation worked

For example, the following statement tests for the end-of-file condition:

```
if (myfile.eof())  { error(); }
```

340

Suppose that you opened a printer for output, and after trying to print to it, you wanted to test to see whether an error occurred. The following program fragment would do so:

```
if (prnt.fail())  {
   cerr << "* Printer error! **\n";
   cerr << "Please correct the problem and press ENTER.";
   cin >> en;  // Waits for the Enter keypress
   prnt.clear();  // Clears the status so that you can try again
}
```

Now that you have seen the common member functions and their arguments, the next section contains some program examples for your review.

Sample I/O Programs

The next program shows how to append to the data file created in an earlier program.

APPEND.CPP. Appends to a data file.

```
// Filename: APPEND.CPP
// Appends to a data file.
#include <fstream.h>

void main()
{
   fstream afile;  // Creates a file object
   afile.open("MYDATA.DAT", ios::app);

   afile << "Line 3 in the file.\n";
   afile << "Line 4 in the file.\n";

} // File object goes out of scope
  // You can afile.close() if you want to
```

Before the program executes, MYDATA.DAT looks like this (from the program named SEQOUT.CPP):

```
Line 1 in the file.
Line 2 in the file.
```

The program appends two more lines to the file so that it looks like this:

```
Line 1 in the file.
Line 2 in the file.
```

```
Line 3 in the file.
Line 4 in the file.
```

The following program demonstrates random file I/O. The program writes the letters of the alphabet to a disk file, then reads two letters, I and Q, from the file. The program must open the file in both input and output mode so that seekg() can find the two characters to read after writing the alphabet.

ALPH.CPP. Stores the alphabet in a file and then reads two letters from it.

```cpp
// Filename: ALPH.CPP
// Stores the alphabet in a file and
// then reads two letters from it.
#include <fstream.h>
#include <stdlib.h>
void main()
{
   fstream alphfile;

   alphfile.open("ALPH.DAT", ios::in | ios::out);
   if (!alphfile)
      {
          cerr << "\n*** Error opening file ***\n";
          exit(0);
      }
   for (char ch='A'; ch<= 'Z'; ch++)  {
     alphfile << ch;  }  // Writes the alphabet

   alphfile.seekg(8L, ios::beg);  // Points to the ninth letter
                                  // (8 past the beginning)
   alphfile >> ch;  // Reads the current character
   cout << "The first character is " << ch << "\n";

   alphfile.seekg(16L, ios::beg);  // Points to the 17th letter
                                   // (16 past the beginning)
   alphfile >> ch;  // Reads the current character
   cout << "The second character is " << ch << "\n";

   alphfile.close();
}
```

Here is the program's output:

```
The first character is I
The second character is Q
```

The next program is a rewritten version of the preceding one. When the letters I and Q are found, the letter x is written over the I and the Q. The seekg() function is used to back up one byte in the file to overwrite the letter just read.

CHANGEAL.CPP. Stores the alphabet in a file, reads two letters from it, and changes each letter to x.

```cpp
// Filename: CHANGEAL.CPP
// Stores the alphabet in a file, reads two letters from
// it, and changes each letter to x.
#include <fstream.h>
#include <stdlib.h>
void main()
{
   fstream alphfile;

   alphfile.open("ALPH.DAT", ios::in | ios::out);
   if (!alphfile)
      {
         cerr << "\n*** Error opening file ***\n";
         exit(0);
      }
   for (char ch='A'; ch<= 'Z'; ch++)  {
      alphfile << ch;  }  // Writes the alphabet

   alphfile.seekg(8L, ios::beg);  // Points to the ninth letter
                                  // (8 past the beginning)
   alphfile >> ch;  // Reads the current character
   // Changes the letter to an x
   alphfile.seekg(-1L, ios::cur);  // Backs up one character
   alphfile << 'x';  // Overwrites with the x

   alphfile.seekg(16L, ios::beg);  // Points to the 17th letter
                                   // (16 past the beginning)
   alphfile >> ch;  // Reads the current character
   // Changes the letter to an x
   alphfile.seekg(-1L, ios::cur);  // Backs up one character
   alphfile << 'x';  // Overwrites with the x

   alphfile.close();
}
```

The file named ALPH.TXT looks like this when the program finishes:

ABCDEFGHxJKLMNOPxRSTUVWXYZ

The programs in this chapter include the file I/O inside main() just to get you comfortable with the specifics. Of course, you would put these routines inside C++ classes for true C++ programs. Not only would you clean up main(), but you also would compartmentalize your code, making it easier to debug. Your objects then would write themselves to disk, read from disk, and so forth.

Summary

You now have the fundamentals for C++ file input and output. As soon as you have mastered this chapter's fundamentals, you should read your compiler's reference manual to determine the other member functions supplied. All the C I/O functions still work if you include the proper header files, but you will have less work to do if you get used to the C++ methods.

One of the most time-consuming tasks of writing programs is error handling. This chapter explained some basics of C++ file error handling, but there is much more that you will want to know that you can find only in your compiler manuals. Often, you need to know not only that an error occurred, but also which operating system error number was triggered.

At this point, you have mastered about all there is in C++ up to version 3.0. There are some very advanced concepts that you will want to pick up as you advance through the C++ programming ranks, but you now understand all the fundamentals of the language. Because of OOP, C++ takes a while to learn, even if you are a C programmer. Learning the language as you have done is quite an accomplishment. The more you program in C++, the more difficult you will find regular procedural languages to be.

The next chapter offers an explanation of *templates,* a new AT&T 3.0 feature. Although you can (very roughly at times) simulate templates with the preprocessor directives, templates extend that power much further and aid you when you write extensible programs.

19

TEMPLATES

"A space shuttle? Great idea. We'll build it once and reuse it."

Templates offer a very flexible way to reuse code for more than one purpose. You know the basics of code reuse already. At its primitive level (primitive by OOP standards), you reuse code by writing a function that performs the same job several times in a program. Instead of writing the code to print your name and address in three different places in the program, you put the code in a function only once, then call the function three times.

OOP offers a better approach. You can put code inside a member function and let the objects take care of calling the right functions when they need to, as you learned with polymorphism.

Beginning with the AT&T 3.0 standard, C++ offers a feature called a *template* that extends code reuse even further. Beginning C++ programmers often put off learning about templates. Because templates are such a new addition to the language, C++ programmers might assume that templates are an advanced feature. Although templates are powerful, they are very easy to master.

You must have a compiler that conforms to AT&T C++ version 3.0 to use templates.

In this chapter, you will learn about:

- The need for templates
- The basics of template functions
- The basics of template classes

The Need for Template Functions

Templates enable you to write an outline of a function. This outline is called a *template function.* Instead of specifying data types as a normal function would require, you can specify arguments for the data types.

The ability to specify function arguments is not new to you. Until now, however, you have specified object arguments. The function's argument types remained fixed. For example, the following function contains an argument list. It does not matter what values you pass to it, as long as you pass it a floating-point value followed by a character value.

ARG.CPP. A function that receives a floating-point argument followed by a character argument.

```
// Filename: ARG.CPP
// Function that receives a floating-point argument
// followed by a character argument

void function(float salary, char stype)
{
   cout << "Your salary is $" << salary << endl;
   cout << "Your employee salary type code is " << stype << endl;
}  // Function returns nothing
```

You know that salary and stype act only as placeholders. They tell C++ the following:

"The calling code will send function() two values. One will be a floating-point value and one will be a character value. No matter what the floating-point value is named in the sending function, refer to it as salary here. Even if the sending function sends a

floating-point literal, refer to it as salary here. No matter what the character value is named in the sending function, refer to it here as stype, even if the sending function sends a character literal."

So far, this review is fundamental and might seem like a waste of time. After all, you did not get this far without understanding the basics of functions and argument lists. It is important to realize, however, that you really can think of argument lists as just placeholders. Argument lists are simply places where the receiving function can grab values from the sending code, rename those values into a local-like variable, and use the new names.

The job of a placeholder is also shown in a #define's macro code. As Chapter 2, "C++ Data and Program Basics," points out, using inline functions is *much* safer than using defined macros when you want to streamline smaller function calls. Nevertheless, defined macros illustrate even more clearly (because they do not work with data types but are preprocessor directives) how arguments are nothing more than placeholders for the defined code. For example, in this CUBE macro:

You cannot pass data types in regular function argument lists.

```
#define CUBE(x) ((x)*(x)*(x))
```

the argument x is there just to tell the preprocessor the following:

"If you see the word CUBE in the code that follows, look at whatever is inside the parentheses for some text. Take that text, label it x, and replace the CUBE code with ((x)*(x)*(x)), putting the text in place of the x's."

Because the defined macro is a preprocessor directive, it does no type checking. Macros are the epitome of true placeholder substitution.

Neither regular functions nor macros enable you to pass data types recognizable by the receiving code. Although you can send a macro's data type and the macro will make the substitution, macros are blind to anything going on in the true C and C++ program.

Sometimes it would be useful if you could actually send data types to a function and let the function work with whatever data you sent. For example, you might want to write a function that takes any numeric data value, no matter what the data type is, and returns the absolute value (the positive equivalent) of it to the calling function.

The following code will *not* work, but it shows what you might need:

```
// Invalid function, but it attempts to receive both
dtype absval(dtype x)  // a value and the value's type
{
   return (x <= 0) ? -x : x;
}
```

If this were possible, you could get the absolute value of a floating-point variable like this:

```
dist = absval(float dist);   // Not allowed
```

and you could get the absolute value of a double floating-point variable like this:

```
ddist = absval(double ddist);   // Not allowed
```

and you could also get the absolute value of an integer variable like this:

```
idist = absval(int idist);   // Not allowed
```

Neither C nor C++ allows such function calls. You might be thinking about the overloaded functions available in C++. As Chapter 5, "C++ Function Advantages," discusses, you can write a function several times, using several different argument lists, and the C++ compiler will figure out which function to call based on the data type of the arguments you pass. Overloaded functions work well. Without them, you would have to write several functions that basically do the same thing, and intelligent object constructors would be impossible to write. Nevertheless, overloaded functions just are not quite what is needed here. You still have to write the code, basically duplicates of each other, of every overloaded function you need. It would be nice if one function would suffice for several different data types.

Also, defined macros, although they would enable you to create a macro that worked with any data type, just are not intelligent enough to use safely.

Template functions act like overloaded functions with less work on your part.

Therefore, the designers of C++ sought to find a way that would let you write a single function (instead of having to overload several similar functions) that would operate on data that you send to the function. Instead of the blind macro substitution, these intelligent functions would allow for type checking and operate like true functions. Template functions offer the solution. Now that you've seen the need for template functions, the next section explains their use.

Using Template Functions

The `template` keyword and angled brackets, < and >, signal template functions. You will find a line similar to the following before a template function:

```
template<class T>
```

The `class` keyword does not necessarily have anything to do with C++ classes. It is a signal to C++ that the next identifier (in this case `T`, but it could be any legal C++ identifier or list of identifiers, separated by commas) represents a data type in the function code that follows. The next few lines will be a function that becomes the `template` function. The `template` statement basically tells C++ that T represents *any data type* in the next function. The following program provides code that uses a template function to return the absolute value of any built-in data type passed to it.

TEMPABS.CPP. A template for returning the absolute value of a built-in data type.

```
// Filename: TEMPABS.CPP
// Template for returning the absolute
// value of a built-in data type
#include <iostream.h>
#include <iomanip.h>

template <class T>

T absv(T value)  // T is a type in the template
{
    return ( (value <= T(0)) ? -value : value );
};

void main()
{
    int i = -15;
    long int l = 47;   // Already positive
    float f = -2.78;
    double d = -59483.456677;

    cout << setprecision(2);  // Two-decimal-place output
    cout << "Integer: absv(-15) is " << absv(i) << endl;
    cout << "Long integer: absv(47) is " << absv(l) << endl;
    cout << "Floating-point: absv(-2.78) is " << absv(f) << endl;
    cout << setprecision(6);  // Six-decimal-place output
    cout << "Double: absv(-59483.456677) is " << absv(d) << endl;

}
```

The program's output is as follows:

```
Integer: absv(-15) is 15
Long integer: absv(47) is 47
Floating-point: absv(-2.78) is 2.78
Double: absv(-59483.456677) is 59483.456677
```

In the `template` function, the `T` becomes (to the compiler) the data type of whatever value is passed to `absv()`. To the compiler, when you pass a floating-point value to `absv()`, the function becomes this:

```
float absv(float value)  // T is a type in the template
{
    return ( (value <= float(0)) ? -value : value );
};
```

The compiler generates code for as many different functions as it needs to satisfy the calls made to it. Therefore, the template function and its definition must reside in the same source file, generally in header files. (You can separate a `template` prototype from its implementation code, but they must reside within the same source file.) The actual mechanism that the compiler uses to fill in the `template` function is not important. You must remember only that C++ will assume that `T` is whatever data type the argument is that you pass to the function. Even the typecast works. Because the function will be comparing `float`s, `int`s, and any other data type to 0, you must typecast the 0 so that it matches the data type of the value you compare it to.

Template Functions with Classes

The `template` function program you saw earlier worked with built-in data types. The typecast assured that it would. This, however, is C++, and you know that you want your template functions to work with `class` data as well as with built-in data types.

Of course, templates work with `class` objects, but you must be careful. If you were to pass a `class` variable to the previous `template` function, you would have to make sure that you overloaded the `<=` operator so that it worked with your `class` objects.

The next program does just that. It defines a `Mileage` class for travel to cities that surround yours. It then defines a `max()` `template` function that returns the maximum of the two numbers you pass to it. Because the `max()` function compares its two arguments using the `>=` operator, you must overload the `>=` operator so that it works with the `Mileage` class. Nothing special has to be done for `max()` to work with built-in data types because `>=` is already defined for them.

TEMPMILE.CPP. A template demonstration for returning the maximum value of a built-in data type, even `class` objects.

```cpp
// Filename: TEMPMILE.CPP
// Template demonstration for returning the maximum
// value of a built-in data type, even class objects
#include <iostream.h>
#include <string.h>

class Mileage  {
   char cityname[20];
   int milesaway;
public:
   Mileage(const char *, const int);
   friend ostream& operator<<(ostream &, Mileage &);
   friend int operator>=(const Mileage, const Mileage);
};

Mileage::Mileage(const char * c, const int m)  // Constructor
{
   strcpy(cityname, c);
   milesaway = m;
}

ostream& operator<<(ostream & out, Mileage & m)
{
   out << "City: " << m.cityname << "\n";
   out << "Miles from home: " << m.milesaway << "\n";
   return out;
}

int operator>=(const Mileage m1, const Mileage m2)
{
   return ( (m1.milesaway >= m2.milesaway) ? 1 : 0 );
}

template <class T>

T max(T a, T b)  // T is a type in the template
{
   return ( (a>=b) ? a: b );
};

void main()
{
   // Sets up some objects
   Mileage town1("Miami", 542);
```

continues

TEMPMILE.CPP. continued

```
    Mileage town2("Oklahoma City", 1034);
    Mileage town3("New York", 2437);
    Mileage town4("Memphis", 106);

    cout << "\nOf the 1st two towns, the following ";
    cout << "is farthest away\n";
    cout << max(town1, town2);

    cout << "\nOf the 2nd two towns, the following ";
    cout << "is farthest away\n";
    cout << max(town3, town4);

    cout << "\nTake some time to get away.\n";
}
```

Here is the program's output:

```
Of the 1st two towns, the following is farthest away
City: Oklahoma City
Miles from home: 1034

Of the 2nd two towns, the following is farthest away
City: New York
Miles from home: 2437

Take some time to get away.
```

If you were to expand this program to do other things, you could still use max() for any built-in data type. If you added additional classes, you would only have to overload >= to work the additional classes.

 TIP You can overload template functions just as you can overload other functions as long as the argument lists differ.

Template Classes

If you find that you need to write several similar classes, you might consider using a template class. To create a template class, precede the class name with the template specification. For instance, the following describes a template class named Holder:

```
template<class T> class Holder {
   T num;
public:
   Holder();
   ~Holder();
   void printit(T &);
   void add(T &);
   void takeout(T &);
};
```

> A template class is a description that the compiler can use to build a more specific template class.

Many C++ programmers use template classes to hold class data. Many C++ compilers now come with class libraries called *container classes*. These container classes are nothing more than many template class data structures such as linked lists, stacks, and queues. Because the compiler designers cannot predict your exact class descriptions ahead of time, they use template classes. When you want to store many Employee classes (or whatever) into a linked list, you do not have to write your own linked list class. You only have to pass the Employee object to the appropriate linked list container, and the template does the work.

Container classes hold objects.

The more container classes your compiler supplies, the less you will need to write your own template classes. Understanding the way the template classes work, however, improves your understanding of containers. You also might find yourself writing your own containers someday for some kind of advanced data structure.

Consider the following skeleton of the Holder template class implementation.

```
template<class T> class Holder {
   T num;
public:
   Holder();  // Constructor
   ~Holder();  // Destructor
   void printit(T &);
   void add(T &);
   void takeout(T &);
   int  full(T &);
   T doubleit(T &, T &);  // Two parameters are okay
};

template<class T> Holder<T>::Holder()  {
   //
```

```
    // Implementation code
}

template<class T> Holder<T>::~Holder()  {
    //
    // Implementation code
}

template<class T> Holder<T>::printit(T &)  {
    //
    // Implementation code
}

template<class T> Holder<T>::add(T &)  {
    //
    // Implementation code
}

template<class T> Holder<T>::takeout(T &)  {
    //
    // Implementation code
}

template<class T> int Holder<T>::full(T &)  {
    //
    // Implementation code
}

template<class T> int Holder<T>::doubleit(T & t1, T & t2)  {
    //
    // Implementation code
}
```

Try to envision the compiler's job when it gets the following class variable definitions:

```
Holder<float> salaries;  // Creates a class for this type
Holder<char *> employee;  // Creates a class for this type
```

When C++ sees these variable definitions, it generates the proper class code needed to support a Holder class of floating-point values and a Holder class of character pointers. For the first line with a float template argument, the compiler generates a class similar to the following:

```
class Holder {
    float num;
public:
    Holder();  // Constructor
    ~Holder();  // Destructor
```

354

```
   void printit(float &);
   void add(float &);
   void takeout(float &);
   int  full(float &);
   T doubleit(float &, float &);  // Two parameters are okay
};

Holder::Holder()  {
   //
   // Implementation code
}

Holder::~Holder()  {
   //
   // Implementation code
}

Holder::printit(float &)  {
   //
   // Implementation code
}

Holder::add(float &)  {
   //
   // Implementation code
}

Holder::takeout(float &)  {
   //
   // Implementation code
}

int Holder::full(float &)  {
   //
   // Implementation code
}

int Holder::doubleit(float & t1, float & t2)  {
   //
   // Implementation code
}
```

This code is similar to the actual class C++ generates when it encounters a class definition for the template class. If you supplied five different template class variable definitions, using five different types of data values, C++ would generate five different sets of Holder classes, each one ready for one of the five specific data types. Typing one template class definition is much easier than typing all five class definitions. Let the compiler do the work for you.

355

Some C++ programmers make a distinction between class `template` and `template` class. They say that a class `template` is the source code you write when you write a `template`, and a `template` class is the resulting generated class when C++ generates the class after seeing your variable definitions.

Summary

Now that you understand `template` functions and classes, you might not have much need to use them. A lot depends on your programming needs. If you are satisfied with the container classes supplied with your compiler (which, in reality, are just `template` classes that hold objects), you might not need to use them at all. `template` classes benefit you when you need two or more classes, with each `class` differentiated only by data types.

   `template` functions might be more beneficial to you than `template` classes. There might be many times when you need to write a function that needs to work on several different types of data to accomplish the same task for each.

YOUR OOP
C++ FUTURE

"Ready, set, program!"

You now have all the knowledge you need to move from C to C++. C++ offers so many more natural ways of programming than C or the other procedural programming languages do. The only way to master C++ is to use it. Don't start big; write a few simple programs, slowly building and adding features. If you program for a living, don't attempt to convert all your existing C code into C++ code. There is no reason to do that, but there is good reason to begin using C++ for all your *new* code development.

Begin programming in OOP gradually if you feel most comfortable doing so. You are not used to encapsulating code and data together, so take it slowly at first. You do not have to dive right into inheritance and all the problems (albeit minor ones) that inheritance brings to budding C++ programmers who need to write base `class` constructor initialization lists. Nevertheless, the only way to learn inheritance is to use it, so don't be afraid to try some if your application warrants it.

Programming in C++ is an iterative process. You will not always get the inheritance hierarchy correct the first time (nor the hundredth). That's okay. C++ makes it easy for you to change your code, add to code, and remove code. You might forget to virtualize a base

class, or you might slip up and use `malloc()` in one place, then `delete` in the next (you'll find out soon enough that you've mixed an old function with a new keyword). If it takes you a while to find problems that such error-prone code produces, it will be a lesson learned for a lifetime—or at least until the next time you write a program!

Have fun with C++. You will be surprised, because it will sneak up on you. After you program in C++ for a while, two things happen to almost everyone who uses the language:

1. You will find yourself writing programs much faster than you are used to doing now. Even with the syntax of a new language to sidetrack you at first, you still will produce more readable, accurate, and maintainable code than you ever did before you used C++.

2. You will find yourself forgetting how to use regular C and the other procedural languages. Unlike with a procedural language, in which it is easy to fall into a nonstructured, throw-it-together style, it becomes difficult *not* to use object-oriented programming elements after you begin using them.

C++ Policies

If a C programmer learned only the non-OOP differences between C and C++, they would facilitate the C programmer's move to C++. The fact that C++ is termed "a better C" has merit. C++ purists do not always like the label "a better C." They want C++ to be the language of choice because of the entire C++ language—not just because it contains constructs that are better than C's, but because C++ stands on its own as a language of choice.

Throughout this book, you have read many philosophies, tips, and notes about C++ programming. There are never any hard and fast rules for using any programming language. If one language made everybody happy, there would be only one programming language instead of the tens of languages in popular use today. Nevertheless, there are some preferred C++ styles of coding:

- You no longer need `#define` because `const`, `inline`, and templates produce more accurate code with the same or better results.

- Don't think of your data as being stand-alone variables on which your program operates. Your C++ data is now active. Your C++ data now knows what it can do (via member functions). Instead of performing an action on a data object, you pass a message to your objects, telling them what you want *them* to do.

- When you have to track many "things," whether the things are people, inventory items, car sales, salaries, or stocks, the things probably are good class candidates. Create `class` descriptions for the things and write member functions that manipulate those things.

- Avoid public data of any kind. Limit (or even better, eliminate) your use of global variables and public data members. Write access member functions that return all the data member values needed in the program to hide their access.

- If a function needs to modify a data member, make that function a member function if possible. You cannot do this with some overloaded operator functions, as discussed in Chapter 12, "Operator Overloading." The few exceptions to this rule should be `friend` functions. Member functions and `friend` functions signal to you and to the rest of the program that the data is hidden and limited except through controlled access.

- Limit your use of `friend` functions as much as possible. Novice C++ programmers tend to write too many `friend` functions when those functions should have been member functions of the class or placed in a derived class.

- Stay away from all the I/O functions prototyped in the stdio.h header file. Get used to C++'s `cout` and `cin` I/O objects and the extractor (`>>`) and insertion (`<<`) operators. Not only are the C++ operators more efficient, but they are easier to use and are overloadable.

- Forget about `malloc()`, `free()`, and all the derivatives that associate with them. The `new` and `delete` operators are built into the C++ language, recognize the sizes of the data they are working on, and are safer and easier to use. Use a `set_new_handler()` exception function to handle possible heap problems.

- Use inheritance when some of your data relates to other data in is-a relationships and use composition for the has-a relationships. Inheritance limits the amount of code you have to rewrite and makes large programming projects (and small ones) much more manageable.

- Pass by reference when you are thinking about passing by address. In C, "passing by address" is analogous to "passing by reference." In C++, they mean two very different things.

- Take advantage of operator overloading. If you have to add two `class` members, output `class` members, or do any other operation that is analogous to an operator, overload that operator to work with the class. Do not write an overloaded operator for every operator for every class, because you might not need every operation performed on an object. Overload the operators you know you will need. Additional overloaded operators are easy to add if you need them later.

359

- Try your best to stay away from multiple inheritance. Single inheritance suffices for almost any application you will write.

- Be sure to write constructors and destructors for the classes that need them (almost all do, as it turns out). Always write base `class` destructors for `virtual` classes (see Chapter 17, "Virtual Functions"). Constructor and destructor functions are probably the least-understood aspect of C++ for beginning C++ programmers. The bottom line is that C++ knows how to create built-in data variables. It has to guess at your `class` and `struct` data types, and C++ is not always a very good guesser. Now that you understand base `class` constructors and `virtual` function destructors, review them and write some programs that use them. They are like brain surgery—easy to do as soon as you learn all about them. (Actually, constructor initialization lists are somewhat simpler for beginning C++ programmers than brain surgery, or at least a little less risky.)

- Check your compiler manual for the available container classes. Container classes are really template classes that hold your objects no matter what they look like.

The Object's in Your Court

There was once an author who was invited to speak at a monthly would-be writers' group. The author was told in advance that the group met to encourage the members to write, to teach them writing tips, and to share their thoughts on writing. The author walked to the podium and looked around at the hopeful eyes staring at him. He offered them as much of an encouraging smile as he could muster and said, "If you really wanted to write, you'd be home in front of your keyboards right now." He felt bad about his bluntness, but he knew that most of their problems were caused by a lack of effort and nothing else.

This book is not going to end with a similar quote such as, "If you really wanted to learn C++, you'd be at the keyboard right now." For one thing, you already are a programmer and you probably spend so much of your time programming that you are lucky to have found time to finish this book. Nevertheless, the way to learn C++ is to program as much as possible in C++.

Good luck, and start your keyboards!

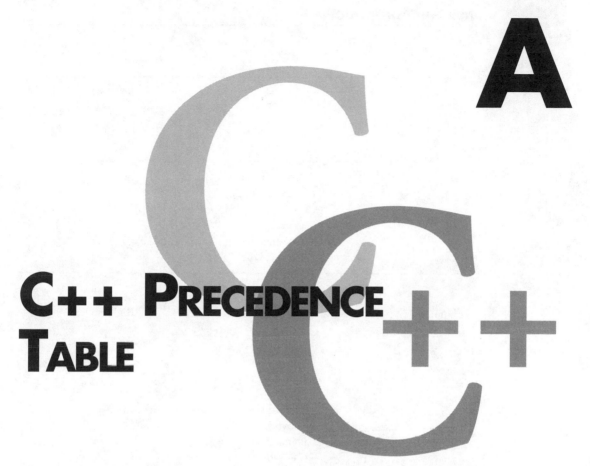

C++ PRECEDENCE TABLE

A

Because of the confusion in most precedence tables, the postfix ++ and – – and the prefix ++ and – – do not appear here. Their precedence works the same in C++ as it does in C. The postfix operators usually appear in level 2, and the prefix operators appear in level 3. In practice, perform prefix before all other operators except for the scope resolution operator, and perform postfix right before the statement continues to the next executable statement in the program. C++ purists will cringe at this description, but it works 99.9 percent of the time, while the "technically correct" placements of these operators simply confuse programmers 99.9 percent of the time.

Precedence Level	Symbol	Description	Associativity
1	::	C++ scope access/ resolution	Left to right
2	()	Function call	Left to right
	[ ]	Array subscript	
	→	C++ indirect component selector	
	.	C++ direct component selector	
3			
Unary	!	Logical negation	Right to left
	~	Bitwise (1's) complement	
	+	Unary plus	
	-	Unary minus	
	&	Addresss of	
	*	Indirection	
	sizeof	Returns size of operand in bytes.	
	new	Dynamically allocates C++ storage.	
	delete	Dynamically deallocates C++ storage.	
	type	Typecast	
4			
Member Access	.*	C++ dereference	Left to right
	→*	C++ dereference	
	()	Expression parentheses	
5			
Multiplicative	*	Multiply	Left to right
	/	Divide	
	%	Remainder (modulus)	

Precedence Level	Symbol	Description	Associativity
6			
Additive	+	Binary plus	Left to right
	-	Binary minus	
7			
Shift	<<	Shift left	Left to right
	>>	Shift right	
8			
Relational	<	Less than	Left to right
	<=	Less than or equal to	
	>	Greater than	
	>=	Greater than or equal to	
9			
Equality	==	Equal to	Left to right
	!=	Not equal to	
10	&	Bitwise AND	Left to right
11	^	Bitwise XOR	Left to right
12	¦	Bitwise OR	Left to right
13	&&	Logical AND	Left to right
14	¦¦	Logical OR	Left to right
15			
Ternary	?:	Conditional	Right to left
16			
Assignment	=	Simple assignment	Right to left
	*=	Assign product	

continues

Precedence Level	Symbol	Description	Associativity
	/=	Assign quotient	
	%=	Assign remainder	
	+=	Assign sum	
	-=	Assign difference	
	&=	Assign bitwise AND	
	^=	Assign bitwise XOR	
	¦=	Assign bitwise OR	
	<<=	Assign left shift	
	>>=	Assign right shift	
17			
Comma	,	Sequence point	Left to right

B

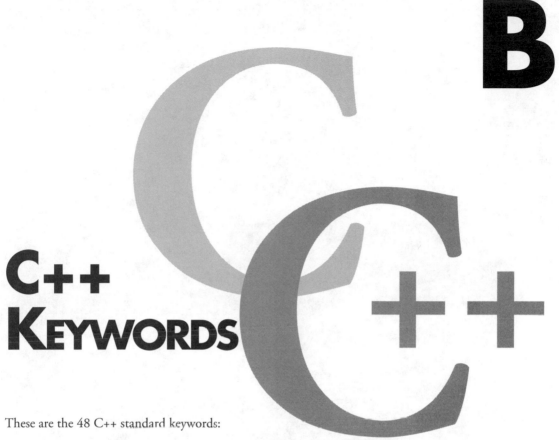

C++ KEYWORDS

These are the 48 C++ standard keywords:

asm*	double	new*	switch
auto	else	operator*	template
break	enum	private*	this*
case	extern	protected*	throw*
catch*	float	public*	try*
char	for	register	typedef
class*	friend*	return	union
const	goto	short	unsigned
continue	if	signed	virtual*
default	inline*	sizeof	void
delete*	int	static	volatile
do	long	struct	while

These keywords are specific to C++. All others exist in both C and C++.

> The catch, throw, and try keywords are reserved for a future version of C++.

ASCII Chart

Dec X_{10}	Hex X_{16}	Binary X_2	ASCII Character
000	00	0000 0000	null
001	01	0000 0001	☺
002	02	0000 0010	☻
003	03	0000 0011	♥
004	04	0000 0100	♦
005	05	0000 0101	♣
006	06	0000 0110	♠
007	07	0000 0111	●
008	08	0000 1000	■
009	09	0000 1001	○
010	0A	0000 1010	■
011	0B	0000 1011	♂
012	0C	0000 1100	♀
013	0D	0000 1101	♪
014	0E	0000 1110	♪♪

continues

Dec X_{10}	Hex X_{16}	Binary X_2	ASCII Character
015	0F	0000 1111	☼
016	10	0001 0000	►
017	11	0001 0001	◄
018	12	0001 0010	↕
019	13	0001 0011	‼
020	14	0001 0100	¶
021	15	0001 0101	§
022	16	0001 0110	─
023	17	0001 0111	↨
024	18	0001 1000	↑
025	19	0001 1001	↓
026	1A	0001 1010	→
027	1B	0001 1011	←
028	1C	0001 1100	FS
029	1D	0001 1101	GS
030	1E	0001 1110	RS
031	1F	0001 1111	US
032	20	0010 0000	SP
033	21	0010 0001	!
034	22	0010 0010	"
035	23	0010 0011	#
036	24	0010 0100	$
037	25	0010 0101	%
038	26	0010 0110	&
039	27	0010 0111	'
040	28	0010 1000	(
041	29	0010 1001	)
042	2A	0010 1010	*
043	2B	0010 1011	+
044	2C	0010 1100	,

Dec X_{10}	Hex X_{16}	Binary X_2	ASCII Character
045	2D	0010 1101	-
046	2E	0010 1110	.
047	2F	0010 1111	/
048	30	0011 0000	0
049	31	0011 0001	1
050	32	0011 0010	2
051	33	0011 0011	3
052	34	0011 0100	4
053	35	0011 0101	5
054	36	0011 0110	6
055	37	0011 0111	7
056	38	0011 1000	8
057	39	0011 1001	9
058	3A	0011 1010	:
059	3B	0011 1011	;
060	3C	0011 1100	<
061	3D	0011 1101	=
062	3E	0011 1110	>
063	3F	0011 1111	?
064	40	0100 0000	@
065	41	0100 0001	A
066	42	0100 0010	B
067	43	0100 0011	C
068	44	0100 0100	D
069	45	0100 0101	E
070	46	0100 0110	F
071	47	0100 0111	G
072	48	0100 1000	H
073	49	0100 1001	I

continues

Dec X_{10}	Hex X_{16}	Binary X_2	ASCII Character
074	4A	0100 1010	J
075	4B	0100 1011	K
076	4C	0100 1100	L
077	4D	0100 1101	M
078	4E	0100 1110	N
079	4F	0100 1111	O
080	50	0101 0000	P
081	51	0101 0001	Q
082	52	0101 0010	R
083	53	0101 0011	S
084	54	0101 0100	T
085	55	0101 0101	U
086	56	0101 0110	V
087	57	0101 0111	W
088	58	0101 1000	X
089	59	0101 1001	Y
090	5A	0101 1010	Z
091	5B	0101 1011	[
092	5C	0101 1100	\
093	5D	0101 1101	]
094	5E	0101 1110	^
095	5F	0101 1111	_
096	60	0110 0000	`
097	61	0110 0001	a
098	62	0110 0010	b
099	63	0110 0011	c
100	64	0110 0100	d
101	65	0110 0101	e
102	66	0110 0110	f
103	67	0110 0111	g

Dec X_{10}	Hex X_{16}	Binary X_2	ASCII Character
104	68	0110 1000	h
105	69	0110 1001	i
106	6A	0110 1010	j
107	6B	0110 1011	k
108	6C	0110 1100	l
109	6D	0110 1101	m
110	6E	0110 1110	n
111	6F	0110 1111	o
112	70	0111 0000	p
113	71	0111 0001	q
114	72	0111 0010	r
115	73	0111 0011	s
116	74	0111 0100	t
117	75	0111 0101	u
118	76	0111 0110	v
119	77	0111 0111	w
120	78	0111 1000	x
121	79	0111 1001	y
122	7A	0111 1010	z
123	7B	0111 1011	{
124	7C	0111 1100	¦
125	7D	0111 1101	}
126	7E	0111 1110	~
127	7F	0111 1111	DEL
128	80	1000 0000	Ç
129	81	1000 0001	ü
130	82	1000 0010	é
131	83	1000 0011	â
132	84	1000 0100	ä

continues

Dec X_{10}	Hex X_{16}	Binary X_2	ASCII Character
133	85	1000 0101	à
134	86	1000 0110	å
135	87	1000 0111	ç
136	88	1000 1000	ê
137	89	1000 1001	ë
138	8A	1000 1010	è
139	8B	1000 1011	ï
140	8C	1000 1100	î
141	8D	1000 1101	ì
142	8E	1000 1110	Ä
143	8F	1000 1111	Å
144	90	1001 0000	É
145	91	1001 0001	æ
146	92	1001 0010	Æ
147	93	1001 0011	ô
148	94	1001 0100	ö
149	95	1001 0101	ò
150	96	1001 0110	û
151	97	1001 0111	ù
152	98	1001 1000	ÿ
153	99	1001 1001	Ö
154	9A	1001 1010	Ü
155	9B	1001 1011	¢
156	9C	1001 1100	£
157	9D	1001 1101	¥
158	9E	1001 1110	P$_t$
159	9F	1001 1111	ƒ
160	A0	1010 0000	á
161	A1	1010 0001	í
162	A2	1010 0010	ó

Dec X_{10}	Hex X_{16}	Binary X_2	ASCII Character
163	A3	1010 0011	ú
164	A4	1010 0100	ñ
165	A5	1010 0101	Ñ
166	A6	1010 0110	a
167	A7	1010 0111	o
168	A8	1010 1000	¿
169	A9	1010 1001	⌐
170	AA	1010 1010	¬
171	AB	1010 1011	½
172	AC	1010 1100	¼
173	AD	1010 1101	¡
174	AE	1010 1110	«
175	AF	1010 1111	»
176	B0	1011 0000	░
177	B1	1011 0001	▒
178	B2	1011 0010	▓
179	B3	1011 0011	│
180	B4	1011 0100	┤
181	B5	1011 0101	╡
182	B6	1011 0110	╢
183	B7	1011 0111	╖
184	B8	1011 1000	╕
185	B9	1011 1001	╣
186	BA	1011 1010	║
187	BB	1011 1011	╗
188	BC	1011 1100	╝
189	BD	1011 1101	╜
190	BE	1011 1110	╛
191	BF	1011 1111	┐

continues

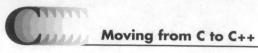

Dec X_{10}	Hex X_{16}	Binary X_2	ASCII Character
192	C0	1100 0000	└
193	C1	1100 0001	┴
194	C2	1100 0010	┬
195	C3	1100 0011	├
196	C4	1100 0100	─
197	C5	1100 0101	┼
198	C6	1100 0110	╞
199	C7	1100 0111	╟
200	C8	1100 1000	╚
201	C9	1100 1001	╔
202	CA	1100 1010	╩
203	CB	1100 1011	╦
204	CC	1100 1100	╠
205	CD	1100 1101	═
206	CE	1100 1110	╬
207	CF	1100 1111	╧
208	D0	1101 0000	╨
209	D1	1101 0001	╤
210	D2	1101 0010	╥
211	D3	1101 0011	╙
212	D4	1101 0100	╘
213	D5	1101 0101	╒
214	D6	1101 0110	╓
215	D7	1101 0111	╫
216	D8	1101 1000	╪
217	D9	1101 1001	┘
218	DA	1101 1010	┌
219	DB	1101 1011	█
220	DC	1101 1100	▄
221	DD	1101 1101	▌

Dec X_{10}	Hex X_{16}	Binary X_2	ASCII Character
222	DE	1101 1110	▌
223	DF	1101 1111	■
224	E0	1110 0000	α
225	E1	1110 0001	β
226	E2	1110 0010	Γ
227	E3	1110 0011	π
228	E4	1110 0100	Σ
229	E5	1110 0101	σ
230	E6	1110 0110	μ
231	E7	1110 0111	τ
232	E8	1110 1000	Φ
233	E9	1110 1001	θ
234	EA	1110 1010	Ω
235	EB	1110 1011	δ
236	EC	1110 1100	∞
237	ED	1110 1101	ø
238	EE	1110 1110	∈
239	EF	1110 1111	∩
240	F0	1111 0000	≡
241	F1	1111 0001	±
242	F2	1111 0010	≥
243	F3	1111 0011	≤
244	F4	1111 0100	⌠
245	F5	1111 0101	⌡
246	F6	1111 0110	÷
247	F7	1111 0111	≈
248	F8	1111 1000	°
249	F9	1111 1001	•
250	FA	1111 1010	·

continues

Dec X_{10}	Hex X_{16}	Binary X_2	ASCII Character
251	FB	1111 1011	√
252	FC	1111 1100	η
253	FD	1111 1101	2
254	FE	1111 1110	∎
255	FF	1111 1111	

 The last 128 ASCII codes listed in this table, numbers 128 through 255, are specific to the IBM PCs and IBM compatibles.

GLOSSARY

abstract base class A class that contains one or more `virtual` functions from which other classes derive through inheritance.

alias Two or more objects that refer to the same memory location (a second name for another variable).

ANSI American National Standards Institute, the committee that approves computer standards. The ANSI committee is now working to adopt a C++ standard.

argument The value sent to a function or a procedure. This can be a constant or a variable and is enclosed in parentheses.

ASCII Acronym for American Standard Code for Information Interchange. ASCII is a common PC system for collating characters.

automatic variable A local variable that loses its value when its block (the one in which it is defined) ends.

base class The first class in a series of derived classes.

binary A numbering system based on only two digits. The only valid digits in a binary system are 0 and 1. See also *bit*.

binary zero Another name for null zero.

bitwise operator   A C++ operator that manipulates the binary representation of values.

block   One or more statements treated as though they are a single statement. A block is always enclosed in braces, { and }.

bug   An error in a program that prevents the program from running correctly. The term originated when a moth short-circuited a connection in one of the first computers, preventing the computer from working!

byte   A basic unit of data storage and manipulation. A byte is equivalent to eight bits and can contain a value ranging from 0 to 255.

child class   In an inheritance hierarchy of classes, a child class is any class derived from another class.

class   A C++ user-defined data type that consists of data members and member functions. Its members are `private` by default.

class variable   An instance of a class.

code   A set of instructions written in a programming language. See *source code.*

comment   A message in a program, ignored by the computer, that tells users what the program does.

compile   The process of translating a program written in a programming language such as C++ into machine code that your computer understands.

composition   The process of creating classes from existing classes.

constant   Datum defined with the `const` keyword that does not change during a program run.

constructor function   The function executed when the program declares an instance of a class.

copy constructor   A constructor function that creates and initializes a new `class` variable from an existing `class` variable.

data   Information stored in the computer as numbers, letters, and special symbols such as punctuation marks. This also refers to the characters you input into your program so that the program can produce meaningful information.

data hiding   The `private` members of a `class` or a `struct` whose access is limited to the `class` functions.

data member   A data component of a `class` or a `struct`.

data processing   What computers do. They take data and manipulate it into meaningful output. The meaningful output is called *information.*

debugging   The process of locating an error (bug) in a program and removing it.

declaration   A statement that declares the existence of a data object or a function.

default   A predefined action or command that the computer chooses unless you specify otherwise.

default argument list   A list of argument values, specified in a function's prototypes, that determines initial values of the arguments if no values are passed for those arguments.

definition   A statement that defines the format of a data object or a function. A definition reserves memory.

dereference   The process of finding a value to which a pointer variable is pointing.

derived class   A class created through inheritance from another class.

destructor   The function called when a class instance goes out of scope.

DOS   Disk Operating System.

dynamic memory allocation   The process of allocating memory from the available memory area at runtime.

early binding   Resolving function calls at compile time. All function resolution code must be available to the compiler.

element   An individual variable in an array.

encapsulation   The process of binding both class code and data into a single object.

execute   To run a program.

extraction operator   The >> operator that reads stream input.

file   A collection of data stored as a single unit on a floppy or hard disk. Files always have a filename that identifies them.

filename   A unique name that identifies a file.

fixed-length record   A record in which each field takes the same amount of disk space, even if that field's data value does not fill the field.

function   A self-contained coding segment designed to do a specific task. All C++ programs must have at least one function called main(). Some functions are library routines that manipulate numbers, strings, and output.

global variable   A variable that can be seen from (and used by) every statement in the program.

hardware   The physical parts of the machine. Hardware has been defined as "anything you can kick," and it consists of the things you can see.

header file   A file that contains prototypes of C++'s built-in functions.

hexadecimal   A numbering system based on 16 elements. Digits are numbered 0 through F, as follows: 0, 1, 2, 3, 4, 5, 6, 7, 8, 9, A, B, C, D, E, F.

hierarchy of operators   See *order of operators*.

information   The meaningful product from a program. Data goes into a program to produce meaningful output (information).

inheritance   The process of deriving classes from other classes without the programmer's having to copy and maintain the code in two separate places.

initialization list   A data member initialization list, separated by commas, that precedes a constructor function body.

inline function   A function that compiles as `inline` code each time the function is called.

input   The entry of data into a computer through a device such as the keyboard.

insertion operator   The << operator that sends output to a stream.

instantiation   Defining a `class` object. When you define a `class` variable, you instantiate that variable (you create an instance of the class).

integer variable   A variable that can hold an integer.

I/O   Acronym for Input/Output.

late binding   Resolving function references at runtime and not at compile time.

link editing   The last step that the C++ compiler performs when preparing your program for execution.

literal   Datum that remains the same during program execution.

local variable   A variable that can be seen from (and used by) only the block in which it is defined.

loop   The repeated execution of one or more statements.

machine language   The series of binary digits that a microprocessor executes to perform individual tasks. People seldom (if ever) program in machine language. Instead, they program in assembly language, and an assembler translates their instructions into machine language.

maintainability   The computer industry's word for the ability to change and update programs written in a simple style.

manipulator   A value used by a program to inform the stream to modify one of its modes.

math operator   A symbol used for addition, subtraction, multiplication, division, or other calculations.

member   A piece of a structure variable that holds a specific type of data, or a `class` variable that holds a specific type of data or a function acting on that data.

member function   A function defined inside a class.

memory   Storage area inside the computer, used to temporarily store data. The computer's memory is erased when the power is turned off.

message   Calling a member function using a `class` object.

modular programming   The process of writing your programs in several modules rather than as one long program. By breaking a program into several smaller program-line routines, you can isolate problems better, write correct programs faster, and produce programs that are much easier to maintain.

modulus   The integer remainder of division.

MS-DOS   An operating system for IBM and compatible PCs.

multiple inheritance   Deriving classes with more than one parent or base class.

null string   An empty string with an initial character of null zero and with a length of zero.

null zero   The string-terminating character. All C++ string constants and strings stored in character arrays end in null zero. The ASCII value for the null zero is 0.

object   A C++ variable, usually used for `class` variables defined in the class as having both data and member functions.

object code   A "halfway step" between source code and executable machine language. Object code consists mostly of machine language, but it is not directly executable by the computer. It must first be linked in order to resolve external references and address references. See also *source code*.

object-oriented programming   A programming approach that treats data as objects capable of manipulating themselves.

octal   A numbering system based on eight elements. Digits are numbered 0 through 7, as follows: 0, 1, 2, 3, 4, 5, 6, 7.

operator   Works on data and performs math calculations or changes data to other data types. Examples include the +, -, and sizeof() operators.

order of operators   Sometimes called the *hierarchy of operators* or the *precedence of operators*. It determines exactly how C++ computes formulas.

overloading   The process of writing more than one function with the same name. The functions must differ in their argument lists so that C++ can identify which one to call.

parameter   A list of variables enclosed in parentheses that follows the name of a function or a procedure. Parameters indicate the number and type of arguments that are sent to the function or procedure.

parent class   In an inheritance hierarchy of classes, a parent class is any class from which you derive another class.

passing by address   When an argument (a local variable) is passed by address, the variable's address in memory is sent to and assigned to the receiving function's parameter list. (If more than one variable is passed by address, each of their addresses is sent to and assigned to the receiving function's parameters.) A change made to the parameter in the function also changes the value of the argument variable.

passing by copy   Another name for *passing by value*.

passing by reference   Passing an alias value. Passing by reference replaces most needs for passing by address (in regular C, they mean the same thing).

passing by value   By default, all C++ variable arguments are passed *by value*. When the value contained in a variable is passed to the parameter list of a receiving function, changes made to the parameter in the routine do not change the value of the argument variable. Also called *passing by copy*.

path   The route the computer travels from the root directory to any subdirectories when locating a file. The path also refers to the subdirectories that MS-DOS examines when you type a command that requires it to find and access a file.

pointer   A variable that holds the address of another variable.

polymorphism   Greek meaning "many forms." Polymorphism generally refers to the process of C++ objects deciding which functions to call at runtime.

precedence of operators   See *order of operators*.

preprocessor directive   A command, preceded by a #, that you place in your source code that directs the compiler to modify the source code in some fashion. The two most common preprocessor directives are #define and #include.

private class member   A class member inaccessible except to the class's member functions.

program   A group of instructions that tells the computer what to do.

programming language   A set of rules for writing instructions for the computer. Popular programming languages include BASIC, C, Visual Basic, C++, and Pascal.

protected class member   A class member inaccessible except to the class's member functions or to inherited members.

prototype   The definition of a function that includes its name, return type, and parameter list.

public class member   A class member accessible to any function.

pure virtual function   A virtual function that contains no code but is used to act as a guide for other derived functions through inheritance.

random-access file   Records in a file that can be accessed in any order you want.

relational operator   An operator that compares data. It tells how two variables or constants relate to each other. It tells you whether two variables are equal or not equal, or which one is less than or more than the other.

scientific notation   A shortcut method of representing numbers of extreme values.

sequence point/comma operator   This operator ensures that statements are performed in a left-to-right sequence.

sequential file   A file that has to be accessed one record at a time, beginning with the first record.

single-dimensional array   An array that has only one subscript. Single-dimensional arrays represent a list of values.

single inheritance   Deriving classes with only one parent or base class.

software   The data and programs that interact with your hardware. The C++ language is an example of software.

sorting   A method of putting data in a specific order (such as alphabetical or numerical order), even if that order is not the same order in which the elements were entered.

source code   The C++ language instructions, written by humans, that the C++ compiler translates into object code. See also *object code*.

standard input device   The target of each `cout` and output function. Normally the screen, unless rerouted to another device at the operating system's prompt.

standard output device   The target of each `cin` and input function. Normally the keyboard, unless rerouted to another device at the operating system's prompt.

static data member   A member that exists only once no matter how many `class` variables you define.

static member function   A function that has access only to `static` data members of a class.

static variable   A variable that does not lose its value when the block in which it is defined ends. See also *automatic variable*.

stream   Literally a stream of characters, one following another, flowing among devices in your computer.

string   One or more characters terminated with a null zero.

string constant   One or more groups of characters that end in a null zero.

string delimiter   See *null zero*.

string literal   Another name for a *string constant*.

structure   A unit of related information containing one or more members, such as an employee number, employee name, employee address, employee pay rate, and so on.

subscript   A number inside brackets that differentiates one *element* of an array from another.

syntax error   The most common error a programmer makes. Often a misspelled word.

template   A `class` model that other C++ classes can generate from.

typecast   Temporarily converting one object to another data type.

unary operator   The addition or subtraction operator used before a single variable or constant.

variable   A datum that can change as the program runs.

variable-length record   A record that takes up no wasted space on the disk. As soon as a field's data value is saved to the file, the next field's data value is stored after it. Usually there is a special separating character between the fields so that your programs know where the fields begin and end.

variable scope   Sometimes called the *visibility of variables,* this describes how variables are "seen" by your program. See also *global variables* and *local variables.*

virtual base class   A base class that is shared by multiply-inherited classes.

virtual function   Allows polymorphism by defining a function called by an object at runtime (late binding) instead of at compile time (early binding).

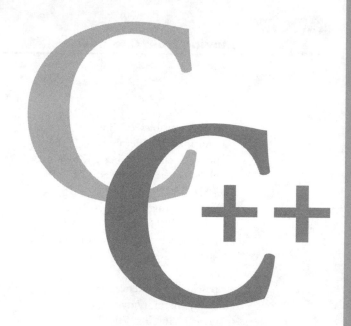

INDEX

F

GLOC1.CPP program, 29-30
GLOC2.CPP program, 30
good( ) member function, 340

H

.h header filename extension, 16
hardware, 380
header files, 380
    fstream.h, 331
    iostream.h, 38-45
        format flags, 51-52
        overloaded operator functions,
          196-197
heap, 69
hex numeric base manipulator, 45-47
hexadecimal numbering system, 380
hiding data, 92, 117, 378
    and structures, 95-96
    error checking, 96-97
.hpp header filename extension, 16

I

I/O (input/output), 380
    error messages, displaying, 44-45
    file, 331-332
        error checking, 340-341
        random, 337-344
        sample programs, 341-344
        simple, 332-336
    input member functions, 326-328
    iostream.h header file, 38-45
    manipulators, 45-46
        character control, 48-49
        format control, 49-53
        numeric base, 46-48
    objects, 39

operators, overloading, 196-201
output member functions, 328-331
stream class, 324-325
stream operators, 40
ifstream derived class, 331-336
inf file object, 333
information, 380
INHCONST.CPP program, 262-268
INHER1.CPP program, 251-252
inheritance, 236-237, 380
    base class access, 245-247
    constructor initialization
      lists, 260-261
    dominance rule, 255-257
    importance of, 239-241
    limitations, 270-271
    member functions, calling, 255-257
    multiple, 238-239, 271-273, 381
        deciding to use, 277
        troubleshooting, 273-276
        virtual base classes, 273-276
    overriding inherited
      access, 268-270
    private class members, 243-245
    protected class members,
      244-245
    public class members, 241-242
    restricting inherited members, 278
    single, 238, 383
        SmallTalk programming
          language, 239
    with constructor
      functions, 261-268
    with virtual functions, 306-310
    without virtual functions, 303-305
INHERNOV.CPP program, 303-305
INHERV1.CPP program, 306
INHERV2.CPP program, 307-310
INHERV3.CPP program, 311-313
initialization list, 380

W

Order Your Program Disk Today!

You can save yourself hours of tedious, error-prone typing by ordering the companion disk to *Moving from C to C++*. The disk contains the source code for all the complete programs and many of the shorter samples in this book.

You get code that shows you how to use most of the features of C++. Samples include code for keyboard control, screen control, file I/O, template functions, classes, constructors, virtual functions, and more.

Disks are available in 3 1/2-inch format. The cost is $12 per disk. (When ordering outside the U.S., please add $5 for extra shipping and handling.)

Just make a copy of this page, fill in the blanks, and mail it with your check or postal money order to:

Greg Perry, C to C++ Disk
P.O. Box 35752
Tulsa, OK 74153-0752

Please *print* the following information:

Number of Disks:_____@ $12.00 =_____

Name:_____

Street Address:_____

City:_____State:_____

ZIP:_____

(On foreign orders, please use a separate page to give your mailing address in the format required by your post office.)

Checks and money orders should be made payable to **Greg Perry**.

(This offer is made by Greg Perry, not by Sams Publishing.)